the series on school reform

Patricia A. Wasley
Coalition of
Essential Schools

Ann Lieberman
NCREST

SERIES EDITORS

Joseph P. McDonald
Annenberg Institute
for School Reform

PROFESSIONAL DEVELOPMENT AND PRACTICE SERIES

Authentic Assessment in Action

Studies of Schools and Students at Work

LINDA DARLING-HAMMOND
JACQUELINE ANCESS
AND BEVERLY FALK

National Center for Restructuring
Education, Schools, and Teaching
Teachers College, Columbia University

Teachers College, Columbia University
New York and London

Published by Teachers College Press, 1234 Amsterdam Avenue, New York, N.Y. 10027

Excerpt on page 181 from *Brown Bear, Brown Bear, What Do You See?* by Bill Martin, Jr. Illustrated by Eric Carle (1983). Copyright © 1967 by Bill Martin, Jr. Copyright © 1983 by Henry Holt and Co., Inc. Reprinted by permission of Henry Holt and Co., Inc.

Library of Congress Cataloging-in-Publication Data

Darling-Hammond, Linda, 1951–
    Authentic assessment in action : studies of schools and students
at work / Linda Darling-Hammond, Jacqueline Ancess, and Beverly
Falk.
        p.   cm. — (The series on school reform)
    Includes bibliographical references and index.
    ISBN 0-8077-3439-X (cloth : acid-free paper). — ISBN
0-8077-3438-1 (paper : acid-free paper)
        1. Competency based education—United States—Case studies.
    2. Educational evaluation—United States—Case studies.   I. Ancess,
Jacqueline, 1943–   .   II. Falk, Beverly.   III. Title.   IV. Series.
    LC1032.D37 1995
    379.1'54—dc20   94-46491

ISBN: 0-8077-3438-1 (paper)
ISBN: 0-8077-3439-X

Printed on acid-free paper
Manufactured in the United States of America
02 01 00 99 98 97 96 95   8 7 6 5 4 3 2 1

CONTENTS

FOREWORD

HOW'M I DOING

"How'm I doing?"

Such is the reasonable question posed by any student, of any age. It is also a critical question. Unless I know how I am "doing," I cannot adjust the regimen of my learning. If I am getting "it," fine. If I am not, I must rearrange my effort.

Good schools not only frequently tell their students "how they are doing" but get the youngsters into the habit of asking the question for themselves. The expectation of illuminating feedback—indeed aggressively searching it out—is a universal characteristic of an educated person.

The quality of that feedback must be incisive and apt. Telling the kid, "You got a 57 on Friday's test . . . you gotta do better . . ." is not much help. Indeed, that 57 may tell us more about the test than the test taker. Understanding that one has not done well on a test is the barest beginning of why one did not do well. The learning is in the substance and barely in the score.

The substance of a youngster's problem may emerge only by looking at that student's work over time and by querying him directly. "Carlos, read this poem to me. . . . of what does that remind you . . . shut your eyes and take these words and put them into a picture in your mind . . . what do you see. . . ." One plumbs Carlos' understanding by careful and persistent questioning and observation. Only thus can one help him to understand, and thereby to learn.

Knowing how the students "are doing" is necessary equipment for the teacher and the parent as well. Why does Dorothy consistently miscompute when a zero is part of the arithmetic problem? Why and how does Carlos appear to misread these poems? Unless one knows how and why the student's mind is working, it is difficult to teach him—or to parent him—well.

In recent years all sorts of other folks have wanted to know how the students were doing. Indeed, the collection of scores is now a major commercial industry and their promulgation a cause for media attention. Americans now even adjust their views of themselves in relation to other countries by how well our students are doing. The aggregation of those scores of 57 (or whatever) has become part of American politics. Indeed, in some quarters the aggregation has become the principal representation of education. Being educated is having high scores.

"Assessment" thus has many functions. It is only as good as its instruments, and it is defensible only to the extent that it actively forwards and enhances a child's learning.

It was in recognition of this view of assessment that a growing number of concerned schoolpeople have freshly defined their work. They have put at the center of their teaching the persistent answering of the student's question "how'm I doing?" and they labor to persuade that student to make a habit of asking it herself, always. They struggle to get the deepest possible assessment, a rich understanding of that youngster's intellectual struggle, and they document her progress. They make the assessment as "authentic" as possible, taking the measure of the child's real work over time (not just the tokens of that work, the grades on a few hours of formal testing) and embedding that assessment, as the teaching before it, in powerful but familiar intellectual contexts which are comprehensible to the child.

They have deliberately kept their teaching plans flexible to adapt to where the student was, to take account of the most informed judgment of how that student was "doing." For teaching they have combined and interweaved the imperatives both of the disciplines they address and the heads and hearts of the students.

They have committed themselves to involve the student and his family in this effort. There are no secrets here, no trick questions, no confidential files. The means and standards of assessment are everyone's property, not some sort of technical mystery to be implicitly trusted by families.

It is far easier to keep school in a more superficial way, with the curriculum marched through on a schedule designed a year in advance without regard to any particular pupils save an age group. It is easier to lean wholly on an assessment system designed by others which tests but a few things, and these rarely. It is certainly much easier not to have to explain to parents the basis for the test "scores" ("the grading is done elsewhere by experts . . ."). And it is easiest of all to blame "poor scores" on the kids, without having then to use those same "scores" to help the students learn.

Some schools have decided to take the more difficult route. They have reconnected learning, teaching, and assessment in powerful ways, ones which raise all sorts of central questions about education. What *are* high standards? Who decides what they are? How can one tell them when one sees them? To what extent do we care how our students perform in life beyond the classroom and testing room? They have taken on the repercussions of the public display of shoddy student work, a matter usually left embedded in arcane scores. They have not flinched from taking responsibility for each child's learning: no buck passing here.

It was five such schools that Linda Darling-Hammond and her colleagues have studied and which form the basis for this important book. The issue of assessment comes first, but we see in the following case studies how it becomes powerfully enveloped in the processes of learning and teaching, of informing students, teachers, parents, and others of "how the children are doing." The portraits explicitly and implicitly suggest a deep, fair, and defensible way to answer the question "How'm I doing" in a manner that helps this child and eventually every child.

Theodore R. Sizer
Brown University

PREFACE

This book examines how five schools have developed "authentic," performance-based assessments of students' learning, and how this work has interacted with and influenced the teaching and learning experiences students encounter in school. Case studies of two elementary and three secondary schools describe how they are using a number of different strategies for personalizing instruction, deepening students' engagement with subject matter, and assessing learning in rigorous and holistic ways. The case studies examine how authentic assessment supports changes in curriculum, teaching, and school organization and how it is, in turn, embedded in and supported by these aspects of school life. The cases document the changes in student work and learning that can accompany new approaches to assessment when these are embedded in a school-wide effort to create learner-centered education.

With all of the burgeoning interest in alternative forms of assessment, there is yet very little rich description of how schools develop and use strategies such as portfolios, projects, performance tasks, and other documentation of student accomplishments to inform instruction and to stimulate greater learning. This volume begins to develop a school's eye view of authentic assessment, aiming to illuminate how it can enrich life in classrooms and focus the energies of students, teachers, and other members of the school community on deep learning demonstrated through applications and performances. It is not our intent to investigate either the measurement properties of these assessments or their effects on student performance as captured by other measures, though we touch on these matters as they arise in the course of our inquiry. Instead, we hope to help capture the kinds of work students and schools engage in as they use teaching, learning, and assessment strategies that together support high levels of accomplishment, on challenging "real world" tasks.

The case studies examine how the introduction of authentic forms of assessment interacts with other aspects of teaching and learning in schools undergoing change. Yet to be answered are questions concerning how these strategies can be further developed and shared with other schools, how they can be used to provide useful, comprehensible information to various school publics, and how existing policies, which currently pose difficult tensions and barriers, can be restructured to support this kind of teaching, learning, and assessment. We hope future research and the development of practice will aid efforts to seek answers to these questions. Most of all, we hope this work supports teachers in their ongoing efforts to work with students in supportive, engaging, and authentic ways.

ACKNOWLEDGMENTS

Work on the three secondary school case studies included in this volume was supported in part by a grant to the National Center for Restructuring Education, Schools, and Teaching (NCREST) at Teachers College, Columbia University, from the National Center for Research on Vocational Education, located at the University of California at Berkeley and funded through the U.S. Department of Education. The findings and conclusions are, of course, our own and do not represent the views of the Department. Additional funding for the research was provided through NCREST from its major funder, the DeWitt Wallace Reader's Digest Fund. We are grateful for their support. Versions of the individual case studies have been published separately by NCREST.

Helpful reviews on earlier drafts of several of the case studies came from Walt Haney, Lorrie Shepard, Pat Wasley, and an anonymous reviewer. Their comments contributed much to our thinking and enriched our research. Patrice Litman and Nicole Amelio helped in the production of the report. We thank them for their assistance.

We would also like to acknowledge the staff, students, and parents at The Bronx New School, Central Park East Secondary School, Hodgson Vocational Technical School, International High School, and P.S. 261, who not only gave of their time and insights in the construction of these studies, but who together make these schools the lively and engaging places they are—and who provide living proof that an exciting, challenging, and successful education can be a reality for all children.

Authentic Assessment in Action

Studies of Schools and Students at Work

1

AUTHENTIC ASSESSMENT IN CONTEXT: THE MOTIVATION FOR CHANGE

As students prepare for graduation at Central Park East Secondary School (CPESS), a high school of 450 students in an East Harlem neighborhood in New York City, their attention is not focused on assembling Carnegie units or cramming for multiple choice Regents examinations as it is for many students in other high schools around New York. Instead, they work intensively during their 2–3 years in the CPESS Senior Institute preparing a portfolio of their work that will reveal their competence and performance in 14 curricular areas, ranging from science and technology to ethics and social issues, from school and community service to mathematics, literature, and history. This portfolio will be evaluated by a graduation committee composed of teachers from different subjects and grade levels, an outside examiner, and a student peer. The committee members will examine all of the entries and hear the students' oral "defense" of their work as they determine when each student is ready to graduate.

Across the East River in Long Island City, students at International High School are engaged in the development of their own portfolios and projects. All of International's students enter as recent immigrants speaking little or no English; they learn both subject matter and language skills while intensely engaged in collaborative project work. International's emphasis on collaborative learning and on performance projects is combined with a number of strategies that regularly involve students in self- and peer-assessment. In their interdisciplinary classes and outside internships, students create products that integrate what they have learned and that enable them to assess and continually improve their own performance and that of their peers. As they will need to do to be successful in the world outside school, these students work in teams, striving to meet personal and group goals in an environment of continual self-reflection and feedback.

Several states away, in suburban Delaware, students at Hodgson Vocational Technical High School are also hard at work on an interdisciplinary senior project that combines their vocational and academic work in a product they design and produce, accompanied by a research report and an oral presentation they deliver to a team of their teachers. Houses built to scale are created alongside dentures, satellite dishes, geological models, designer clothes, and antique beds. The history, social uses, science, and technology associated with these products are the subject of carefully documented research and of a major presentation that serves as an exhibition of their readiness to graduate into the worlds of work and further study.

Part of the growing movement to establish means for more authentic assessment of student learning, these three high schools are developing ways to focus students' energies on challenging, performance-oriented tasks that require analysis, integration of knowledge, and invention—as well as highly developed written and oral expression—rather than focusing merely on recall and recognition of facts. These strategies are called "authentic" because they require that students demonstrate what they can do in the same ways that workers do in out-of-school settings: by performing tasks that are complex and that require production of solutions or products. Rather than taking multiple choice tests in which students react to ideas or identify facts, these students engage in science experiments, conduct social science research, write essays and papers, read and interpret literature, and solve mathematical problems in real-world contexts.

For their graduation portfolio at CPESS, for example, students develop a project that demonstrates their knowledge of scientific methodology by using it in a particular field. They engage ethical and social issues by participating in a debate, writing an op-ed article, or analyzing a film or novel that raises important moral issues. In each case, they demonstrate their ability to see multiple viewpoints, weigh conflicting claims, and defend their views with credible evidence. Literary essays and historical analyses, along with documentation and evaluation of their internship experiences, add to the wealth of evidence accumulated about students' attainment of valued school—and societal—goals.

Other forms of authentic assessment, particularly in the early grades, involve teachers in observing and documenting their students' work and learning. At P.S. 261 in Brooklyn, teachers use the *Primary Language Record,* an assessment tool initially developed in England, to document how and what their young students are reading, writing, and speaking about in the authentic contexts in which they live and learn. Rather than administering standardized multiple choice tests that are several steps removed from actual literacy activities, these teachers watch their students at work; evaluate the children's oral reading, writing samples, and conversations; hold conferences with parents and students about their literacy development inside and outside school; and confer with one another about how to best serve student needs over time.

At The Bronx New School, students keep portfolios during grades K through 6 that include samples and other records of their work in all subject areas, along with teacher observations and reading logs. Teachers keep running records of oral reading and miscue analyses that evaluate their students' reading strategies. Narrative reports to parents supplement these assessment tools, providing rich descriptions of what students are doing and how they are progressing. These assessments enable teachers to evaluate progress, design useful learning opportunities, and involve parents, other teachers, and the˙ students themselves in assessing and supporting their growth and development.

These three high schools and two elementary schools are among the thousands across the country that are engaging in assessment reforms that will enable them to look at students through more instructionally useful lenses and to engage students in more meaningful and satisfying work. Teachers and principals in these schools launched efforts to move beyond traditional grades and standardized tests for a number of reasons. They wanted ways to look at students that would tell them more about *how* students learn, as well as *what* they have learned—ways that would help them support learning more effectively. They wanted their students to engage in more complex and challenging tasks that would allow students to integrate what they were learning, to generate their own knowledge, and to create their own products. They wanted strategies that would allow teachers to work collectively as a faculty, thinking and acting more collaboratively on behalf of common, school-wide goals and ideas about learning and sharing their knowledge about students with one another so as to support students' work across departments and throughout the grades.

All five schools are members of the Coalition of Essential Schools,[1] which is committed to evaluating student work through exhibitions of real performance rather than through more artificial testing approaches. Among the assessment strategies described in these schools are some that emphasize the production of products and others that emphasize the ability to engage in intellectual, interpersonal, or intrapersonal processes; some that engage students in lengthy tasks over long periods of time and others that are more time bound; some that focus on problem solving and others that focus on problem framing; some that emphasize tasks commonly thought of as "vocational," or targeted toward identifiable future work, and others that emphasize tasks commonly thought of as "academic," or centered around skills needed for school success; some that evaluate children's learning and development by looking at the children in action and others that assess performance by looking at their work.

In some cases, these assessments are so firmly embedded in the curriculum that they are practically indistinguishable from instruction. This is one salient characteristic of an "authentic assessment": it is designed to provide the student with a genuine rather than a contrived learning experience that provides both the teacher and student with opportunities to learn what the student can do. The demonstration of learning occurs in a situation that requires the application and production of knowledge rather than the mere recognition or reproduction of correct answers. Authentic assessments are also contextualized: that is, rather than assembling disconnected pieces of information, the tasks are set in a meaningful context that provides connections between real-world experiences and school-based ideas. These assessments are connected to students' lives and to their learning experiences and are representative of the kinds of "real world" challenges encountered in the fields of study students explore (Archbald & Newman, 1988; Wiggins, 1989). Together, these case studies permit us to take an in-depth look at how such strategies not only allow much richer evaluations of students and their capabilities, but also support and transform the processes of teaching and learning.

WHY ARE ALTERNATIVE ASSESSMENTS BEING CREATED?

Increasingly, local schools, school districts, and states are experimenting with these methods and with other alternatives to standardized testing for assessing student learning and performance. Persuaded that traditional standardized tests fail to measure many of the important aspects of learning, and that they do not support many of the most useful strategies for teaching, practitioners are introducing alternative approaches to assessment into classrooms—approaches that help teachers look more carefully and closely at students, their learning, and their work.

Much like the kinds of assessment that prevail in most other countries around the world, in which multiple choice testing is much less common, these approaches include essay examinations, research projects, scientific experiments, oral exhibitions and performances in areas like debating and the arts. They also include portfolios of students' work in various subject areas, along with individual and group projects requiring analysis, investigation, experimentation, cooperation, and written, oral, or graphic presentation of findings. Often the assessment occasion requires students to respond to questions from classmates or from external examiners, thus helping them learn to think through and defend their views, while allowing their teachers to hear and understand their thinking (Archbald & Newman, 1988; Coalition of Essential Schools, 1990).

One of the reasons for these efforts to develop alternative forms of assessment is a growing consensus among educators, researchers, and policymakers that most currently used American tests do not tap many of the skills and abilities that students need to develop in order to be successful in later life and schooling. Mounting evidence demonstrates that commonly used, standardized, norm-referenced, multiple choice tests fail to tap both "higher order skills" and students' abilities to perform "real world" tasks (Resnick, 1987a, b; Sternberg, 1985). Moreover, the heavy use of these tests as arbiters of many school decisions appears to be driving instruction away from the development of those performance skills and thinking abilities increasingly needed in most workplaces and in postsecondary education (Bailey, 1989; Carnevale, Gainer, & Meltzer, 1989), as well as for daily life and citizenship in a complex, democratic society.

These concerns are partly due to the limits of widely used American testing methods, described more fully below. The concerns are also related to the increasing demands for a kind of education that encourages students to do more than memorize information and use algorithms to solve tidy problems—an education that prepares students to frame problems, find information, evaluate alternatives, create ideas and products, and invent new answers to messy dilemmas.

The capacities required of students in the world they are growing up in today are more demanding than those required of most citizens and workers in the more simple and stable world of the past. A growing number of jobs in our information economy require highly developed intellectual skills and technological training. Even "low-skilled" jobs require technical training and flexibility. In addition, most industries are restructuring the way they organize work so that cooperative planning and problem-solving have now become "basic skills," replacing simply following directions on an assembly line. Citizens must be able to access resources and perform complicated tasks at high levels of literacy just to survive in today's world. Workers must anticipate changing occupations several times over the course of a lifetime, adapting to ever changing technologies and job demands and inventing solutions to productivity problems rather than relying on a manager to tell them what to do (Drucker, 1986; Hudson Institute, 1987).

These kinds of skills and abilities are not based on the kinds of thinking and performance that are evaluated in most U.S. testing programs. Because of the way multiple choice, norm-referenced tests are constructed, they exclude a great many kinds of knowledge and types of performance we expect from students, placing test takers in a passive, reactive role, rather than one which engages their capacities to structure tasks, produce ideas, and solve problems (National Research Council, 1982).

In response to these concerns, new forms of assessment are being promoted, developed, and used in schools, school districts, and states across the country. The new assessments rely on tasks that are valued in nonschool settings as well as in-school settings, focusing on students' abilities to produce a wide variety of products and performances, to manipulate concrete materials as well as symbols, to frame and solve messy problems with many possible solutions, to effectively express themselves orally and in writing, and to work in groups as well as individually.

Concerns About Traditional Standardized Testing

U.S. schools administer a wide array of standardized tests to children of all ages and grades. These are used to determine readiness for school and placement in grade and class levels; to assess academic achievement levels and place students in different programs, groups, or tracks; and to diagnose potential learning problems. Increasingly common criticisms of the nature and uses of these tests were summarized in a recent report by the New York Public Interest Research Group, which noted the narrowness of what they measure, their lack of accuracy for decision making, and their lack of useful diagnostic information for teaching (Harris & Sammons, 1989). Some of the problems identified with widespread use of standardized tests are described below.

Standardized Tests Are Limited Measures of Learning

Multiple choice tests do not evaluate student performance on actual tasks, such as reading, writing, or problem-solving in various subject areas, and they are poor measures of higher order thinking skills. These kinds of tests require that students respond to predetermined problems by recognizing a single answer, rather than by producing their own products and wrestling with complex, ambiguous problems (National Research Council, 1982). Because the questions contain only one correct answer, they reward the ability to think quickly and superficially (National Assessment of Educational Progress [NAEP], 1981). They do not measure the ability to think deeply, to create, or to perform in any field. They are unable to measure students' abilities to write coherently and persuasively, to use mathematics in the context of real-life problems, to make meaning from text when reading, to understand and use scientific methods or reasoning, or to grasp and apply social science concepts (Darling-Hammond, 1991; Medina & Neill, 1988).

Most traditional standardized tests do not reflect current understandings of how students learn. They are based on an outmoded theory of learning that stresses the accumulation and recall of isolated facts and skills. They do not reflect current knowledge that people learn in meaningful and purposeful contexts by connecting what they already know with what they are trying to learn (Gardner, 1983; Kantrowitz & Wingert, 1989; Resnick, 1987a). "Thinking skills" are the foundation for building "basic skills," not the other way around, as many testing programs assume. Furthermore, real skills must be demonstrated in complex performance contexts, not on tasks demanding only recognition of discrete facts. By focusing on rote skills rather than on conceptual learning, the tests often miss the forest for the trees.

Overuse of Such Tests Narrows the Curriculum

Because test scores are used for so many different purposes, they often exert great influence on what is taught, leading to a narrowed curriculum. Teachers are pressured to teach only what is tested, and to teach these things in the particular forms and formats used by the tests. This leads to an overemphasis on superficial content coverage and rote drill on discrete skills at the expense of in-depth projects and other thought-provoking tasks that take more time. It also leads to classwork in which students spend their time on test-like tasks, such as answering multiple choice or fill-in-the-blanks questions, rather than on more challenging types of work, like writing essays, conducting research, experimenting, reading and discussing literature, debating, solving difficult problems, and creating products (Boyer, 1983; Darling-Hammond & Wise, 1985; Darling-Hammond, 1990a, 1991; Goodlad, 1984; Kantrowitz & Wingert, 1989; National Association for the Education of Young Children [NAEYC], 1988).

Standardized Tests Are Poor Diagnostic Tools

Because most traditional standardized tests provide only a limited measure of a narrow aspect of learning or development, they are poor predictors of how students will perform in other settings, and they are unable to provide information about why students score as they do. Because they record only final answers and report only numerical scores, mass-administered, standardized tests do not provide information about how children tackle different tasks or what abilities they rely on in their problem solving. This promotes a view of children as having deficits that need to be remediated rather than as having individual differences, approaches to learning, and strengths that can be supported and developed. It also fails to provide enough information about areas of difficulty to inform instructional strategies for addressing them (Bradekamp & Shepard, 1989; NAEYC, 1988).

An additional factor contributing to the inadequacies of standardized tests for diagnostic and placement purposes is that they do not reflect or capture the diversity of students' backgrounds and experiences. Because they often contain assumptions and facts that are grounded in the context of the dominant culture—and fail to include relevant forms of knowledge from other cultures—the tests place students from nondominant cultures at a disadvantage in demonstrating what they know and can do (Garcia & Pearson, in press; Medina & Neill, 1988). This leads to consistent inaccuracies in identifying students for special education and remedial education. These placements then tend to further limit the curriculum to which students are exposed (Darling-Hammond, 1991; Oakes, 1985).

Influences of Tests on Teaching and Learning

These shortcomings of American tests were less problematic when they were used as only one source among many other kinds of information about student learning, and when they were not directly tied to decisions about students and programs. However, as test scores have increasingly been used to make important educational decisions, their flaws have become more damaging. As schools have begun to "teach to the tests," the scores have become ever poorer assessments of students' overall abilities, because classwork oriented toward recognizing the answers to multiple choice questions does not heighten students' proficiency in areas that are *not* tested, such as analysis, complex problem solving, and written and oral expression (Darling-Hammond & Wise, 1985; Haney & Madaus, 1986; Koretz, 1988). Because teachers must emphasize those things that tests measure, current approaches to testing often limit the kinds of teaching and learning opportunities provided in classrooms.

The results of this phenomenon can be seen in U.S. students' performance. Since about 1970, when standardized tests began to be used for a wider variety of accountability purposes, basic skills test scores have been increasing slightly while assessments of higher order thinking skills have declined in virtually all subject areas. Officials of the National Assessment of Educational Progress (NAEP), the National Research Council (NRC), and the National Councils of Teachers of English and Mathematics (NCTE and NCTM), among others, have all attributed this decline in higher order thinking and performance skills to schools' emphasis on tests of basic skills. They argue that, not only are the test scores inadequate measures of students' performance abilities, but the uses of the tests have actually corrupted teaching practices.

More than a decade ago, the NAEP attributed its finding that only about 5%–10% of high school students can actually explain or defend their points of view to the fact that most reading tests emphasize short responses and lower level cognitive thinking (NAEP, 1981). A more recent NAEP report summarized the status of high school students' performance as follows:

> Sixty-one percent of the 17-year-old students could not read or understand relatively complicated material, such as that typically presented at the high-school level. Nearly one-half appear to have limited mathematics skills and abilities that go little beyond adding, subtracting, and multiplying with whole numbers. More than one half could not evaluate the procedures or results of a scientific study, and few included enough information in their written pieces to communicate their ideas effectively. Additionally, assessment results in other curriculum areas indicate that high school juniors have little sense of historical chronology, have not read much literature, and tend to be unfamiliar with the uses and potential applications of computers. (Educational Testing Service [ETS], 1989, p. 26)

International comparisons of students' performance in mathematics and science tell a similar story. U.S. students score at about the median of other countries at 5th grade, dip below the average by 8th grade, and consistently score near the bottom by 12th grade, especially on tasks requiring higher order thinking and problem solving. An international mathematics study found that, in line with American testing demands, instruction in the U.S. is dominated by textbooks and lectures followed by individual seatwork, with little use of other resources such as computers, calculators, or manipulatives. The researchers concluded that these "strategies geared to rote learning" represent

> a view that learning for most students should be passive—teachers transmit knowledge to students who receive it and remember it mostly in the form in which it was transmitted. . . . In the light of this, it is hardly surprising that the achievement test items on which U.S. students most often showed relatively greater growth were those most suited to performance of rote procedures. (McKnight et al., 1987, p. 81)

These findings were confirmed by a U.S. study of the influence of testing on mathematics and science teaching. An item analysis of the most widely used standardized tests at grades 4, 8, and 12, supplemented by a survey of over 2,000 teachers, found that more than 95% of the math test questions tested low level conceptual knowledge and low level thinking, as did over 70% of the questions on science tests. In districts that use the tests for a wide array of decisions, teachers reported themselves least able to adopt innovative curriculum materials designed to support higher order thinking and performance skills. Over 60% of the teachers interviewed described negative effects of the tests on curriculum and student learning, ranging from fragmentation and narrowing of the curriculum to lack of opportunities for in-depth study (Madaus et al., 1992).

At the start of the current reform movement, two major studies of American education called attention to this problem. Ernest Boyer's (1983) study of American high schools found an overabundance of teaching consisting of the transmittal of "fragments of information, unexamined and unanalyzed." Boyer notes:

> The pressure is on to teach the skills that can be counted and reported. As one teacher said, "We are so hung up on reporting measured gains to the community on nationally normed tests that we ignore teaching those areas where it can't be done." (p. 90)

Similarly, John Goodlad (1984) found in his massive study of more than 1,000 American classrooms that, for the most part, the curriculum appeared to call for and make appropriate only some ways of knowing and learning and not others. He found that students listen, read short sections in textbooks, respond briefly to questions, and take short-answer or multiple choice quizzes. They rarely plan or initiate anything, create their own products, read or write anything substantial, or engage in analytic discussions. And there are few incentives for their teachers to pursue these approaches.

A recent study of the implementation of California's new mathematics curriculum demonstrates that when a curriculum reform aimed at problem solving and the development of higher order thinking skills encounters an already mandated, rote-oriented basic skills testing program, the tests win out (Darling-Hammond, 1990b). As one teacher put it:

> Teaching for understanding is what we are supposed to be doing . . . [but] the bottom line here is that all they really want to know is how are these kids doing on the tests? . . . They want me to teach in a way that they can't test, except that I'm held accountable to the test. It's a Catch 22. (Wilson, 1990, p. 318)

These studies indicate how important it is for schools to choose their "accountability tools" carefully. Clearly, if performance measures are actually to support meaningful learning, they must assess and encourage valuable kinds of teaching in classrooms.

What Alternatives Are Being Developed?

Many educators and researchers are seeking to overcome the problems of standardized testing by developing alternative assessment practices that look directly at students' work and their performances in ways that can evaluate the performances of students, classes, and whole schools. These alternatives are frequently called "authentic" assessments because they engage students in "real world" tasks rather than in multiple choice exercises, and evaluate them according to criteria that are important for actual performance in that field (Wiggins, 1989). Such assessments include oral presentations or performances along with collections of students' written products and their solutions to problems, experiments, debates, and inquiries (Archbald & Newman, 1988). They also include teacher observations and inventories of individual students' work and behavior, as well as of cooperative group projects (NAEYC, 1988).

These kinds of assessment practices directly measure actual performance. They are intended to provide a broad range of continuous, qualitative data that can be used by teachers to inform and shape instruction. They aim to evaluate students' abilities and performances more fully and accurately, and to provide teachers with information that helps them develop strategies that will be helpful to the real needs of individual children.

The "new" assessments more closely resemble assessment in many other countries, which is substantially different from the kind of multiple choice testing common in the United States. Not unlike some of the Advanced Placement tests taken by a small minority of American high school seniors, high school students in most European countries complete extended essay examinations, often coupled with oral examinations, in a range of subjects requiring serious critical thought. The French *Baccalaureat* examination, for example, asks philosophical questions like: "What is judgment?" and "Why should we defend the weak?"—a far cry from the kind of thinking required of most American students who fill in, with number two pencils, fixed response bubbles aimed at identifying a single right answer.

Other countries' assessments also often include practical performance events requiring students to plan, implement, and/or evaluate various tasks, such as the use of scientific procedures or the conduct of a social research project. Some assessments involve the guided development of cumulative portfolios of student work that shape learning opportunities and classroom evaluation over the course of a year or more. Graduation candidates in England submit such portfolios, along with written examinations in three of their chosen areas of specialty. The other exhibitions and oral examinations in which they participate are designed to provide many and varied opportunities for them to display their best work, while allowing their teachers and outside examiners opportunities to probe the nature and quality of their thinking.

In most of these countries, educators have long been actively involved in assessment development rather than relying on commercial testing companies to determine content and manage test administration. Faculties convene to develop and score the assessments. Teachers are involved in examining their own students and also those of teachers in other schools. In many cases, much of the assessment process is internal, in the sense that it is under the control of the teacher and directly tied to ongoing instruction. In these ways, the act of assessment improves knowledge, practice, and shared standards across the educational enterprise as a whole, among both the professional faculty and the students.

What Makes Assessment "Authentic"?

What separates these assessment strategies from traditional forms of testing in the United States? According to Wiggins (1989), authentic assessments have four common characteristics. First, they are designed to be truly representative of performance in the field. Students actually *do* writing—for real audiences—rather than taking spelling tests or answering questions *about* writing. They *conduct* science experiments, rather than memorizing disconnected facts about science. The tasks are contextualized, complex intellectual challenges involving the student's own research or use of knowledge in "ill-structured" tasks requiring the development and use of meta-cognitive skills. They also allow appropriate room for student learning styles, aptitudes, and interests to serve as a source for developing competence and for the identification of (perhaps previously hidden) strengths.

Second, the criteria used in the assessment seek to evaluate "essentials" of performance against well-articulated performance standards. These are openly expressed to students and others in the learning community, rather than kept secret in the tradition of fact-based examinations that are kept "secure." Knowing the tasks and the standards is not "cheating" when a task requires an actual performance, rather than the recognition of a single right answer from a list, and when the task is intrinsically valuable and inherently complex. Learning and performance are both supported when teachers and students know ahead of time that an assessment will focus, for example, on students' demonstrated ability to evaluate competing viewpoints and use evidence in developing a persuasive essay concerning a topic of social importance.

The criteria suggested by such a task represent a performance standard because they are based on explicit and shared school-wide aims, and they are multifaceted, representing the various aspects of a task, rather than reduced to a single dimension or grade. Because the criteria are performance oriented, they guide teaching, learning, and evaluation in a way that illuminates the goals and processes of learning, placing teachers in the role of coach and students in the role of performers, as well as of self-evaluators.

As suggested above, self-assessment plays an important role in authentic tasks. A major goal of authentic assessment is to help students develop the capacity to evaluate their own work against public standards, to revise, modify, and redirect their energies, taking initiative to assess their own progress. This is a major aspect of self-directed work and of the self-motivated improvement required of all human beings in real world situations. Because performance standards take the concept of progress seriously—making the processes of refinement and improvement of products a central aspect of the task and its evaluation—they also allow students of all initial levels of developed competence the opportunity to see, acknowledge, and receive credit for their own growth.

Finally, the students are often expected to present their work publicly and orally. This deepens their learning by requiring that they reflect on what they know and frame it in a way that others can also understand. It also ensures that their apparent mastery of an idea, concept, or topic is genuine. This characteristic of authentic assessment serves other goals as well—signaling to students that their work is important enough to be a source of public attention and celebration; providing opportunities for others in the learning community—students, faculty, and parents—to continually examine, refine, learn from, and appreciate shared goals and achievements; and creating living representations of the purposes and standards of the learning community, so that they remain vital and energizing.

WHAT HAPPENS WHEN SCHOOLS ENGAGE IN
AUTHENTIC ASSESSMENT?

A number of schools, including members of the Coalition of Essential Schools (see Sizer, 1984; 1992), are engaged in creating authentic assessments of student learning. In addition, a growing number of states, including Vermont, California, Connecticut, Maryland, New York, and Texas, are developing new approaches to assessment that will transform state-wide testing. Teachers in Vermont have developed student portfolios in writing and mathematics as the basis of their state's assessment system. Connecticut and New York have begun to develop performance-based assessments that require students to perform a science experiment or solve a real world problem using mathematical and scientific concepts, rather than complete a multiple choice test. California, Maryland, and several other states have developed writing assessments that engage students in complex writing tasks requiring several days of work, including revisions, as part of the examination process. Districts as different from one another as affluent Shoreham-Wading River, New York; urban Pittsburgh, Pennsylvania, Rochester, New York, and Albuquerque, New Mexico—and rural towns in states as far apart as Vermont and Arizona—are also creating authentic assessments to take the place of standardized testing.

Initiatives such as these are an attempt to make schools genuinely accountable for helping students acquire the kinds of complex, integrated skills and abilities they will need to use in the world outside of school. As the Coalition of Essential Schools (1990) explains:

> Of course we want students who are curious, who know how to approach new problems, who use reading and writing across the disciplines as a natural part of that process, who are thoughtful, able, and active citizens. And to get them we (should) make those goals known from the start, test for them regularly, and correct a student's course when necessary. (p. 2)

Those engaged in these efforts argue that keeping track of student growth and development in these "authentic" ways enhances professional development by encouraging teachers to think more deeply about their teaching, its objectives, methods, and results. Because students are involved in developing, exhibiting, and evaluating their own work, it also helps them to develop a sense of responsibility and ownership of their work and encourages them to regularly analyze and reflect on their progress. Authentic evaluation encourages an intelligent, rich curriculum, rather than the narrowed one fostered by teaching and coaching for multiple choice tests. It provides the opportunity for assessment to be directly aligned with educational values, goals, and practices.

The Schools We Studied

Though the schools described in this book were not originally selected to represent a particular reform strategy, as it turned out they are all affiliated with the Coalition of Essential Schools. Our search for places where school-wide authentic assessment practices had been in development for a number of years found the Coalition to be an important catalyst for schools' efforts.

The three secondary schools were selected in part because they have developed programs that integrate academic and vocational education, involving students in internships and other career development activities as well as in assessments that engage them in complex, extended, and often collaborative tasks evaluated by "real world" performance criteria. One of them, Hodgson Vocational Technical School, is in Delaware, a "Re: Learning" state that has been working with the Coalition and other states to rethink local practice and state policy simultaneously. The other four schools are members of the Center for Collaborative Education (CCE), a group of over 35 New York City schools that constitute the Coalition's affiliate in New York, and include the Coalition's first group of elementary schools. The growing CCE network supports the collective learning of schools that are working together to deepen their practice and create new forms of accountability. These partnerships create opportunities for schools to work together on the difficult problems of change, to learn from one another, and to innovate within a learning network that provides intellectual and moral resources for their efforts.

All of the schools serve substantial populations of minority and low-income students, as well as students who have previously been classified as "at-risk" by traditional standardized tests. As their successes, described later on in this book, attest, these schools demonstrate that all children *can* learn when they are well taught in schools that both nurture and challenge them. Students at Central Park East Secondary School are predominantly African American and Latino students from the surrounding low-income East Harlem neighborhood; nearly one third had been classified for special education prior to entering CPESS. Hodgson, in Delaware, serves a heterogeneous population of vocational education students drawn county wide from rural, suburban, and small city communities. Here, too, nearly a third are classified for special education. International High School accepts only recent immigrants, mostly Latinos and Asians, who score below the 20th percentile on New York City's language achievement battery. P.S. 261 and The Bronx New School serve "typical" New York City school populations—a multiracial, multiethnic, multilinguistic mix of students from low-income, working class, and middle class neighborhoods striving to hold family and community together under the stresses of city life.

Though they are different in their programs and emphases and in the populations of students they serve, these schools have in common a commitment to the nine principles of the Coalition (see Figure 1.1). These principles focus on creating schools in which teaching and learning are personalized, student experience is honored, and standards for achievement are both high and made highly attainable by the way the school is organized. The schools' associations with the Coalition are both a result of and a stimulus for ongoing efforts to create school environments that take students' lives and learning seriously, and that enable teachers to come to know the minds of students well and to focus on developing deep understanding and "habits" of mind.

The case studies are based on classroom observations and interviews with staff, students, and parents. They examine:

- How the schools' assessment strategies work in the classroom, in the lives of the students, and in the life of the school as a learning organization
- How various assessment strategies were developed and introduced, how they have evolved, and how they continue to be revised
- What problems have been experienced in using these new forms of assessment
- What effects staff and students feel the assessments have had on instruction and other school activities
- What changes, if any, in classroom organization and student activities have occurred as a result of the assessment strategies
- What effects the assessments may have had on student learning— as suggested by the results of the assessments themselves as well as by other types of indicators.

Our analysis pays particular attention to the ways in which these changes in curriculum and assessment may lessen the disjunctures between what students do in school and what they can expect to do in social settings and workplaces where they are asked to work with others, and to listen and communicate well with co-workers, customers, and fellow citizens. We also examine whether and how the assessments help students learn to use many different strategies for diagnosing problems and improving their work.

The most important question the case studies seek to answer is the extent to which the use of these approaches to assessment encourage schools to adopt goals and develop practices that allow for more authentic teaching and learning. In each of these cases, we conclude that students are indeed working on much more complex tasks, with more outside-of-school relevance, with much greater success than they would otherwise. And in all five, the indicators of student accomplishment—inside and outside school, in both "academic" and "vocational" arenas—are impressive.

Figure 1.1. The Common Principles—
The Coalition of Essential Schools—Brown University

---

1. The school should focus on helping adolescents learn to use their minds well. Schools should not attempt to be "comprehensive" if such a claim is made at the expense of the school's central intellectual purpose.

2. The school's agenda should be simple: that each student master a limited number of essential skills and areas of knowledge. While these skills and areas will, to varying degrees, reflect the traditional academic disciplines, the program's design should be shaped by the intellectual and imaginative powers and competencies that students need, rather than necessarily by "subjects" as conventionally defined. The aphorism "Less is More" should dominate: curricular decisions should be guided by the aim of thorough student mastery and achievement rather than by an effort merely to cover content.

3. The school's goals should apply to all students, while the means to these goals will vary as those students themselves vary. School practice should be tailor-made to meet the needs of every group or class of adolescents.

4. Teaching and learning should be personalized to the maximum feasible extent. Efforts should be directed toward a goal that no teacher have direct responsibility for more than 80 students. To capitalize on this personalization, decisions about the details of the course of study, the use of students' and teachers' time, and the choice of teaching materials and specific pedagogies must be unreservedly placed in the hands of the principal and staff.

5. The governing practical metaphor of the school should be student-as-worker rather than the more familiar metaphor of teacher-as-deliverer-of-instructional-services. Accordingly, a prominent pedagogy will be coaching, to provoke students to learn how to learn and thus to teach themselves.

6. Students entering secondary school studies are those who can show competence in language and elementary mathematics. Students of traditional high school age but not yet at appropriate levels of competence to enter secondary school studies will be provided intensive remedial work to assist them quickly to meet these standards. The diploma should be awarded upon a successful final demonstration of mastery for graduation—an "Exhibition." This Exhibition by the student of his or her grasp of the central skills and knowledge of the school's program may be jointly administered by the faculty and by higher authorities. As the diploma is awarded when earned, the school's program proceeds with no strict age grading and with no system of "credits earned" by "time spent" in class. The emphasis is on the students' demonstration that they can do important things.

7. The tone of the school should explicitly and self-consciously stress values of unanxious expectation ("I won't threaten you but I expect much of you"), of trust (until abuse), and of decency (values of fairness, generosity, and tolerance). Incentives appropriate to the school's particular students and teachers should be emphasized, and parents should be treated as essential collaborators.

(cont'd.)

Figure 1.1. (cont'd.)

---

8. The principal and teachers should perceive themselves as generalists first (teachers and scholars in general education) and specialists second (experts in but one particular discipline). Staff should expect multiple obligations (teacher-counselor-manager) and a sense of commitment to the entire school.

9. Ultimate administrative and budget targets should include, in addition to total student loads per teacher of eighty or fewer pupils, substantial time for collective planning by teachers, competitive salaries for staff, and an ultimate per pupil cost not to exceed that at traditional schools by more than 10 percent. To accomplish this, administrative plans may have to show the phased reduction or elimination of some services now provided students in many traditional comprehensive secondary schools.

In addition to helping teachers and the students themselves evaluate what the students can *really* do, the assessments are highly motivating for students. Sizer points out that they are as much inspiration as measurement: "Giving kids a really good target is the best way to teach them. . . . And if the goal is cast in an interesting way, you greatly increase the chances of their achieving it" (Coalition of Essential Schools, 1990, p. 1).

As a testament to Sizer's claim, every one of the first class of graduates of both International High School in 1988 and Central Park East Secondary School in 1991 was accepted to postsecondary education, and more than 90% of them were accepted to 4-year colleges, a rate more than twice as high as surrounding area high schools. One CPESS student explained his and his classmates' success in terms of the authenticity of goals set and performances achieved: "This environment gives us standards. It makes us look at ourselves in the mirror and feel proud of our accomplishments." When assessment allows students to achieve challenging goals in authentic ways, it creates more than just high scores—it creates confident and capable learners.

The Importance of Contexts for Learning

It is important to recognize that in Coalition schools, exhibitions of learning and other forms of authentic assessment are but one part of a broader set of efforts to restructure education. This is equally true in most other schools that are deeply engaged in authentic assessment development. The integrated nature of school change efforts is important for understanding the possibilities and essential contexts for assessment reforms. None of the practices described in this volume could stand on their own as a single intervention in the lives of schools or students. None of them would stimulate the kinds of deep learning students exhibit without analogous changes in curriculum and teaching, school organization, and opportunities for teachers' collaborative work. In a very real sense, assessment is a part of instruction in these schools: it provides a catalyst for conversations about the quality of teaching and learning, and the nature of the school experience. Rather than "driving" instruction, it evolves from teachers' own development as learners and professionals, and from their ideas about learning and curriculum, which create the basis for assessment and are then informed in turn by occasions for examining student work.

As a result, these assessment strategies are alive and evolving. In fact, the particular tangible procedures or products for assessment—whether portfolios, senior projects, exhibitions, scoring guides, observational forms, or evaluation processes—are means to an end, rather than ends in themselves. They serve as catalysts to bring together teacher and student, student and student, teacher and parent, student and parent, teacher and teacher around examinations of student work and questions of goals and standards. It is the *action* around assessment—the discussions, meetings, revisions, arguments, and opportunities to continually create new directions for teaching, learning, curriculum, and assessment—that ultimately have consequence. The "things" of assessment are essentially useful as dynamic supports for reflection and action, rather than as static products with value in and of themselves.[2]

Furthermore, the context in which assessment is embedded is extremely important. It is clear that the ways in which these schools have restructured schedules and relationships among staff and students are essential to the success of their curriculum and assessment practices. Longer class periods, advisement systems that create strong bonds between students and teachers over time, extended time for faculty collaboration and participation in assessment occasions, structures and practices that create real connections to parents and communities, schools small enough to allow democratic decision making and continual consultation—all of these are factors that enable students and teachers to undertake this challenging work and to find ways to be successful. Layered on top of traditional school structures, curriculum mandates, texts, and teaching practices, these assessment strategies would fail, as would the teachers and students engaged in using them. Thus, these stories must be read whole—as pictures of assessment practices in the context of redesigned work for teachers and students and restructured school organizations; indeed, as deeply embedded, integral components of complex environments teachers have created to help them understand and support their students' learning.

In the chapters that follow, we explore how authentic assessment strategies—embedded in the deeper set of relationships, purposes, and learning opportunities created by these schools—help teachers and students pursue high standards without dysfunctional standardization. We describe how these schools' strategies have helped create a common, collective framework for assessing students' work that also accommodates differing student experiences, interests, and modes of performance. We discuss the ways in which these assessment strategies strive to balance objectivity and subjectivity by using common criteria and multiple viewpoints while considering the context of the work and the development and experience of the student.

Each of these contexts and strategies is different. Chapter 2 describes a highly developed portfolio system for graduating students at Central Park East Secondary School in New York City. This system structures the last two years of high school for these students and covers all aspects of the curriculum, providing new kinds of information for colleges and employers—as well as for teachers and students—to consider. Chapter 3 describes the Senior Project at Hodgson Vocational Technical School in Delaware, a cross-disciplinary capstone assessment prior to graduation that links academic and vocational learning for students and integrates these parts of the school's curriculum for faculty as well. Chapter 4 describes a more informal but pervasive approach to assessing the work of bilingual students at International High School through a variety of projects and portfolios used in interdisciplinary courses structured around collaborative learning and performance. These assessments in secondary schools share a concern for preparing students in the light of "real-world" standards for the work they will encounter when they leave school.

The two elementary school case studies raise other concerns for the development of young children from a variety of home, community, and language backgrounds in settings that will support their growing awareness, competence, and self-confidence in school-based tasks. Chapter 5 describes the use of a strategy for supporting and assessing students' literacy development in a more thorough and authentic fashion than traditional standardized tests. The *Primary Language Record* (*PLR*) provides an approach to structured documentation that many schools are hoping will both support better literacy instruction and provide an alternative to tests they feel are undermining teaching and learning in the early grades. The case study treats the introduction of the *PLR* at P.S. 261, a large "regular" public school in New York City. Chapter 6 describes a more wide-ranging set of strategies for documenting and assessing children's learning at The Bronx New School, a small alternative school in New York that, because it started from scratch, could build virtually all of its reporting and assessment practices around its learner-centered values.

Chapter 7 looks at some of the cross-cutting lessons and concerns illuminated across the case studies. Throughout the book, we examine how assessment can become a dynamic vehicle for school development by spurring ongoing curricular development, professional discourse, and mean-

ingful dialogue among parents, students, and school staff about educational goals and values. Together, the cases document how authentic assessment
can enhance genuine accountability by expanding a school's capacity to be
responsive to student needs and responsible for student learning that is
meaningful in the world outside, as well as inside, school.

NOTES

1. Although the Coalition of Essential Schools began as a secondary school initiative, a group of elementary schools in New York City have become members
through the Center for Collaborative Education, a Coalition affiliate that includes both
secondary and elementary schools.

2. We are indebted to an anonymous reviewer for drawing out this implication of
our work.

2

GRADUATION BY PORTFOLIO AT CENTRAL PARK EAST SECONDARY SCHOOL

Edward*[1] is midway through the presentation of his science portfolio to his graduation committee—his advisor, two other faculty members, and a younger student at Central Park East Secondary School (CPESS). Behind him on the chalkboard are the names of three popular antacids—Milk of Magnesia, TUMS, and Mylanta—along with their chemical names and equations showing how they break down in the presence of acids. A tall, lanky young man with a shy smile, Edward is stalking back and forth, pointing to various parts of the equations, explaining how he found in his experiment that Milk of Magnesia neutralized more acid than did Mylanta or TUMS, but that another group in his class found that baking soda neutralized acid more effectively than did any of these three.

He stops, leaning intently over the desk before him, and queries in an urgent tone: "Now, I asked myself, 'How can this be? How can baking soda perform better than all these others, yet they are doing so much better on the market?'" This is the key moment of an authentic learning experience— the moment when a student challenges himself with a self-initiated question that he is driven to find the answer to.

Edward goes on to explain that when he did further research, he discovered that the American Medical Association does not recommend the use of baking soda because it creates a salt that raises blood pH, and is therefore sometimes harmful to your health. In the remainder of his research, he evaluated the health effects of the different salts produced by each of the other products to reach an answer to the question with which he titled his report: "How do you spell relief?"

When he finishes his presentation, the committee asks a wide range of questions about Edward's experiment, his research process, his conclusions, and other questions that could be investigated following on the heels of the ones he explored. He leaves the room while they deliberate, and then returns to hear how they have evaluated his presentation and portfolio item. The committee members illustrate the basis for their evaluations with con-

crete examples of criteria Edward has met in fulfilling this graduation requirement. Committee member Mardi Tuminaro,[2] a CPESS teacher, tells Edward:

> I gave the paper an "18" [out of 20]. I thought it was a wonderful
> paper. It went beyond the scope of the initial experiment; it provided
> evidence of literature research in addition to the experiment; it was
> clear that you knew what you were doing in the experiment; and I
> loved the way it was written. . . . I gave you a "4" [out of 5] on the
> presentation, because I was somewhat disappointed in your ability to
> explain pH, although I felt that you handled the rest of the presenta-
> tion and questions quite well.

Committee member and CPESS co-director Paul Schwarz follows with
his evaluation: "I loved it. I gave it a '20' across the board. I thought the
paper was clear; it was personal and yet it also acknowledged the work of
the group. It went beyond the problem that you initially stated in terms of
investigating side effects. I understood what you were talking about." And
on a more personal note, he adds: "It brought back some old chemistry
memories!"

As the committee laughs about whether those old memories were likely to have been positive ones, Edward's obvious pride in his accomplishment shows in the irrepressible smile playing at the corners of his mouth.
Being told by respected partners precisely why and how one's work is
interesting, valued, and understood is a confidence-building and compe-
tence-building experience for any of us, and one most teenagers rarely
have the opportunity to encounter. As part of the graduation exercises at
CPESS, it is one that every senior will experience on several occasions over
a year or more, as each of 14 portfolio entries is carefully evaluated, and
as 7 of them are presented before the graduation committee for this kind
of roundtable discussion and assessment.

Edward is a member of the first graduating class of Central Park East Secondary School, which was founded in 1985 by Deborah Meier after she had
successfully created three alternative elementary schools in the same East
Harlem neighborhood. CPESS is an extraordinary secondary school, committed to authentic and learner-centered education, and a school which has
developed an approach to assessing student performance that is itself active,
authentic, and learner-centered. The CPESS graduation portfolio establishes
high standards without standardization, and it creates a dynamic vehicle for
ongoing curriculum development, professional discourse, and meaningful
dialogue among parents, students, and school staff about educational goals
and values. It also allows for a much deeper and more effective accountability for student growth, learning, and preparation to succeed after high
school than most schools provide. The assessment system, embedded as it
is in an organization structured for caring and striving for academic rigor, suc-

ceeds at motivating and deepening student learning rather than deperson-
alizing students and their work.

A HIGH SCHOOL STRUCTURED FOR SUCCESS

Central Park East Secondary School has been carefully designed from its
inception to support students and teachers in their work together. The
school is small and intimate by city standards: its 450 students, in grades
7–12, are largely drawn from the local community, and many attended one
of the three alternative elementary schools out of which CPESS grew. The
students and their parents choose CPESS from among other junior high
schools in District 4's choice system, but the school does not screen students
to create an elite student body. In 1991, when the research for this case
study was conducted, 85% of the students were from Latino and African-
American families, mostly in the neighboring East Harlem community; 60%
qualified for free or reduced-price lunch; and 25% were eligible for special
education services. CPESS shares a building with two other schools, but
maintains its own character and values in the midst of the overwhelming
size, density, and impersonality that tend to characterize New York City Public Schools.

The CPESS information booklet characterizes the commitments that
have guided the school since it was started in 1985:

> In 1985 we promised to be more than a place to "stick it out." Our students
> do stay with us—our drop-out rate is tiny. Our advisory system and small
> class size insure that every student is well known by staff so that they can
> be taught to use their minds well and so that staying in school is the expect-
> ed norm. There are no cracks at CPESS for students to fall through. . . .
> Beyond sticking it out we promised to be a place where learning would
> be challenging, where students would get excited about their work in the
> here and now so they would be prepared to face the future with strength,
> skills and confidence. . . . Finally, we made a promise that CPESS would
> be a caring environment—a place where the answer to the question "Who
> cares?" is answered by a resounding "Everyone!" Everyone does care at
> CPESS and we promise that caring—about each other and about educa-
> tion—will always be our signature. (Central Park East Secondary School
> [CPESS], n.d.)

Visited by over 2,000 educators and others each year, the school has set
a standard for urban education that works for kids: In a city with a graduation rate of only 55% in 5 years, CPESS graduates well over 90% of its ninth
graders within 5 years[3] and does so to much more demanding standards
than most schools. The school also sends more than 90% of its graduates on
to college right after graduation, with others entering college after working

for a year or two. In the first three graduating classes, students have gone on to Ivy League schools, like Columbia, Brown, Vassar, and Wesleyan, as well as to many campuses in the State University of New York system, to in-state private colleges, like Syracuse and New York University, and to historically black colleges, like Spellman and Hampshire. As we describe later, students find when they reach these campuses that they hold their own admirably, that they have indeed learned to use their minds well, and that they are confident in doing so.

With these extraordinary outcomes, one might conjure an image of a school that is idyllic and problem-free. Yet CPESS is not a fairy tale school. Meier (1992) describes how the community copes with the realities of urban education—the police finding crack vials near the front door (left by the dealers who ply their trade in front of the school); teens who must traverse hostile territory to and from school; young women who become pregnant; children who see friends and parents die from gunshots and AIDS. Co-director Paul Schwarz notes:

> We are supported. There's a synergy and a community that lifts us up.
> But we're real, too. There is anger and there are problems. It's real
> and messy and noisy. We all struggle with the same issues. You strug-
> gle every day with teaching and students. We have all the issues any
> institution would have with 450 adolescents.

The struggles are more successful because the school is structured to create a community that can, in turn, create bonds of caring that withstand the stresses that can otherwise easily overwhelm students, their families, and their teachers. The small size and communal nature of CPESS are an important key to its ability to create strong bonds with students and parents—the basis of genuine accountability. As Meier explained in a *New York Times* editorial:

> A good school can't work without greater trust and support from families.
> But trust comes from parents, teachers and students knowing each other over
> a period of time. . . . Trust builds and issues that arise get settled handily.
> Accountability to parents, as well as to the community, is a less knotty prob-
> lem. (Meier, 1989)

That the school is small enough to permit such familiarity and trust is deliberate. Research and experience demonstrate that smaller, more personal schools are more effective in heightening achievement, in graduating students, in creating good interpersonal relationships, and in providing leadership opportunities to students (Fowler, 1992; Gottfredson & Daiger, 1979; Green & Stevens, 1988; Haller, 1992; Howley, 1989;

Howley & Huang, 1991). Most important, these schools are more effective in allowing students to become bonded to important adults in a learning community, which can play the role that other communities and families find more and more difficult to fulfill. CPESS has consciously created such a learning community, and its assessment practices are a crucial element in what constitutes the community's core—its focus on meaningful learning.

Accountability for Meaningful Learning

A commitment to authentic teaching, learning, and assessment at CPESS is part of its approach to accountability. It shares this commitment with other members of the Coalition of Essential Schools, a network of restructuring secondary schools to which CPESS belongs. This commitment to authenticity leads to a naturally integrated approach to academic and vocational instruction and to instruction across the disciplines. Tracking has never been a part of the curriculum structure at CPESS. There is neither an academic track nor a vocational track for students. Intellectual and experiential work are part of the common core for everyone. Application of knowledge in real world contexts that are personally and socially relevant is the proving ground for all forms of learning at the school.

Among the principles that guide CPESS and the Coalition of Essential Schools are several that serve as a foundation for these practices.

1. *Less is more.* It is more important to understand some things well than to know many things superficially. Schools must focus on the essential skills, areas of knowledge, and habits of mind that are central to students becoming well educated members of society.
2. *Student as worker.* Learning is not an observer sport. Students must be active participants and active citizens, discovering answers and solutions, and learning by doing rather than by simply repeating what texts or teachers say.
3. *Goal setting and assessment.* High standards are set for all students. Students should be evaluated on the basis of their performance, not hours spent or credits earned. Performance assessment should be as direct and authentic as possible. Graduation should be based on demonstrated mastery over clearly stated competencies related to the school's goals.
4. *Personalization.* Schools should be personalized to the greatest extent possible. Learning units should be organized so that students and adults remain together in small communities over several years so they can get to know each other well. (CPESS, n.d.; Center for Collaborative Education [CCE], n.d.)

As we describe below, the school makes good on these commitments through its policies, its structures, and its practices, ranging from curriculum through assessment and including organizational arrangements and relationships between and among students, teachers, and parents.

THE RATIONALE FOR PORTFOLIO-BASED GRADUATION

In 1987, three years before the first cohort of CPESS students would reach their senior year, Deborah Meier, the school director, and Haven Henderson, who would become the Senior Institute director, went to Racine, Wisconsin, to examine the system of portfolio assessment entitled "Rites of Passage" (ROPE), developed a decade earlier by an alternative public school called Walden III. They spoke to students, parents, and staff, and observed the program in action, confirming their interest in adopting a similar performance-based assessment grounded in active learning experiences for students. A major attraction was that the performance-based exhibitions in the Walden model created the "real live audience for schoolwork" that Meier and Henderson sought.

The CPESS committee returned to New York and shared the ROPE system with the rest of the staff. During the next 2 years, the staff, along with parents, other educators, and the Coalition of Essential Schools, worked to create their own assessment system and the *Senior Institute Handbook,* which lays out the philosophy of the school and its relation to the graduation requirements:

> The fundamental aim of CPESS is to teach students to use their minds well and prepare them to live productive, socially useful, and personally satisfying lives. . . . The curriculum affirms the central importance of students learning how to learn, how to reason, and how to investigate complex issues that require collaboration, personal responsibility and a tolerance for uncertainty. Students graduate only when they have demonstrated an appropriate level of mastery in each area. (CPESS, 1991)

Since its inception, CPESS has been focused on developing an environment for learning that permits students to construct their own knowledge, develop their capacities for independent reasoning and action, and develop "habits" of mind and behavior that will enable them to be competent, responsible citizens. The portfolio system of graduation supports all of these goals, and because of its focus on creating a corpus of high quality work, it is especially conducive to the development of sustained habits of thought and work. The projects require research and planning; they demand that students organize their time and their thoughts; commit to an in-depth process of inquiry, critique, and reflection on a variety of topics and on their own work; acknowledge and participate in standard-setting; and find their own voice in the process.

As one recent graduate described the effect of the portfolio work on her current abilities:

> It's worth all the work you do in 12th grade. It prepares you for college. The outcome is that we're able to tell somebody what we think. We can think critically, go in-depth, and research things on our own. We can express our viewpoint and back it up.

Darwin Davis, a father of one of the first graduates and chair of the parent association, concurs that the portfolio process supports the school's most ambitious goals for students.

> The portfolio is an attempt—a successful attempt in my view—to document the *variety* of student skills, not just math skills or just reading skills which too often other schools focus on to the detriment of other learning skills and other learning areas. It was an extraordinary amount of work to produce those 14 portfolio items. One student explained it this way at one of the CPESS assessment conferences: "My mother just completed her Ph.D. and she had one dissertation. We had 14." . . . It took that same kind of work: Those students invested their time, their energy, their smarts, their peers, and their committee in producing 14 different portfolio items, which reflected their ability, what they'd learned [and] where they wanted to go in their lives.

Students' intellectual development at CPESS is guided by five "Habits of Mind," which embody the goals of the school and permeate the entire curriculum. They are:

1. Weighing evidence: How do we know what we know? What is the evidence and is it credible?
2. Awareness of varying viewpoints: What viewpoint are we hearing, seeing, reading? Who is the author and what are her/his intentions?
3. Seeing connections and relationships: How are things connected to each other? Where have we heard or seen this before?
4. Speculating on possibilities: What if . . . ? Can we imagine alternatives?
5. Assessing value both socially and personally: What difference does it make? Who cares? (CPESS, 1990)

In classrooms throughout the school, the Habits of Mind are prominently displayed. These modes of inquiry guide the assessment of student work throughout CPESS and appear as criteria incorporated into assessment instruments for the required Graduation Portfolio. In developing its graduation requirements, CPESS staff engaged in a process of "planning backwards" (McDonald, 1993), asking first, "What kind of graduate do we want?" then, "How do we get there?" and, finally, "How will we know when we have arrived?" This third question has led CPESS to develop graduation requirements—and structures within which students prepare for these requirements and for later life—that reflect the values and goals of the school for what students ought to know and be able to do.

These goals are to enable students to be well prepared for all aspects of life in a complex and changing world. They are not academic, on the one hand, or vocational, on the other. Nor are they predetermined by what role or job students see themselves as assuming in the future: Although students' goals are important as entry points to their interests and motivations, they do not differentiate or limit students' curriculum options. The school's goals are to enable students to live empowered lives in which they can continue to learn whatever they need to be successful at whatever they care about—and to be contributors in their fields of work as well as to their local communities. As this extract from a CPESS newsletter notes about the Habits of Mind:

> What we set about looking for was a set of "intellectual habits" that make us good at handling important ideas. It's these "habits of mind" that make us life-time learners and useful citizens. What are these mental habits? It seemed to us that well-educated people have a habit of asking certain kinds of questions. We spent a lot of time trying to come up with the ones that were most powerful. We wanted the ones that were used by a top-notch auto mechanic, computer technician, writer, doctor, or lawyer. We were looking for habits that are needed by historians as well as mathematicians. We were looking for the habits that keep citizens from being conned by "experts," and that serve us well at home as well as at work. We wanted habits that held up well in college, as well as the streets. We invented five. We could have found many more, but we liked these best. We hope you do too. (CPESS, 1991, Oct.)

THE SENIOR INSTITUTE

While the aims of the school express an idea of the kind of graduate CPESS wants, the Senior Institute is an important aspect of how the school hopes to get there. The Senior Institute is the division of the school that in most traditional structures would be identified as grades 11 and 12,[4] and it is consciously designed to serve as a transitional stage of increasing self-responsibility prior to entry into the "adult" world of college or work. The increasing independence afforded the students is intended to help them learn to manage their affairs while there is still a safety net.

The Foundation for the Senior Institute

There are a number of structural features of the school that support students and teachers in their work in the years prior to and throughout the Senior Institute (see Figure 2.1). In divisions I and II, students pursue a common core curriculum, featuring 2 hours daily in each of two team-taught inter-

Figure 2.1

Central Park East Secondary School Structure

Grades 7/8 - Division I

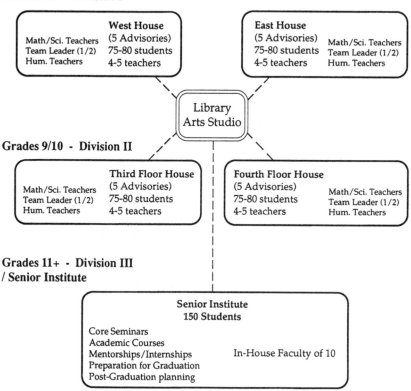

West House		**East House**
Math/Sci. Teachers — (5 Advisories)	(5 Advisories) — Math/Sci. Teachers	

West House
Math/Sci. Teachers
Team Leader (1/2)
Hum. Teachers
(5 Advisories)
75-80 students
4-5 teachers

East House
(5 Advisories)
75-80 students
4-5 teachers
Math/Sci. Teachers
Team Leader (1/2)
Hum. Teachers

Library
Arts Studio

Grades 9/10 - Division II

Third Floor House
Math/Sci. Teachers
Team Leader (1/2)
Hum. Teachers
(5 Advisories)
75-80 students
4-5 teachers

Fourth Floor House
(5 Advisories)
75-80 students
4-5 teachers
Math/Sci. Teachers
Team Leader (1/2)
Hum. Teachers

Grades 11+ - Division III / Senior Institute

Senior Institute
150 Students

Core Seminars
Academic Courses
Mentorships/Internships   In-House Faculty of 10
Preparation for Graduation
Post-Graduation planning

Division I & II Daily Schedule

8-9am	Spanish	**Note:** One day per week for
9-1	2 Hours each of Humanities and Math/Science	school/community service occu-
1-2pm	1/2 hour educational options and 1/2 hour lunch	pies the first 2 - 1/2 hours of the
2-3	1 hour Advisory	day for students while faculty
3-5	Extended day options	meets for curriculum planning.

disciplinary courses—humanities/social studies and mathematics/science—along with an hour-long Spanish course and a one-hour advisory. These courses take place within houses of 4–5 teachers and 75–80 students, each of which, along with the advisories, helps to personalize students' experience of the school. Students remain with the same teachers and peer group within their house for two years, until they "move up" to the next division.

The advisory is one of the school's key strategies for ensuring that students cannot "fall through the cracks." Each professional staff member works over a period of 2 years with a group of 15 students and their families, providing academic and personal supports of many kinds. The advisory period is used as a study time, an opportunity for quiet reading and writing, for discussion of health, social, and ethical issues, and for one-on-one and group advising and counseling. The advisor is the "expert" on the student, meeting frequently with the family and with other teachers to ensure communication about the student's needs and progress, to "tap the family's expertise" (CPESS, n.d.) and to guide the student through courses, exhibitions, and graduation requirements.

Students in divisions I and II also spend 2 ½ hours weekly in a community service program, tutoring younger students, working with senior citizens, and working in community settings, like museums and other nonprofit organizations. While these experiences help them to understand the adult world, explore occupations, and develop a sense of social responsibility and initiative, the community service time also allows their teachers to spend at least one morning per week engaged in team planning, so that the school's promises about high-quality curriculum and teaching in a caring environment can be fulfilled.

Putting Students at the Helm

These opportunities prepare students for the much more demanding and student-directed work they will encounter in the Senior Institute. While there is a set of core seminars that all students take, much of the work in the Senior Institute is structured around a process of negotiation aimed at simultaneously achieving each student's goals plus the school's goals. Students can design their course of study within the broad guidelines of the core requirements of literature, social studies, mathematics, science, and Spanish. The school offers a variety of literature courses; history, political science, sociology, and economics; biology, physiology, and chemistry; advanced geometry and algebra, trigonometry and statistics; and courses in art and video, as well as in Spanish.

In addition, each student participates in a work-related internship and attends at least two courses on college campuses. Some of these are regular college courses; others are courses offered for high school students at campuses like Lang College, Columbia University's Teachers College, and others. These two curricular components place students outside the school in the "adult" arenas of work and college, where they are evaluated by "real world" standards. Rather than trying to create courses or tests that would seek to predict, probably poorly, whether or not students are likely to succeed in college or in employment settings, the Senior Institute places them in these situations in which they are evaluated and can then test themselves directly against the actual criteria for performance that such experiences call for. This is authentic teaching, learning, and assessment in its most immediate and genuine form.

Tamika,* for example, currently enrolled in a college course on Greek Mythology, understands from her experience what the standards in college are likely to be:

> I am reading *The Iliad* by Homer, and the readings are very hard. I have to go over it twice to really get the idea of what's going on. It really does help to reread a few times. Everything is hard, [for example] writing papers like college kids do. At CPESS you draft a lot, but not as much as they do. They draft and draft and draft. I'm thinking, "When I get to college, it's going to be exactly like this." And at least I'll have an advantage. I'll know what they're going to expect.

The Internship: Crossing the Divide

The Senior Institute internships, which follow on the heels of the community service experiences in the lower grades, are placements in work settings totaling 100 hours over the course of a semester. Students work in a wide range of settings: as office helpers at banks, publishers, and other businesses; as photographers and writers for nonprofit organizations; as elementary school teacher aides, veterinarian aides, computer programmers, and so on. A concurrent seminar is conducted on related issues, such as work policies and practices that students can explore at the worksite and then discuss with their peers.

Senior Institute teacher Joe Walters credits the internship with helping students really begin to make the transition to young-adult decision makers. Internships require students to take responsibility and look at themselves in terms of the role they play within the context of an institution for which they are working. They keep a log and make a presentation at the end. This process helps them develop their ideas about careers and the world of work in the real world.

Whether or not students will be enrolling in college, they are better prepared for their futures in tangible and intangible ways. Joe Walters offers two examples:

> One of my advisees is doing carpentry at CoopTech. He said from the beginning that he was not interested in going to college. He really likes it, and he's developing connections with people on the outside. He most likely will be employed in looking into how he's going to get into the union.

Another of Joe's students wants to be an architect. In the course of planning for his future, this student took the initiative in checking out a program at a school Joe had recommended as having a good program. By doing so, he learned that that particular school did not offer a degree in architecture, so he began to expand his search on his own, not reliant on adult guidance to help him pursue his interests.

Students see their accomplishments in the internship as extending far beyond that particular experience. Steve* explains how the internship builds confidence and competence:

> With the community service program and internships and all the things that we do outside of the school, this makes us look at ourselves and say, "Wow! I worked with little kids who couldn't do such and such, and when I was finished with them, they were on their way to doing it. I did a good job in that place." Things like that show that you are good at doing other things.

Assessment in the Senior Institute

The completion of 14 portfolio requirements, along with the coursework and internships described above, is the glue of the Senior Institute's curriculum. The portfolio requirements help students accomplish authentic work in each of the areas the school values, and helps them to do so in ways that fundamentally connect to the students' own experiences, interests, values, and goals, preparing them to take charge of their own lives. The requirements describe tasks that students are expected to tackle and standards they are expected to meet, both within and outside the bounds of traditional coursework. The curriculum is grounded in multiple assessment opportunities and encourages students to learn to reflect on and evaluate their own work and experiences. Because the requirements are performance-based, the criteria are open and constantly discussed, and the work is viewed as always in process and improving, students thus have control over their ability to succeed. They learn that time and effort, self-discipline, and organization make the difference in being able to achieve their goals.

These qualities are, of course, the kinds of "generic," work-related skills frequently identified in recent discourse about the changing needs of American industry and the changing demands of the workforce. The capacity to structure one's work, find resources, and use them for accomplishing complex tasks is at the heart of these school reform demands, and at the core of CPESS's goals and curriculum. As the portfolio requirements demonstrate, defining school outcomes in terms of such qualities also blurs traditional distinctions between vocational and academic work, and expands the definitions of both. CPESS graduates are preparing themselves to "do" history or science as vocations as much as they are preparing themselves to work with computers, photography, child care, or other areas traditionally thought of as vocational-technical training. All areas are approached from a performance-oriented stance—and all are open to all students as areas for further academic and vocational exploration.

Parent Darwin Davis articulates how CPESS deliberately structures an educational experience that addresses what the broader society really wants from schools:

> What's ironic is if you ask an employer, a politician, a school professional, a student, a parent, a principal what they would expect a student to be after completing the academic process, most of the qualities that are enumerated speak to the ability to work with other people, to synthesize information, to think a problem through, to solve issues, to work collectively, maybe to benefit the environment, the community, or some other idealistic goal, very few of which are typical subjects or issues that are addressed in your normal school setting. CPESS has been able to combine the best of both worlds—that individual who can work with other people, who is a problem solver, who is a leader in their own right, but who is academically grounded as well.

Structures for Learner-Centered Practice

In order for students and faculty to be able to undertake such ambitious goals, CPESS is organized so that teaching and learning time is structured much differently than it is in traditional schools. Teachers, especially Senior Institute teachers, have time for their roles as advisor, mentor, tutor, coach, and assessor because CPESS allocates almost all of its staff to the classroom rather than to administrative slots or to roles peripheral to the classroom (there are, for example, no counselors or specialists), thus affording more "teacher power" on a budget that is not equivalently larger. In addition, it uses external learning experiences—such as coursework at local colleges and required internships—in lieu of some classes.

These strategies allow Senior Institute teachers to spend about half of their time advising students rather than teaching classes. They teach traditional courses about 12 hours per week, spending another 5 hours weekly leading their 12-member advisories, and many more hours working on portfolio development and graduation committee meetings with their individual advisees.[5] Given that Senior Institute advisors accompany their advisees on college visits—as well as supporting them through courses and internships, helping them conceptualize their portfolios and locate resources, and serving as facilitator, backstop, and cheerleader—their student-focused time is a critical investment in students' later success, and in the success of the portfolio process.

Another structural feature that supports student success is teachers' ability to work with students in a way that integrates content and enables them to come to know students well over time. As math/science teacher Edwina Branch explains about her move to CPESS from a traditional school setting:

I was teaching physics in a traditional high school and at the time I was enjoying the kids but I wasn't enjoying the situation. I wasn't enjoying the Regents curriculum and the pressure of having the kids pass that test. I remember thinking, "I wish I taught the kids math. If I had them for a longer period of time and if I had them for both math and science, then maybe I could make sure." Then I read about CPESS and I read *Horace's Compromise* and it was very validating. You should have kids for a longer period of time. It just made sense to me. When I got the opportunity to come to CPESS, I came and it was great. But then the things I had—the Regents exam, the textbook, the tests I could give at the end of the chapter were not enough. . . .

Having created the conditions under which students can learn well and deeply, CPESS has been propelled to find ways of evaluating that learning that are also more useful and more telling.

THE PORTFOLIO

During the 2 (or sometimes 3) years in the Senior Institute, students complete portfolio requirements[6] across fourteen categories and present their completed portfolio to a graduation committee comprised of the student's faculty advisor, another faculty member, a third adult of the student's choosing, and another student. Of the fourteen portfolio items, seven are presented orally before the Graduation Committee, four from the core subjects (asterisked below). The other seven entries are evaluated independently, and the student may be asked about them during the Graduation Committee hearing. While the final review is based on the individual student's accomplishments, certain portfolio requirements can be based on group work. The portfolio requirements include the following:

1. *Post Graduate Plan:* Students must outline their current purpose for earning a diploma; as the Handbook notes, "Reflecting on purposes helps to set goals." Long- and short-range career and life goals, financial concerns, living arrangements, and indicators of progress—such as examinations, interviews, letters of reference, and so on—must be included in this section. The Post Graduate Plan is begun at entry to the Senior Institute and provides direction for all of the student's subsequent work in the Senior Institute. It is revised as needed and revisited for evaluation at the time of graduation.

2. *Autobiography:* Autobiographies provide another opportunity for students to reflect on their lives and to plan for the future. A project of the student's choosing is required. It may examine family history, special events or relationships, or values or beliefs in any of a variety of media—written or oral narrative, essay, art, video, drama, music, or other forms selected by the student.

3. *School/Community Service and Internship:* Opportunities for working and serving others are part of student experiences each year, starting in 7th grade. Students must develop a formal resume of their past work and employment experiences, along with a project that demonstrates what they have learned from one or more of these experiences. Projects can include essays, videos, work samples, reference letters, or other demonstrations of their accomplishments, combined with evidence of what they have learned.

4. *Ethics and Social Issues:* Students can demonstrate their capacity to see multiple perspectives, weigh and use evidence, and reason about social and moral issues in any of a number of ways—by staging a debate, writing an editorial, discussing important issues raised in a novel or film, or creating another project that demonstrates these capacities.

5. *Fine Arts and Aesthetics:* Creative expression and creative appreciation are both evaluated. Students must create a "hands-on" exhibition of performance in any of the arts, and must offer evidence of knowledge or understanding in an aesthetic area by studying or critiquing a work, an artist, or a field of artistic expression.

6. *Mass Media:* Students must show that they understand how different forms of media work and how they affect people and their thinking, including the CPESS habits of mind. This understanding can be demonstrated through many types of projects or activities—ranging from essays to exhibits or media presentations—and must include a relevant bibliography.

7. *Practical Skills:* In line with CPESS's commitment to preparing students for all aspects of life, they must show evidence of working knowledge in a number of areas—ranging from health and medical care to employment, citizenship, independent living, computers and technology, and legal rights—in a variety of ways, ranging from securing a driver's license to registering to vote to demonstrating the ability to operate a computer.

8. *Geography:* A faculty-designed test and a student-designed performance assessment are used to evaluate knowledge about geography and the ability to use tools such as maps and globes.

9. *Second Language and/or Dual Language:* All students must demonstrate competence to work in a language other than English as a speaker, listener, reader, and writer.[7] In addition, all students must describe their personal experience with dual language issues and be prepared to discuss a key social or cultural issue associated with language use.

10. *Science and Technology:** Students must demonstrate knowledge in traditional ways—a summary of the work they have completed in high school and passage of a faculty-designed or state competency test—as well as in performances that demonstrate use of scientific methodology (e.g., conducting and documenting an experiment) and awareness of how science is used in the modern world (e.g., by staging a debate or conducting research on a scientific development, analyzing social costs and benefits).

11. *Mathematics:** Students must demonstrate basic skills knowledge by

passing a state competency test and a faculty-designed test. In addition, they must demonstrate higher order thinking abilities by developing a project using mathematics for political, civic, or consumer purposes (e.g., social science statistics or polling, evaluation data, architectural blueprints) and either scientific or "pure" mathematics (e.g., using mathematics in a scientific application and/or studying a mathematical topic or problem for its own sake).

12. *Literature:** Students prepare a list of texts they have read in a wide range of genres to serve as the basis for discussion with the Graduation Committee. They also submit samples of their own essays about literary works or figures, demonstrating their capacity to reflect on and communicate effectively about literary products and ideas.

13. *History:** In addition to passing a state competency test or faculty-designed test in history, students must prepare an overview of the areas of history they have studied in secondary school and a time line of major events and persons. They must also demonstrate understanding of historical work by conducting historical research using primary as well as secondary sources and developing a bibliography. They apply the Habits of Mind by drawing connections between and among past and present events, weighing and using evidence, speculating on other possibilities, and evaluating how history is used or abused in current debates.

14. *Physical Challenge:* Students demonstrate and/or document their participation and proficiency in any team or individual competitive or non-competitive sport or activity over the past four years. The goal is to encourage the development of life-long health habits and attitudes of independence, interdependence, personal responsibility, and sportsmanship.

A more extensive final senior project is also required in an area of particular interest to the student, which may be one of the portfolio items explored in greater depth.

There is no one way to complete these requirements, nor is there only one way to present them. Work completed to meet one requirement can be used to fulfill other requirements. Students can use work that they began in Division II, developing it further during their years in the Senior Institute. Because knowledge and skills are constructed and demonstrated in many different ways, CPESS encourages diverse modes of presentation: research papers, videos, constructions, and original theater pieces, as well as individual and group projects. As students prepare a wide array of products and presentations for their portfolios, they develop competencies in the analytic, creative, and practical domains and have opportunities to work cooperatively and communally. The portfolios become a vehicle for developing as well as assessing their abilities.

Quality, depth of understanding, and a demonstration of mastery of the particular subject area and the habits of mind are the major criteria for evaluating all of the portfolio items. Figure 2.2 illustrates how the habits of mind have been incorporated into a rubric for scoring portfolio items, with descriptors of levels of mastery ranging from "needs more work" to "exceeds our standards." Another scoring system has been developed for evaluating the oral presentations (see Figure 2.3). These evaluations ultimately result in a grade of "minimally satisfactory," "satisfactory," or "distinguished" for each portfolio entry. These standards, and the criteria by which work will be evaluated, are available to the students, who use them to guide their efforts, beginning in the lower divisions of CPESS.

The fourteen portfolio areas attempt to accommodate the tensions between breadth and depth. They provide breadth by their number, but within each area students complete in-depth projects. The portfolio is also intended to reflect cumulative knowledge and skill in each area—with the expectation that much work will be interdisciplinary, and thus will fall into more than one area for evaluation.

A Glimpse at a Portfolio

Marlena's* transcript illustrates how all of these efforts came together in a challenging and personally compelling body of work during her Senior Institute years. The first page of her transcript (Figure 2.4), though nontraditional in format, gives us most of the traditional information colleges would seek about her course-taking and test scores. She took a strong mathematics and science sequence during those two years, including precalculus and Pascal 1 and 2, chemistry 1 and 2, genetics, and several science courses at Hunter College, as well as required courses in literature, social studies, and her internship. In addition, she passed all of the Regents Competency Tests required by the State of New York, along with the City University of New York (CUNY) placement tests, and also secured creditable scores on the SAT and College Board Achievement Tests.

The second page of the transcript (Figure 2.5) provides a more personalized glimpse of Marlena's work, listing the titles of her fourteen portfolio entries. How these intersect and express her interests and views can be seen by looking inside the portfolio, a weighty collection of papers contained in a large accordion folder. Her science and technology portfolio, "Construction of Expression Vectors with Phosphatases 1 & 2A," reports on an experiment on cancer-causing cell transformations conducted as part of her internship in a Minority Research Apprenticeship Program at Hunter College. Marlena's sophisticated treatment of the complex set of procedures she undertook and her fearless discussion of oncogenes and other aspects of cell biology depict a young person well-launched on a scientific career. In the section on materials and methods she explains her procedures, which are accompanied by detailed lab sheets and findings:

Figure 2.2. Habits of Mind

Student: _____

Advisor: _____

Portfolio Item: _____

	VIEWPOINT	CONNECTIONS
	Encompasses Wide Knowledge Base But Is Focused • Clearly identifies, addresses key questions & ideas. • Demonstrates an in-depth understanding of the issues. • Presents position persuasively and discusses other views when appropriate.	The Whole Is Greater Than the Sum of the Parts • Explains signficance of problems/issues beyond the project. • Conjectures, predicts, and explains observations where appropriate. • Organized so that all parts support the whole. • Contains useful transition. • Concludes in a satisfying way.
EXCEEDS 4	Paper demonstrates an in-depth understanding of the issues. Presents position very persuasively, and clearly discusses other views when appropriate.	This paper has a helpful beginning and concludes in a satisfying way. • It is organized so that all parts support the whole. • It makes effective transitions. • It makes larger connections.
MEETS 3	Paper shows a good understanding of position taken and is focused. Discusses other positions when appropriate.	The paper has a clear beginning and ending. • It is organized so that most parts support the whole. • It makes transitions. • It attempts to make larger connections.
AP- PROACHES 2	A position is implied but not clearly stated. Focus is inconsistent.	The paper has a beginning and an ending. • Connections of parts to the whole are sometimes made. • Some transitions are made.
NEEDS MORE 1	Lacks focus, does not present a position. Lacks direction.	The text does not have either a beginning or an ending (one or both). • It is not yet able to connect the parts to the whole.

Figure 2.2 (cont'd.)

Date: _____

Title of Paper: _____

Reader: _____

Score: _____

EVIDENCE	VOICE	CONVENTIONS
Credible/Convincing	Engaging	Legible and Intelligible
• Generalizations & ideas supported by specific relevant and accurate information, which is developed in appropriate depth. • Contains discussion of strengths and weaknesses of evidence. • Cites appropriate resources. • Uses graphs, formulas, figures, and equations accurately.	• Lively, interesting use of language. • Awareness of reader (explains concepts so they are understandable to the lay person). • Student uses own language.	• Excellent appearance; • Correct format. • Varied sentence structure. • Good mechanics and standard notation. • Appropriate, broad vocabulary and word usage.
Generalizations & ideas supported by specific, relevant and accurate information. The above is developed in appropriate depth and contains clear discussion of the evidence: its strength and weaknesses.	Lively interesting use of language. Awareness of audience.	Excellent appearance, correct format (including bibliography, footnotes, references, etc., where applicable), varied sentence structure, good mechanics (spelling, punctuation, capitalization, paragraphing), appropriate broad vocabulary and word usage.
Evidence supports main ideas with specific, accurate, relevant information consistently throughout the paper. Paper includes an attempt to discuss evidence.	Appropriate language, style, and tone chosen.	Neat, legible, minimal number of mechanical and syntactical errors which do not interfere with understanding, appropriate paragraphing, and transition. Correct use of vocabulary. Appropriate format.
Includes some evidence relevant to the topic but which is inconsistently applied and not well-developed throughout the paper. Many general statements and opinions without specific evidence. May contain some discussion of evidence.	Shows some awareness of reader and attempts to inform. Language, style, or tone confused.	Sentence structure needs variation. Limited vocabulary and word choice uses, mechanical errors which interfere with understanding.
Mostly general statements. Little specific evidence relating to the topic.	Little awareness of readers. No particular language, style, or tone adopted.	Sentence structure needs development; mechanics, (spelling, punctuation, etc.) interfere with understanding; incorrect use of words; sloppy appearance; difficult to read; omits words and phrases.

Figure 2.3. Oral Presentation Examination form

Student: _____

Advisor: _____

Title of Paper: _____

Portfolio Item: _____

Committee Member: _____

Score: _____

1. Student gives 5- to 7-minute presentation.
2. The Committee questions student.
3. The Student leaves the room.
4. The Committee discusses and rates the oral presentation.
5. The Committee discusses grids.
6. The Student is recalled to begin next presentation.
7. The Committee gives feedback at the end of all presentations.

RATINGS		Articulation Categories: •Student gives effective, clear, convincing presentation of the subject. •Concepts are explained to indicate thorough understanding of ideas and their ramifications. •Clarity of expression and credible evidence are offered. •Student shows creativity, style and poise. •Student gives intelligent response to questions.	
EXCELLENT presentation	5	Student is very convincing and addresses all categories.	
GOOD presentation	4	Student presents material well and articulates all but one or two of the categories.	
ACCEPTABLE presentation	3	The presentation needs to be more informed, in one or more areas, although not substantially.	
APPROACHES acceptable level	2	The presentation may be improved with more attention given to the weaknesses which leave the audience unconvinced.	
NEEDS more	1	The student's presentation was generally weak in most areas.	
SCORE			

Comments: _____

Figure 2.4 Student transcript

Central Park East Secondary School
1573 Madison Avenue, N.Y. N.Y. 10029
Tel: (212) 860-5933
    (212) 410-5216 (counselor)
Fax: (212) 876-3494
ETS Code: 332964

Coalition of Essential Schools
Community School District 4
NYC Board of Education

Last Name	First Name	Middle		Soc Sec #	OSIS #

Street Address			Borough	State	Zip Code

Parent/Guardian		Date of Birth	Sex

Previous High School (if any)	Date of Enrollment at CPESS	Expected Graduation Date

TRANSCRIPT OF COURSES

The following courses were taken in preparation for the Portfolio. Please refer to the Curriculum Bulletin for course descriptions and grading information. CPESS gives grades only on completion of a course of study, which requires demonstration of minimum competence. Courses are interdisciplinary and students demonstrate a variety of skills; grades therefore represent a range as follows:

Dist   = **Distinguished Work**   **Sat** = **Satisfactorily met requirements**
MinSat = **Minimally met requirements**   **Audit** = **Course not taken for evaluation**
** =   **College Course** (see Curriculum Bulletin for details)

Division II (9th) 1988/89

Humanities (Lit., History, Art)	Sat+
Math	Sat+
Science	Sat+
Advisory	Dist
Community Service	Dist

Division II (10th) 1989/90

Humanities (Lit., History, Art)	Dist
Math	Dist
Science	Dist
Advisory	Dist
Community Service	Dist
Spanish	Dist

Senior Inst, Fall 1990

Sci Foundations, Hunter	C**
Precal & Pascal 1	Sat
Lit: Autobiography	Sat
Internship	Sat+

Senior Inst, Spring 1991

Precal & Pascal 2	Sat+
Chemistry 1	Dist
Linquistics: 1000 Words	Sat+
Civil Rights History	Dist

Senior Inst, Fall 1991

Chemistry 2	Dist
Mass Media	Sat+
Lit: Essay	Sat+
Science Research, Hunter	Dist

Senior Inst, Spring 1992

Genetics	Dist
Rethinking Columbus	Sat
Science Research, Hunter	Dist

Standardized Tests

Regents Competency Tests

Reading	Pass
Writing	Pass
Math	Pass
Science	Pass
US History	Pass
Global Studies	Pass

Languages

Spanish	Pass

CUNY Placement Tests

Reading	Pass
Writing	Pass
Math	Pass

SAT's   3/91

Math	600
Verbal	430

Other Tests

ACH ENG	520
ACH MATH	530
ACH CHEM	550

Signature, Principal   Date

SEAL MUST BE AFFIXED

Figure 2.5 Transcript of portfolios

Central Park East Secondary School
1573 Madison Avenue, New York, NY 10029   **(212) 860-8936**

TRANSCRIPT OF PORTFOLIOS

Please refer to the Curriculum Bulletin for Portfolio requirements. A Portfolio is graded on the basis of all items within it as well as knowledge and skill defended before the student's Graduation Committee. Listed below is the title of the student's major work in each area as well as the cumulative grade. Individual portfolio items are available on request.

Dist	=	**Distinguished Work**	**Sat** =	**Satisfactorily met requirements**
MinSat	=	**Minimally met requirements**	** =	**Final Project (in depth study)**

The Portfolio

	Grade	Date (completed/ projected)
Post Graduate Plan	Sat	12/90
Autobiography	Sat	12/13/91
Practical Skills & Knowledge (Life Skills)	Dist	3/1/92
Internship Brookhaven National Lab & Hunter College, NY	Dist	1/3/91
Ethics, Social Issues, & Philosophy Controversy of Afrocentric Schools	Dist	2/28/92
Literature Influences on Malcolm X's life	Sat+	3/92
History Events affecting the Controversy of Afrocentric Schools	Sat	2/28/92
Geography Geography of the West Indies	Sat+	6/5/92
Language other than English Spanish: English only versus Dual Language	Sat+	1/3/92
Mathematics Mathematical models--Lines & Sines	Dist	3/16/92
Science & Technology Construction of Expression vectors with Phosphatases 1 & 2A	Dist	4/92
Fine Arts & Aesthetics Opera: *Die Fledermaus & The Marriage of Figaro*	Sat	12/13/91
Mass Media Entertainment of News? Our Children's Education	Sat+	2/24/91
Physical Challenge Aerobics	MinSat	6/17/92

Review Date:

Plasmid prep is used to grow large quantities of DNA. The objective is to get the plasmid DNA into the bacterial cells, and then to test whether the cell contains the DNA. The cells with the DNA will not be affected by the antibiotic; these cells with DNA will live in the presence of antibiotics. The attachment is the procedure in doing the plasmid prep.

The next procedure is to isolate the phosphatase fragments. First cut DNA with restriction enzymes. Then run *minigel* to separate by size, cut out fragment of interest and purify (*electrolute*).

The next steps are important ones in getting constructs of phosphatases 1 and 2a. Prepare vector for insertion of phosphatases. Then do a *ligation,* which is the joining of DNA strands, in order to have sense and anti-sense strands of mRNA. Double stranded RNA degrades, and the task is to reduce the quantity of the phosphatase proteins to see if in fact these proteins play a role in signal transduction in transforming cells.

In her internship portfolio, we learn why Marlena is so conversant with this kind of research. There Marlena describes three different internships in science that she undertook over two years at Brookhaven National Laboratory, Hunter College, and Columbia University. She also tells us that she has just been accepted to the New York Academy of Science's Research Training Program for the spring semester of her senior year. The internship portfolio includes excerpts of lab procedures, along with discussions of what she learned in lectures and during on-site visits, and reflections on its meaning for her life.

A mathematics portfolio includes mathematical models of rainfall and a whale sound wave, with empirical data plotted and models developed under differing assumptions. A discussion of linear and sine functions follows, along with a discussion of the advantages and disadvantages of modeling as a means for predicting trends and patterns:

> The models are very useful in giving general information about what's the difference from start to finish. The models are also inaccurate because they don't show what's happening at every time interval. For instance, the line for rainfall doesn't show that at some point the rate of rainfall has decreased and increased during the data taking. The positive aspects of models out weight [*sic*] the negative aspects because models are used to represent and it is not always important to know every aspect of the data.

This same judicious approach is seen in Marlena's media portfolio, which includes a sophisticated, evidence-based analysis of race, gender, and class stereotyping in prime time television, along with essays on violence in the media and First Amendment debates concerning song lyric censorship. These essays display Marlena's capacity to weigh and balance evidence and competing views in a thoughtful and reasoned fashion. She is able to see both sides of each debate without bias or rancor, and to resolve them in a way that avoids oversimplification.

This capacity to understand competing points of view and to look for common ground also emerges in her practical skills portfolio on conflict resolution, describing her training as a mediator and her experiences mediating conflicts within and outside her school. Here, a theme emerges that is obvious elsewhere in her work and thinking:

> I feel that mediation has helped me in understanding the people around me. . . . I feel that Conflict Resolution helps those who are not mediators to understand others by allowing them to put themselves in the other's position and how they might react so that when the mediation is over there are two winners instead of one.

In other portfolios, Marlena traces the history of segregated education in the U.S. (her history portfolio) and applies it to current debates about Afrocentric schools (her entry for Ethics, Social Issues, and Philosophy); she discusses the *Autobiography of Malcolm X* (Literature) and the geography of the British Virgin Islands, where her family is from (Geography). In her second language portfolio, she discusses the "English only" debate, concluding, on the one hand, that such a policy "goes against what this country stands for," and on the other, that those who would restrict language use should be prepared to provide resources to immigrants for learning English. In these entries we see a young woman who understands the history and effects of discrimination on her life and on that of others, but who is motivated by a humane sense of the possibilities for all people, rather than by resentment or despair.

There are other indicators of her learning that deal with concerns of breadth rather than depth. The Geography entry is accompanied by a geography test in which Marlena accurately identified the oceans, continents, and countries of the world. The Literature entry is accompanied by an annotated bibliography of 24 works she has read, ranging from Shakespeare's *Macbeth,* Dickens' *A Tale of Two Cities,* and Victor Hugo's *Les Miserables* to a substantial series of books by Toni Morrison, Alice Walker, and Maya Angelou.

There are light moments in the portfolio as well, as when Marlena explains her efforts to conquer aerobics with a Jane Fonda tape (physical challenge), and when she reviews *The Marriage of Figaro* and *Die Fledermaus* (arts and aesthetics). After a detailed accounting of the two operas' story lines, Marlena notes that "The plot is out of a typical soap opera: adultery, masquerade, and devilish plots to get someone under their thumb. *Die Fledermaus* and *Le Nozze Di Figaro* are two of the most delightful plays I've seen in a while."

In Marlena's autobiography portfolio—a collection of three essays—these many interests come together and we begin to understand her as a person. In the first essay she speaks about her love for books and how reading has helped her develop her own identity:

> I would say books, and learning to think for myself instead of listening to my "friends," is what made me an independent and diligent worker. . . . Books by Alice Walker, Toni Morrison, and other authors captured my interest and urged me to read and made me grow to be a person that I like. . . . Books have given me a broader look at my surroundings: [especially] being able to enjoy various books on different subject like black families in the 1950s–1970s, in which I could place myself in the family member(s) position.

Wryly, she notes that "I couldn't do that with the characters in *Sweet Valley High.*"

The second essay discusses the importance of a good education and examines the historical restrictions in education that women and minorities have faced. Marlena weighs the arguments for education in terms of economic gain as opposed to gaining a better understanding of people and oneself, concluding, in consonance with one of the CPESS commitments, that "Education is what you make of it and that it is more than school. Real education is the experience you have in order to do well in whatever field you go into."

Her third essay begins with her research experiences in studying cancer-causing genes and leads to a poignant discussion of her relationship with her grandmother, who died from cancer. She concludes with a realization that her decision to seek a career in medical research was a legacy left by her grandmother, who "helped me to develop and see my own strength and potential." And in a comment that suggests her appreciation for the CPESS Habits of Mind she has come to value, Marlena notes that her discussions with her grandmother "became good practice for encounters and experiences I would have. I started to be able to defend my position, my point of view, while being able to accept and understand someone else's."

The portfolio as a whole gives one a sense of Marlena's capabilities and concerns, as well as her knowledge and skills. We come to understand her passions and to sense her deep inner keel—what guides her in her path through life. The portfolio collection also displays a great deal about the kind of education she has received and the kind of thinking and caring she exhibits as a result—her habits of mind and heart. Reading through the collection is an engrossing and a moving experience. Though the entries are carefully scored ("gridded" in the evaluation terminology of the school), after a short time one ceases to attend to the assessments of others, learning much more about the student by engaging the work directly, and considering what it illustrates about who the student is as well as what evidence it presents about what she knows and has done in each exhibition.

Like Marlena, CPESS students bring much of themselves, their passions, and their concerns into their portfolio work. Among the many topics for portfolio entries are the following: "Internship Blues: Dealing with a Scissor-Happy Editor," "The Use of Power in *Antigone*," "The Women in *Othello*," "Slavery: The Struggles and Hardships of Black Women," "Education in South Africa and Cuba," "Geometric Home," "Time Dilation in Einstein's Special Theory of Relativity," a science project entitled "A Comparison of the Effects of Hair Straighteners and Hair Removers on Skin and Hair," "Black-on-Black Crime" (a videotape), and "The Effects of Alzheimer's Disease." The personal concerns students bring with them to these topics translate into a motivation to dig deep and to persevere through the hard work that the challenging projects typically entail.

Reaching a "Portfolio Standard"

During their time in the Senior Institute, students work closely with their advisor and other subject matter teachers on each of the chosen portfolio items and revise them until the student and his/her teacher feel the work meets the standards of the school. The curricular goal is for students to "use their minds well," rather than to memorize bits of information. As a result, the Senior Institute courses emphasize inquiry and offer students a wide range of possible topics for their Graduation Portfolios. Students can also develop portfolios from their internships and college courses, or from other interests that they pursue on an independent-study basis. Regular Senior Institute coursework can focus on or aim for the Portfolio if students want it to. If they structure an assignment from one of their courses appropriately and work hard enough on it, it may reach "portfolio level," thus helping them to achieve their goals more quickly.

Mardi Tuminaro, for example, has structured her human physiology course so as to get students "doing science" as early on in the term as possible. She presents an overview of the course's content first, to inform the students so they can select a topic to research. Students may choose to do a library research paper or an original research project. She has found that students are more intrinsically motivated in this way—rather than by a test-driven curriculum—to complete their portfolio projects. The students actively seek her out for assistance with their portfolio work. The projects provide the students with tangible goals that help them focus their energy on the task they have chosen. Their interest motivates them to raise their own standards for their work.

Branch notes that "developing standards for mathematics or science portfolios makes teachers think about what they're doing in their classrooms." She feels she and her colleagues have revamped the kinds of projects they expect of students so that they are closer to "what we all said we wanted as a standard for the kids," and she uses the scoring grid continually as a way to talk to students about the criteria they should be applying. For Branch, reaching a portfolio standard means applying the standards for authentic work that would be applied by professionals in the fields of mathematics or science. In science, she finds that she engages students in more authentic kinds of experiments:

> The kids have to write up lab reports in the way that I think a scientist should do research. I remember when I did labs when I was in high school: They gave you all the instructions and they had some questions and some little blanks and a little table all set up for you, and you just did exactly what they said to do. It was just going through the motions. I try not to do that. I give them the general gist of what they're supposed to do. I ask them to write their own procedures. I don't tell them what the tables should have in them. If they understand what data they should be collecting, they should be able to figure out what information should be in the table and what graphs they do and just how the procedure would go so that it is the best for the question they are trying to answer.
>
> One of the things I want them to get in the habit of is working so that somebody should be able to recreate what they've done. They have to use clear language when they describe their procedures so that they can explain to somebody else how to do it, because what good scientists do is repeatable. A scientist doesn't just do things in a vacuum on his own. You have to answer to the entire scientific community, which I guess is the science community's mode of assessment. That's their accountability measure.

Students come to understand the standards against which scientists measure their own work as they work on their science portfolios. Keisha's* science portfolio, a portion of which is included in the Appendix, illustrates Branch's success in helping students understand how scientists think. In two separate experiments, she chose to investigate phenomena that affected her daily life and intrigued her: the effects of hair straighteners and hair removers on hair and skin, and the different effects of microwaves and infrared rays on food. Her careful enumeration of materials and procedures, her keen observations, her clear and graphic displays of data, and her thoughtful, evidence-based conclusions demonstrate that she has learned to think scientifically and inquire into phenomena in the way that scientists do. Her ability to generalize these understandings to other kinds of work is also seen in a careful, step-by-step description of the making of a video documentary for her mass media portfolio.

Keisha's portfolio also illustrates how students come to understand the uses of mathematics and science in daily life. Not only in her science portfolio, but also in her discussion of her internship at a brokerage firm, in her design of a house to scale, and in her discussion of the relative effectiveness of birth control devices, she uses an understanding of accounting principles, measurement, and statistics with competence and ease.

Branch explains that she uses mathematical modeling in her courses a great deal, because as an engineering major in college she learned that that's what mathematics is used for in engineering: "to model some real situation. You can use math to model a storm or the stock market. So the projects the kids do are often based on mathematical modeling." This also allows her to make frequent connections between math and science concepts and applications.

There is a practical standard that is also valued at CPESS—the ability to critically evaluate ideas and information and to assess the credibility of sources and their basis in fact. Students' portfolios are full of such analysis across a range of subject areas. Branch describes how she strives to reach this standard in mathematics. She notes that, having seen Ross Perot during a recent, televised presentation display a set of graphs that used distortions in scale to make his points, "I was wondering whether our kids could tell this was manipulative. I think they could. But I don't think most people's mathematics education would have prepared them to argue with anything Ross Perot said."

Understanding things deeply is part of reaching the portfolio standard. That is why the oral defense of portfolios is a critically important part of the process. As Marlena explained, "It makes you understand it more if you have to explain it to someone else." Francisco* noted that since different members of the graduation committee have different strengths and perspectives, you have to be able to explain your work from a number of vantage points, thus requiring even greater understanding of the work. "You have to be a teacher to the other teachers," he observed.

The comments written in the margins of one gridded portfolio provide a sense of the kind of understanding sought by the CPESS faculty. Shawn's* science portfolio, a paper on monochromatic laser light, includes both a theoretical discussion and a computer program he created to model light waves under different conditions of interference. The marginal questions, like those in the oral defense, probe for evidence of deep understanding.

> Why does the light keep its intensity over long distances?
> What is it about laser light that makes it travel in a straight line?
> Why is it important that a laser beam is monochromatic?
> How do you make a laser monochromatic? Can it be adjusted?

This paper received a rating of "distinguished" by the reviewers, as did the oral presentation, with a high degree of reliability among raters on each of the categories of the grid (e.g., all of the raters felt the paper "exceeds standards" for viewpoint [knowledge represented] and voice; all of them rated it slightly lower, as "meets standards," on evidence and use of conventions). The final rating is determined by how well the student displays his understanding in the oral presentation and defense, as well as by what is represented in the paper. In this case, the presentation illustrated Shawn's command of the material, even where his paper was not entirely clear.

As the process of preparing a portfolio unfolds, students learn a great deal about writing, critiquing, and revising their work, since this is generally required before portfolio standards are reached. The advisor gives some insight as to when a piece of work is "ready." However, since the grading criteria are known to the students, self-evaluation is also an integral part of the assessment process. Thus, the process itself is a learning experience for the students, providing them with specific, concrete feedback that they can use to improve their performance.

THE ASSESSMENT SYSTEM IN ACTION

The Senior Institute and its performance-based assessment for graduation are not an add-on to the school curriculum, or a trendy, unconnected top layer. On the contrary, they draw their potential for effectively transporting students to the next stage in their lives from the assessment practices and experiences of the school community—teachers, students, and parents— over the four years prior to entrance into the Senior Institute. During those years, when students are in Divisions I and II (the equivalent of traditional grades 7–10), there are at least two major conferences annually that include the advisor, parents, and student. The conferences center on the student's work, samples of which are presented, along with different teachers' narratives evaluating the students' work and progress. Meier comments: "With the CPESS conference, there is the possibility for a real exchange—the kid is there, the work is there, everything is there to carry on a conversation."

The work in those earlier years also prepares students for what they will later encounter. Keisha notes that "Since seventh grade, we've been doing our own research. It motivates you to do more and to push yourself." Exhibitions were always part of assessment in the lower divisions. In recent years, portfolio assessment has also been developed by teachers in these grades, as a means of having a more cumulative and wide-ranging conversation about students' work and progress. Meier notes:

> After four years of lots of conversation around your work, hopefully kids can say, "I understand what they're trying to get at," and they're buying it. "I know what the rules of the game are, and I know how to be more successful. I know when I need to get more help, I know the range of people who can help me, and I have some goals of my own." Hopefully, when they enter the Senior Institute, that shift has begun to take place.

The graduation committee process extends and expands this conversation and formalizes it through both the student's oral defense and the committee's discussion evaluating the portfolio and presentation. Because students and parents have direct access to and participate in the evaluation process (parents can, and frequently do, sit on graduation committees), and because the process, not just the result, is public and not secret, evaluation and "readiness for graduation" are demystified. Demystification empowers students to succeed while increasing their own responsibility to do so.

Supports for Student Learning

Students attend a retreat in the spring of their final year in Division II as part of their preparation for the major shift they will undertake. Entrance into the Senior Institute is marked by a formal welcoming ceremony the following fall and a parent meeting to discuss what students must accomplish in order to graduate.

This knowledge of what's required and the broad range of strategies for demonstrating competence are empowering for both students and their parents, who can play an important role in the process. Davis articulates the parents' view:

> In your typical school, parents are very disconnected from the process of what their children need to graduate. The requirements for graduation are much clearer in a CPESS kind of setting than they are in a typical school. It's very much different than "Did you pass your final? and Did you turn in all your homework assignments?" . . . [The portfolio process] is somethingthat helps parents see who their children can become. . . . You can be a terrific team organizer; you can be a peer counselor [conflict mediator]. Those are valuable roles that aren't often discovered in the typical school setting. All of these are proactive things the school did to empower parents as well as students.

The advisory system is another empowering aspect of the system. All students at CPESS belong to a 12–15 member advisory group guided over the two years by an advisor, who is any one of the staff members of the school. Advisors meet with their advisory group each day for at least an hour to discuss a variety of issues, ranging from health, family, and community issues to concerns about school. For Senior Institute students, the time is largely spent on homework or portfolio work, as well as on individual counseling or college planning. Virtually all staff members—including the school's co-directors, program coordinators, counselors, and teachers—take responsibility for an advisory group. This keeps all of the adults closely connected to students and their families, and it allows for the personalization—and always available safety net—that CPESS students experience. Keisha explains that her advisor "calls my house and talks to my mother." The advisory group "becomes a close-knit family," ensuring that there is "somebody who cares and somebody to rely on. . . . They will make you do the work."

Getting Focused: The Post-Graduation Plan

The Senior Institute advisor meets with each advisee, and later the family, to draw up a post-graduation plan, often affectionately referred to as "Is there life after CPESS?" The plan includes a time line of the student's key life events from birth to date and continuing 10 years into the future, with a discussion of what kinds of career options the student may want to consider and colleges they may consider attending. Senior Institute teacher Joe Walters talks about the students' initial rush of excitement when they do the post-graduate plan: "We look at career possibilities, maybe doing an interview with someone in a field you're interested in, or researching colleges that have the kinds of programs that you're interested in." Internship placements and a series of advisor-organized visits to colleges around the country,[8] along with participation in college courses, help maintain this excitement and give it direction, focus, and a sense of the possible for students who would never consider options they could have had no chance to envision.

Tarik,* one of the first class of seniors, explains how the school opens up students' horizons:

> I know people who started out with me who at first were saying,
> "No, I'm not going to college." But after being in this school and
> going on these trips and seeing these different colleges and how pos-
> itive it is, by seeing it themselves they get a different perspective. And
> they started to realize that this is what they needed to do if they
> wanted to be a doctor, lawyer, or be in business. You'd be surprised
> how many kids changed their minds over the last five or six years.

Kamil,* a fellow senior, also recalls students who decided to go to college because their experience at CPESS enabled them to "have a higher standard for themselves."

Francisco has considered his talents in art and music and has researched schools that would allow him to pursue these interests. As a student previously identified for special education services, Francisco has struggled with some courses, but his appreciation for his own strengths has enabled him to consider the future without discouragement. He notes in his plan:

> I hope and pray that I will enter to college at the end of next year but
> if I need to take another year I will because I would rather be better
> educated than not to be. I also think that it would be in the best
> interest for me to work on a portfolio of all of my work and I would
> show it to the colleges of my choice. I will accomplish this by talking
> to my art teacher and get [sic] all my work together.

His portfolio includes several entries that are rated "distinguished," including his autobiography, which movingly describes a near-death experience as well as his attachment to music and art, a set of self-portraits, and an audiotape of him playing Beethoven's "Moonlight Sonata"; portfolios in geography and physical challenge; and a College Art Portfolio. As we learn later, Francisco graduated on time and went on to college at one of the several that had been on his list.

Keisha was ahead of the game. Her highly detailed and carefully considered plan notes:

> Because I have met the requirements of all those schools which I plan to apply to, I feel it is possible that I will be finished at the end of the 3rd semester. This will leave the 4th semester for another internship and numerous visits to different colleges.

Her time line informs us that she had received the Intern of the Year award in 10th grade for her performance at Shearson-Lehman Brothers brokerage firm. Her transcript shows that she completed all of her Senior Institute coursework by the third semester, with high marks, especially in mathematics courses, and took another college course during her final semester while defending her last few portfolios. She notes in her post-graduation plan:

> I enjoy mathematics and do very well in that academic field of study. I also enjoy creating things that challenge me to think and really use my mind. As a result I am thinking about pursuing a job in the following fields: Accounting, Engineering, Management, Film Work/Production Co. While three of the four choices above run along the same lines, the last choice is a little different. I find that while I enjoy mathematics, I also enjoy film work. This became visible to me when I took part in the production of a documentary for a class project and once again when I was Production Assistant in a friend's production company. . . . My goal is a Bachelor's degree. It would also be to my advantage to take an internship in that field.

Keisha, too, went off to one of the colleges of her choice, feeling well-oriented toward the new choices and options awaiting her. The planning, all of the students agree, pays off in helping them define and successfully pursue their goals.

The post-graduation plan also helps students select their courses, plan an internship, and think about portfolio possibilities with clear goals in mind that connect to the student's own talents and interests. Students describe in the plan what kinds of projects they hope to undertake and when, mapping out a schedule for completing and defending each of their portfolios. Many options for portfolio projects come up in class. Teachers often provide ideas or respond to student's ideas, explaining what a topic and project would entail so that students select ideas that will interest them and sustain the energy that a completed project requires. Since their work will be judged on the presence and conviction of voice, as well as on mastery of information and analytic skill, student interest and engagement in a portfolio topic is crucial.

Developing the Portfolio

When students must turn their efforts to the development of portfolio items, the excitement often turns to anxiety. It is at this point that the shift from dependence toward increasing independence begins to become apparent, and the interaction between the students and the school community is crucial in determining success and keeping students from falling through the cracks.

After selecting a topic, students begin work on portfolio items by doing research. Different students have different strategies for developing their work. Michael,* a senior, describes his strategy as making an outline with an introduction, body, and conclusion, and "getting a whole lot of information" before he prepares a written draft. Students submit their portfolio projects to the appropriate subject teachers, who return them with comments. Students rework the projects and resubmit them. Monique's* comment reflects the fact that this process has begun to instill a sense of pride in the value of the work that overrides the traditional desire to simply get it done: "After you finish a draft, you hand it in. It's good to hand it in before the deadline because then you get it back in two days with the teacher's comments, and you can work on it again."

The teachers will then evaluate the projects, using the 20-point grid scoring system, and return them again. Michael's advisor "will accept nothing less than 15. If you get a 15 or above, you can bring it to your graduation committee and present it. If you get under 15, you have to rework it." Michael asserts that most students revise their portfolio work three or four times before they present it to their committees.

When portfolio submissions are evaluated by the entire committee, each committee member scores the portfolio on the 20-point grid (a possible 4 points for each of the 5 Habits of Mind); they then put their assessments together for an overall rating of distinguished (18–20), satisfactory (15–17), or minimally satisfactory (12–14). Below this level, the student must revise the portfolio and resubmit it for another evaluation. Oral presentations are evaluated on the 5-point scale shown earlier. Although the grid provides structure and makes criteria explicit, evaluation of the total product is holistic. Evaluators often work back and forth between the individual subscores and the total score to see if their overall judgment of the work is sustained by—and reflected in—their assessments of its various aspects. Ultimately, the committee members must ask themselves, individually and collectively, whether the portfolio is good enough to stand up in what Meier calls the "court of the world."

The value of the grid in making standards and criteria explicit is acknowledged by students and staff alike. Branch notes that "I use the grid all the time as I talk to kids about their criteria." Explicit criteria help the whole school focus on its mission. Branch recalls that when she first came to CPESS:

> Teachers pushed each other to answer "Why are we doing this? And what do we want kids to get out of it?" [The grid] is understood to be something we need as an entire school. . . . I can't imagine right now trying to teach without thinking about assessment all the time. It's easier to be in your own little world and not be accountable to anybody. It's much easier for me to be in this room doing what I want. But it's not the best thing for the kids, and it's not really the best thing for my teaching.

For staff, learning occurs as they evaluate student work and consider how to develop and support it. Noting that the level of conversation about learning at CPESS is leagues beyond what had been the rule in her previous school, Branch observes that she feels sorry for other teachers who do not have the opportunity to participate in such a discourse about teaching and assessment: "Going through the process of creating the grid and all the rest . . . made me what I am. I think that makes all the difference in the world."

Learning by Doing—and Redoing

The process of evaluating and revising and re-evaluating makes the assessment process fundamentally a learning process, one that promotes both self-evaluative capabilities and habits of work—the internalization of standards—for students as well as for staff. For students, tangible improvement in their capacities and skills is another by-product of the process. This is especially obvious with writing. The typical portfolio averages 50–100 pages of typed material, ranging from essays and annotated bibliographies to extensive research papers. Almost all of these are products of a process that includes several revisions en route to the portfolio. As Walters observes, students "who write a lot see a change in their writing. They see their abilities transforming." In addition to the fact that they see their skills improving, students learn that they can take charge of extending their own abilities. This empowers life-long growth and learning, along with the self-confidence needed to tackle new arenas in which practice will be needed before success emerges.

As they begin to make the big shift, many students initially look to their advisors to help make them take responsibility. Resource room teacher Jill Herman says that sometimes the metaphor of "teacher as coach" could more accurately be called "teacher as nag." "I've had kids who will come and say, 'Look Jill, you yell at me. You make me sit down. I want you to make sure that I do this.' " Students comment regularly about the availability of their teachers and their desire to make sure they succeed. As another remarks about her advisor, who is also her chemistry teacher, "She bothers me. She gives me the 'what to do' and I have to do it. And if I don't understand something, she's there, just her and me and she'll explain it to me in a one-on-one."

Students can begin filing and presenting portfolio items as they complete them, whenever they feel ready. Often, getting through the first graduation committee defense is what it takes to get students to feel competent and capable of completing what seems to loom as an interminable amount of work, requiring more self-direction than they have been used to. Joe Walters explains how taking the plunge is frequently both difficult and essential to gathering momentum:

> Some kids who had done well previously had difficulty during the first semester because their exhibitions and portfolios are no longer done only within the context of one course. They have to get ready to present to their committee. . . . I had three kids who did not do their first graduation committee until April of last year. It was interesting to me that once they did that graduation committee and they had those two or three portfolios they were finished with, then somehow they were freed up to say, "Hey, I can really do this." But getting it going to that point of the first committee provoked a fair amount of anxiety.

His description is confirmed by many students. Students are also emboldened to present their work by sitting in on the graduation committees of other students, where they can see the process in action and learn more about how to present and how to evaluate their own work as well as others'. Here is Tamika's analysis of what she learned from participating on a graduation committee:

> I learned how a student's paper is written, that every student writes differently—some get into more depth, some have different viewpoints. . . . Sitting on a graduation committee really told me how to prepare for my graduation committee in the future. You see other persons' mistakes, and you tend not to make that same mistake.

When she participated in a committee rating the presentation of a geometry portfolio, Tamika learned what kind of criteria the teachers used in their assessment: "We talked about how well he explained himself, what he knew about geometry, why did he pick a house this big, why did he pick such a width." When this particular presentation did not pass muster, Tamika also learned about the quality of presentation expected: "I understood that you have to do a really good presentation to pass the portfolio . . . you have to really focus on what you have to say." She applied this knowledge when she made her presentations to her own committee, and developed her capacity to look meta-cognitively at her own work and learning process: "I can present and defend as long as I know what my paper is about. I take notes, look for viewpoints and key words, then I just start talking about what it's about, how did I get this information."

The Committee Process

The portfolio presentation is a key event in the learning process because it crystallizes and deepens the student's command of his or her work. It provides an occasion to demonstrate mastery to significant others and to oneself in a public setting guided by clear standards of performance. And it balances rigorous standards against a need to enable each student to experience eventual success. The presentation is not a one-shot event that makes or breaks a student's chances for graduation. It is rather part of a continuum of work and exhibition that is grounded in an assumption of, and commitment to, continual improvement. If a presentation or portfolio item is deemed "not ready," it does not die; instead, it goes back to the drawing board with specific suggestions for improvement.

The guidelines for a committee meeting allow 5–10 minutes for the student's presentation, 20 minutes for the "defense," when committee members ask the student questions about his/her portfolio, and 10–15 minutes for the committee's discussion and assessment. Students and their parents may request access to the committee's discussion and assessment meeting (CPESS, 1991b, p. 21). Students may re-present if their presentation is not satisfactory, or they may choose to re-present if they decide they would like to earn a higher score. The process maintains high standards while providing multiple opportunities for success.

The assessment process provides a learning experience that builds students' insights and confidence. It becomes what Walters describes as a self-fulfilling prophecy: "As kids get better at defending their portfolios and as they see themselves getting better, they get better." Students, faculty, and parents confirm the power of the oral presentation and defense of the portfolio before the committee. The process that brought Danielle,* a student struggling to overcome a phobia about public speaking, through her first oral defense is a case in point.

Danielle's autobiography, one of her portfolios, begins with a poem: "Who am I? / I am my mother's body, shape, and narrow slit eyes. / I am my mother's daughter . . . / I am my mother's hope that one of her children will graduate from college." This essay develops the theme of her mother's influence, help, and support during her younger years in Catholic school—where she fared badly and learned to be afraid to talk—through her teenage years, when her mother worried about Danielle getting into trouble. When it came time for her oral defense, Danielle's mother was seated before her, along with three other committee members, focused intently on the presentation and on the other portfolio research papers (on the Constitutional rights of women to abortions, the appointment of Clarence Thomas to the Supreme Court, and the meaning of the veil in Middle Eastern Islamic society).

The fluency, voice, knowledge, and detail so apparent in Danielle's written work was absent from her presentation and defense. Danielle read from the note cards she prepared in her advisory under the guidance of her advisor, Henderson. She answered committee members' questions, first with single words and then with single staccato sentences that clung to her short, rapid breaths. But despite her terror, resistance, excuses, tears, and failed manipulations to delay this event, she was presenting and defending with her mother— her lifelong support—witnessing her first attempt to speak in public.

All of the committee members rated the portfolios and presentation privately and then shared their ratings. All were aware of Danielle's fear of public speaking and believed that this presentation was a good start for her. The committee agreed on a rating of acceptable ("MinSat") for the oral presentation, although the portfolios received higher marks. The presentation was acceptable only because it was the first one. There was a discussion of Danielle's fear of public speaking, with her mother providing a history of it, although not an excuse for it, and expressing her gratitude to the other committee members, both for their sensitivity and for their demands. When Danielle reentered the meeting room, Henderson informed her of the committee's ratings. She was relieved and pleased. Henderson explained that she expected more, and offered specific suggestions for the next presentation— "Give an overview. Highlight important points in your paper."

Danielle's mother also expects more. The presentation and defense were not adequate representations of Danielle's ability or effort. She has always been an "A" or "B" student, and her mother expects her to conquer her fears so that she can express herself as she advances in the portfolio process. Danielle's mother is grateful to have had the opportunity to see her daughter present her work. She understands her daughter's pain and struggle—and her progress—and she now has a deeper understanding of what CPESS expects, and the form that the expectation takes. As she gains firsthand knowledge of the skills required, she knows she too can become a more informed support for her daughter.

Walters sees the committee process as a transformational experience for all students:

> I think one of the best things about the portfolio process is the defense before the graduation committee. I see incredible changes among kids. Before they go into their first graduation committee they're so nervous. They find it difficult to develop and defend a portfolio. It's much harder

than a paper and pencil test. Sometimes kids are clear and sometimes they are not about what the process involves. And after they've done one or two of them, there's a transformation on how they feel about the process. They get better at it as they learn the process. And definitely, they do buy into the process. . . . There's a qualitative change between the first-year Senior Institute student and the second-year Senior Institute student. The improvement from the earlier defenses to the later ones is astounding. There's a seriousness that develops over the course of the two years—an ability to focus and stay focused. They get more involved in how much effort and work they put into the later portfolios. All of the teachers say this.

The graduation committee process is extremely powerful in a number of ways. For one thing, it brings focus to the educational experience. As Darwin Davis explains:

It was certainly in my mind the clearest and most focused time that I had as a parent, knowing what the expectations were of my daughter in terms of her academic work and performance. I had a clearer sense of what the expectations were during the process of the assessment, working on the evaluation team, versus any other time in her academic career. It lays it out fairly clearly for the student as well: "This is the goal I must reach. And not only must I reach it but I must be able to convince five other people, some of whom are selected [by the student], that this in fact reflects the capability that I have and I bring to this particular subject area."

The activity around and in the committee makes it one of the most significant learning experiences for the students who are candidates, for other students, for the staff, and for parents. It is in these committee meetings that all the members of the CPESS community can see the fruits of their labors. It is a sort of moment of truth for all parties to the teaching and learning process. There is no escaping what has worked, what hasn't worked, and what needs more work.

Parent participation on the committees becomes a source of learning and feedback for the staff, as well as a powerful affirmation for parents of their children's achievement. As they witness their children demonstrating their knowledge, and as they witness the teaching and learning that determine their children's future, parents are brought into the fold of the secret world of school. This stands in contrast to the practice in most schools, in which parents are given access to their children's education only through proxy grades, reports of things gone wrong, or children's tales.

One parent explains how the parent and student roles on the committee bring a special kind of knowledge to the process:

I think the parents' input is crucial in that they probably have a better sense of the overall child than anybody else—the social strengths that child may or may not have; that ability to express him or herself; that ability to operate under stress and pressures and those kinds of things; and what influences might sway their child in a particular direction, positive or negative. And I think that input is key in the academic role. I think it's also important that there's that peer representative there too because that peer probably has a better grasp of those social relationships, positive or negative, than anybody else. I think each brings a unique perspective.

Part of the power of the graduation committee process is that, as Meier explains, it is itself an expression of the Habits of Mind, and at the same time it strengthens the accountability of members of the community to one another.

It's an act of judgment. It reminds kids that we're making decisions here. You and me, we're making judgments. . . . You've got to persuade us and we've got to persuade you of our case if we give you an assessment different than you think. . . . The notion that everybody's got to make persuasive cases, they've got to bring in their evidence, they've got to prove their point—that's built into the life of the school. It's not just a pedagogical principle. It's actually how we run the school: evidence, perception, all these five Habits of Mind are not just on the side here. They're how everything operates.

Students are neither passive nor powerless in this process. They are encouraged to use their own capacities to persuade the committee of their point of view, of the meaning of their work, and of their convictions about its value. The process is totally open, to them, to their parents, and to their advisor, for scrutiny, for argumentation, and for understanding. No judgment is made lightly or mechanically. The committee takes responsibility for the fairness and thoughtfulness of their own decisions, and for the persuasiveness of their reasoning.

Committees don't always agree. In one case, described by a committee member, the math teacher had one view of a mathematics portfolio, accepting but less than glowing; the parent was even tougher, arguing that his daughter could have applied herself more; while another teacher was more empathetic: "Gee, it's math, after all. I could only do so much of that myself." In these cases, there are attempts at negotiating a settlement while also providing feedback that gives the student a clear direction. "It didn't happen often," the committee member explained, "but there were those logjams where you just didn't have the commonality of view and methodology, so therefore we couldn't make a decision at that point in time. We had to go back and do more homework, so to speak."

Committees take their charge very seriously, so that students can have confidence that they and their work have been well-considered. Students agree that when they choose to ask their parents to serve on the committee, the parent is often the most rigorous critic because he or she knows certain things about the student's capabilities that the staff may not have had a chance to see. Having a mix of faculty with other members allows each to contribute a perspective, to balance each other out, and to seek a fair judgment. And no decision has immutable consequences. There is always the opportunity to revise, revamp, and try again.

This mutual accountability—school to student and student to school—symbolizes the dignity afforded to all members of the CPESS community. Everyone must play by the same rules, and all judgments must derive from the weight and power of evidence. Thus, the committee is a real as well as a symbolic enactment of the school's beliefs and values, and of its commitment to accountability grounded in community. An important aspect of this communal accountability is the sense of responsibility that teachers have for the success of their students. Ultimately, the power of the graduation committee and the portfolio process is that they give both teachers and students challenging goals to work for, and they illuminate areas in which teaching supports are needed to ensure student success.

Monique's experience with her literature portfolio illustrates how this process helps increase students' involvement and commitment. Despite her complaint that the Senior Institute is more demanding of her time than she would like (given a professed interest in boys, fashion, and other social priorities), Monique is proud of the "Distinguished" rating she earned for "The Use of Power in *Antigone*," a book she describes as her favorite in all the world. The outstanding rating was earned, she says, because of "the quality of the writing and the dedication that I put into the paper. It showed that I believed what I was writing about."

AUTHENTIC ASSESSMENT IN THE LIFE OF THE SCHOOL

Authentic assessment practices come alive in a school as part of an organic process of goal-setting, communication, collaboration, and learning. The value of these practices when they are developed from within a school community is that they are owned by all the members and can be a source of continuing inquiry into student learning, as well as a source of reflection on practice.

At CPESS we observe influences on parent–school communications as assessment practices help make concrete the aims of the school and the work of the students. The portfolios and graduation committees provide a useful structure for an intensely educational dialogue between staff and parents, one that truly makes parents partners in supporting their children's growth and learning.

There are other influences on curriculum and classroom practice. The portfolio graduation process has occasioned efforts to deepen and strengthen curriculum throughout the school and to stretch teaching practices to find even stronger connections between challenging intellectual content and students' talents, experiences, and interests. Staff in the Senior Institute are always examining ways to increase supports for student success on the portfolios, while staff in the lower divisions, who also sit on graduation committees, have begun to think about how to lay the groundwork for their students' Senior Institute years.

Because the Senior Institute and its graduation requirements grew organically as the school and its students grew (CPESS added a grade each year as its first cohort of 7th graders progressed), the requirements do not differ in kind from the nature of the work students have experienced before 11th grade. In the lower divisions, exhibitions are used as assessment tools in many classes. For example, in a Division II Math/Science curriculum unit on motion and energy, students know they will study such concepts as velocity, acceleration, and projectile motion using data, equations, graphs, and trigonometric functions to answer several essential questions. These include: "How do things move?" "What is motion?" and "What happens to the motion of two bodies when they interact?" The students will not, however, be able to answer these questions with definitions or pat answers copied out of a text. Instead they will need to prepare a research paper and an oral presentation demonstrating that they understand and can use these ideas for their own purposes. Among the exhibitions they might select are the following:

- Design and analyze an original, realistic amusement park ride
- Analyze the projectile motion of a sports activity (e.g., the trajectory of a basketball)
- Using a particular piece of computer software, analyze the horizontal and vertical velocities of a body in horizontal motion

These kinds of activities help students integrate academic knowledge with hands-on applications of mathematical concepts and scientific principles; they encourage deep learning involving creativity, invention, and analysis; and they help students begin to acquire the habits of mind needed to succeed, not only at CPESS in the lower divisions and the Senior Institute, but in the world beyond.

Exhibitions of this kind have become even more prevalent in Divisions I and II, with teachers helping students begin to work with the kinds of criteria that will be applied in the Senior Institute. In some classes, there is more emphasis on developing research skills—how to find and use sources, how to structure information, and how to think about what else one would need to know in order to fully understand a question. Attention to the teaching of writing has increased as well, along with opportunities to present work products in a variety of forms.

The portfolio takes the concept of an exhibition even further. Portfolio work can include a series of projects that allow even greater intensity of effort and even greater connections to the student's developing sense of self. As Senior Institute teacher Jeremy Engle puts it, the idea is that

> Your work is a window into your Habits of Mind. What's important are the habits of mind, habits of heart, and habits of work. You want to see the entirety of a student's work. You want to ask, "Why did you pick these pieces?" You want to know if kids have a sense that the portfolio reflects them.

At the same time, staff understand that the portfolio reflects their own success at helping students find and develop themselves and their talents. Engle talks about the questions staff raise as they explore and construct the possible meanings and functions of the portfolio for themselves and their students: "What do portfolios mean?" "How do we organize class for portfolios?" "How do we avoid teaching to portfolios as people used to teach to the test?"

In quite remarkable ways, assessment development has served as a vehicle for staff development and for school development. It has provided a concrete, student-centered focus for staff collaboration and shared learning, with student work at the center. The negotiation and use of the standards has served to strengthen shared goals and values, the sense of the school as a whole entity with common direction.

Faculty find that the assessment process raises a slew of broader school questions: What kinds of structures and processes—over the six years of life at CPESS—does the school need in order to ensure that students develop the capacity to produce portfolios of depth and quality? What must happen within existing classes? What must happen outside of classes, in advisories, resource rooms, and elsewhere? Do new courses or technical assistance strategies, such as research writing labs, need to be invented?

In other words, the faculty is fully aware that a new kind of assessment system requires a new kind of system to support student achievement. One cannot assume that students will have the skills to achieve in a new system simply because it is more authentic, any more than one could have assumed that students possessed the skills to succeed under the old system. In fact, the skills they need will likely not have been developed under the standardized testing system that predominates in many schools, and changes in practices and supports for more in-depth learning will almost certainly be required. CPESS has undertaken such changes in the various structures and practices it has developed for advisement, for in-depth, integrated coursework, for collegial work and planning, and for their work with families, described earlier.

As new needs continually emerge and as standards are continually raised by virtue of the learning that occurs within the school, the assumption at CPESS is that collaborative change creates new possibilities. Rather than feeling threatened or defensive by feedback and scrutiny, teachers and students are energized to find solutions to the problems revealed. CPESS staff have participated in innumerable professional development retreats to rethink curriculum, evaluating external standards, such as those offered by the National Council of Teachers of Mathematics (NCTM), and refining their internally generated standards and curriculum plans. They have revised and continue to revise the school schedule so that teachers can provide greater support for students. Herman notes that they have learned that coaching needs to be structured coaching—a combination of leading, supporting, stimulating, locating resources, and helping students find ways of organizing themselves, leaving them enough room so that they can initiate their own work without having so much freedom that they are overwhelmed by the possibilities.

As these issues create a dynamic for change throughout the school, the graduation process has had still broader influences on the school and its work. As faculty work through portfolio evaluations together, they are wrestling with articulating their individual standards for what constitutes good work and useful learning, and they are developing shared standards that drive an overall school development process in unseen but powerful ways. Meier notes that the process of working through portfolio requirements, standards, and evaluations leads to improvement of teaching across the entire school. By tackling the question of graduation standards with authentic examples of student work as the focus of the conversations, "We've created a school that's more collective in its practice."

Branch sees the assessment criteria as the motivating and organizing force for collaborative curriculum planning and for teaching. She argues that the standards for what students should know and be able to do are more useful as guides than are requirements about content coverage.

> If we are clear about the criteria and the standards that we use, if the kids are clear, if the parents are clear, and if we are using them similarly throughout the school, that's the thing the kids need to move on with. . . . I need to build on the assessment process, because the assessment process has to do with what we want the kids to be as thinkers and as doers. If they've been constantly told that problem solving and representation in mathematics is an important thing to do, no matter what I teach them they'll be able to do it because they'll know the process they need to go through to learn something and learn it well. The kids will be more independent in their learning and they'll be able to learn almost anything.

Assessing the Assessments

In the process of developing assessments, a dialectic emerges as educators must balance competing, equally valued goals and must create strategies that address concerns for commonality and fairness, while maintaining flexibility and an appreciation for the uniqueness of students. CPESS has approached these issues head-on, striving to give each side of the dialectic its due and seeking out external review of its assessments to validate and improve its work.

In several sessions during which portfolio ratings were reviewed by staff—along with outside evaluators from local colleges—a number of fundamental questions were raised: Is our system of assessment evaluating the things we think are important for students to know and be able to do? Are we using similar criteria when we assess student work? How are faculty's evaluations affected by knowing a student well? Should students with special needs be held to the same standards as other students? How do we achieve high standards without dysfunctional standardization? How can we assure the school community and external agencies—colleges, employers, the State Department of Education—that our assessment system is valid?[9] Even more important, how can we ensure that the process is useful to student learning and school development?

This last question—How do we ensure that assessment serves our broader goals for student learning?—tackles the important issue of consequential validity: What are the *consequences* for students and schools of using a particular form of assessment? This is a type of validity that psychometricians have recently begun to understand as critical to questions of test development and test use (Shepard, 1993). It is also clearly critical to questions of how assessment can serve to strengthen teaching and learning. If assessments—no matter how fancy—do not call for forms of learning and modes of teaching that are valued by the school community, they will undermine the commitments of students and teachers and the confidence of parents and others to whom the school is accountable. As teachers tackle the question of consequential validity, they take charge of shaping the school and their collective efforts in ever more effective ways.

These fundamental questions and dilemmas have been worked through at CPESS, for the moment, in useful ways. They are also ongoing concerns that continually motivate serious discourse and revisions in teaching, learning, and assessment practices.

Achieving Standards Without Standardization

The CPESS portfolio system uses a common framework with common areas of work evaluated through the use of common criteria and a common process. However, it does not require uniform tasks based on predetermined, standardized "prompts" or responses. The balancing has involved staking out and defining common ground without lodging it in concrete. There are at least two important ways in which this commitment is made real in the organization and in the assessment system.

First, CPESS maintains standards without standardization throughout its school program. Although students are never standardized, schools' efforts to find ways to treat them as though they are result in futile attempts to create homogeneous groups through such strategies as tracking. CPESS does not track students or segregate "special needs" students. The school is built on the premise that standards can be achieved without standardization, and it creates a variety of supports—such as the advisory system, resource room supports, and access to additional tutoring—to enable this to occur. Furthermore, students are encouraged to start from their areas of strength and interest in developing their portfolios. Thus, paradoxically, allowing students to begin from their different starting places helps them ultimately to reach more equivalent standards of performance. Herman notes that the portfolio process works for the students she is responsible for assisting.

> I think this concept of individual assessment is perfect for anyone in special education because that's what special education has always focused on—establishing an individual education plan (IEP). The IEP is all demonstration by mastery. It's natural for us to constantly be finding ways for people to demonstrate that they know something. Our job is to figure out how to reach them, and then to figure out how they can show us that they know what they know.

Second, efforts to standardize assessment often lead to the breaking up of tasks and scoring methods in order to measure each discrete aspect individually. This process aims to focus attention on common dimensions and increase reli-ability, but when carried too far it can decrease validity by decontextualizing and fragmenting ideas and their evaluation, confusing the forest for the trees. The CPESS portfolio assessment system recognizes the need to find manageable units and indicators for evaluation as analytic benchmarks for providing common consideration across students, but it also accommodates a holistic assessment, recognizing that the whole is greater than the sum of the parts—that the overall judgment that a standard has been met is ultimately more important (and more likely to be reliable and valid) than is adherence to more discrete, standardized scoring criteria.

Thus, while there are 14 portfolio areas and analytic scoring criteria based on the five Habits of Mind, the portfolio entries—and the overall portfolio—are also evaluated holistically. The overall consideration of the student and his or her collection of work as a body are not lost. Evaluation of whether standards are adequate—whether they would hold up in the "court of the world," is undertaken through ongoing external review of portfolio samples and of the portfolio process as a whole.

Balancing Objectivity and Subjectivity

In assessment, there is a press to be "objective," that is, to judge or score things evenhandedly and reliably. Traditionally, this has been thought to be better accomplished at some distance from the person whose work is being evaluated, using standard criteria in the same way across cases. At the same time, an understanding of any phenomenon requires a certain amount of subjectivity—that is, personal or contextualized knowledge of the work and of its producer, as well as of one's own valuing system. It is that "subjectivity" that is the basis for creating meaning out of everything we encounter.

There are at least two ways in which CPESS achieves a balance between objectivity and subjectivity: by recognizing context while maintaining commonalities, and by putting together a set of judges who can bring different sets of eyes to the student and the work.

In the first instance, the assessment process recognizes the importance of context—the context of the task and the context of the student—while maintaining the common framework for tasks and standards. A discussion of the task context helps the raters understand what a given piece of work means as a representation of a knowledge domain, as an application of a particular skill or ability, and as a piece of work in the context of the student's school experience (when, why, how it was produced, and for what purpose). The context of the student is also taken into account as the graduation committee discusses what the work means in the context of the student's growth and development; for example, what other desired qualities—like effort, perseverance, or a willingness to stretch into unfamiliar or challenging terrain— were required for this particular student to produce this particular piece of work. At the same time, students' work must fit within the requirements of the portfolio, and is evaluated against common standards, guarding against too much subjectivity in judging readiness to graduate.

The balance between objectivity and subjectivity is also aided by involving some graduation committee members who know the student and his/her work well, and some members who do not; i.e., some who bring intimate knowledge, and some who bring a bit of distance and a different perspective. Typically, a subject matter expert for the portfolio being defended is represented on the committee to evaluate the work against disciplinary standards, along with the student's advisor, who knows the student well and who brings another disciplinary perspective to bear. A third adult on the committee, along with a fellow-student, provide yet another vantage point on both the student and the subject matter. The committee structure guards against bias and creates a kind of objectivity through consciously ensuring multiple lenses, or perspectives, on the work and the student.

Balancing a Developmental View and an Evaluative View

Education is inherently developmental (educators care about supporting people in their process of becoming), yet assessment is inherently evaluative (assessors must assert a value regarding what a person, or at least his or her proffered work, has become). In the developmental sphere, there is no beginning or end; there is only a continuum. The evaluative sphere is time-bound: events and products are seen as the end point of an effort. Often the process of formal evaluation can interfere with development by creating a new psychological frame that inhibits further growth and achievement. When an evaluative message persuades a child that he is "not good enough," it can create a demotivating effect, establishing a prophecy-fulfilling psychology that overwhelms competence and capacity. Yet, without some assessment, the process of development cannot be gauged and supported. Properly framed and understood, information about where a student is in terms of goals for his learning is necessary and empowering for future growth.

The balancing, then, concerns the creation of a developmental frame for evaluation, and an evaluative frame for development. CPESS does the former by constructing the task of portfolio development as an iterative process (products can be worked on further if they are not ready for presentation, or revised and strengthened thereafter) and by decoupling the Senior Institute from the concept of age-grading. Students may complete the Senior Institute in 1, 2, or 3 years. Students who are not finished meeting graduation requirements may nonetheless go on to employment or take postsecondary coursework while they continue to work on their portfolios. Because the standards represent criteria all can ultimately reach, rather than norms and rankings that keep some continually "behind" or "below," they are motivating rather than discouraging as sources of information about competence.

Growth and development continue within the frame of evaluation. CPESS constructs an evaluative frame for development by using exhibitions throughout all the years of secondary school, and by involving staff from all of the divisions in the development of graduation standards and the evaluation of portfolios. As a consequence, those who work with students throughout their years at CPESS carry with them an evaluative frame—an understanding of goals, standards, and criteria—that they can use in supporting their students' development.

Balancing Democracy and "Efficiency"

A key issue for all schools (and districts or states) involved in developing authentic assessments is the question of who should be involved in the process, how many, and with what degree of ongoing negotiation, rethinking, and, ultimately, voice. It may seem more efficient to have a few people create and implement an assessment than to have many insiders and outsiders continually involved in invention, negotiation, reinvention, and ongoing management of the assessment process. It may ultimately seem more efficient to have an external agency create and manage the process so that schools don't have to bother. State-developed tests, or maybe even a national examination board, could be viewed as taking the burden off schools for thinking about what should be assessed and how. Even within schools, there are decisions to be made about the range of involvement and the extent of voice, in light of the need to get the job done. The temptation to take the most "efficient" route, however, undermines the possibilities for school, teacher, and community learning, ownership, and improvement.

CPESS has opted for a very democratic process—involving many members of the school community in developing the assessment system and support- ing the students' work, and involving faculty from across the grades, students, parents, and people from outside the school in conducting the assessments. This democratization of the process has had very important implications for integrating assessment in the life of the school, and for creating, maintaining, and strengthening a collaborative culture with shared goals and values within a strong community. In the governance process, as in the assessment process itself, the whole is greater than the sum of the parts. Involvement creates learn- ing and an internal engine for continual school improvement.

One of the many external review sessions used to evaluate the portfolio and the scoring process produced a clear example of how the public, col- lective nature of the process stimulates deep thinking about goals for learn- ing and teaching. Early on in this process, a group of CPESS staff and local college professors met to score selected papers from some of the school's ear- liest portfolios. They compared their scores and comments to see if they were applying the same standards and to evaluate how the papers would stand up in a collegiate setting. While many of the papers received similar scores from the raters, one did not. That paper, on the subject of the book *Down These Mean Streets,* submitted for the Literature requirement, received a range of scores by 12 inside and outside evaluators that was extremely wide.

The ensuing discussion about the paper centered not only on standards for minimally passing papers but on fundamental issues in teaching and assessment: how to strike a balance between objectivity—a focus on the product—and subjectivity—an understanding of the student; how to balance an evaluative and a developmental approach to assessment; and how to bal- ance the student's responsibility for his work and the school's responsibili- ty for struggling to find ways to help him succeed.

The paper had a number of technical problems: the transitions were not clear, the opening paragraph did not state the purpose, and the stu- dent failed to clearly present critical connections to other works. CPESS faculty member Jose Alfaro looked for its strengths: "I passed it for effort, voice, and struggle with issues. I passed it in the context of the portfolio. I didn't pass it in isolation." Henderson also stressed the student's stretch in completing the work.

I want to emphasize that we are going to keep running into the con- flict between our standards and what we know about our students— their histories, work habits, abilities. This student has a hard time getting things through. This paper is his first effort in completing a book and writing about it. His engagement level is very high because of the subject matter, although his writing needs more work. I graded this paper "minimum pass" because I have confidence in his ability to intellectually discuss the literary meaning of the book before his graduation committee and to make connections between his life, the life of his community, and the book. This is an opportunity for him to succeed. It would set the foundation for future improvement and success in the thirteen portfolios to follow. Without this vote of confidence by the staff, his future remains jeopardized.

Jill Herman expressed the other point of view: "I didn't pass this paper. I gave it a 10. I felt the focus was missing." Pat Wagner asked a developmental question: "How many rewrites did the student do?" Jose responded that "he worked on this paper constantly. It was hard for him to go back and rewrite." Deborah Meier voiced the broader school and teaching issue:

> I think we're not really discussing if this paper meets our standards. It doesn't. I think we haven't figured out how to help him become a better writer. I think we're describing our dilemma as advisors. . . . I think we must evaluate this paper as if we were the outside world. Then we must focus on our role in helping him.

Among the list of observations and questions developed at the end of this session were the following, which elaborate the idea that the assessment process is focused as much on the school as on the student: "A review such as this one should make us more critical of ourselves than our students." "How can we use this portfolio assessment to improve instruction?"

The answers to this question are as many and varied as the occasions for instruction in the school. There is no teacher we spoke with at CPESS who has not found a stimulus to rethink curriculum and teaching, to reshape learning tasks and student supports on the basis of insights from the portfolio process. And the collective nature of the assessment triggers a continual cross-classroom inquiry into ways of improving the webbing that supports students in the interdisciplinary and extracurricular niches that are equally important to their learning. As staff member Betsey McGee, who organized the assessment reviews, notes: "The minutes or summaries of the various assessment review meetings constitute a kind of running record of institutional self-study, and one could rely on them exclusively to shape the coming year's school improvement and staff development activities." In the ongoing work of developing a school, the assessment process is providing an engine for continual examination and renewal.

And the process of reflection also provides grist for continual changes in the assessment system. Each year, as teachers have considered the kinds of performances the portfolio elicits and the information it portrays about students, they have made modifications. After the first year, a raft of questions and suggestions came up as faculty surveyed the completed portfolios and evaluated what they could learn from them—and what else they might like them to represent about students' abilities. For example:

> We need videotapes of a student's graduation committee experiences to give the reviewers a fair picture of a student's portfolio.

> Much of this writing is narrative. I'd like to see the students write essays.

> I wanted to see some of her "scrappy" pieces—what she worked on and struggled with. . . . Maybe we should see "first" and "final" drafts.

In the seeds of these observations and questions lie the continual evolution of teaching, learning, and assessment within the Central Park East Secondary School community. Because of CPESS's role in the Center for Collaborative Education—a network of Coalition schools in New York City, the Coalition of Essential Schools, and the New York State partnership program—the answers to these questions will inform the work of many others striving to work their way through similar issues in their own distinctive ways.

STANDING UP IN THE "COURT OF THE WORLD"

The portfolio process, along with all of the other opportunities for authentic teaching, learning, and assessment at CPESS, influences student learning in a number of ways. First, by the students' own admission, they internalize the habits of mind and the habits of work required by the portfolio. As Paul Schwarz notes:

> Using the word "habit" was important. It's not enough to show that you can do something or that you know something. We say that you have to be in the habit of thinking that way. A major portfolio can't contain just one item. One piece of evidence can't demonstrate a "habit." Of course, having 14 portfolios means you have to show it 14 times in 14 different areas of work. That's even more evidence of a true habit.

As these several different testimonials suggest, the students see the value of what they have learned.

> We've been using [the Habits of Mind] for a while now. It just becomes natural, like a world view. You start to look at what evidence there is. You start to question everything. It all builds up.

It affects your whole life, how you react to it. You start thinking in terms of a deeper level. Kids in this school think about topics like politics and race and other things that normally kids wouldn't think about. I mean, everyone's still interested in music and clothes and that kind of stuff, but there's also another part where kids are serious. They know the reality of the world.

You're going to need it after you move on from high school and college and go into the real world. It's like a basic necessity—like knowing how to brush your teeth. You're always going to have to write for whatever job you do. You want people to understand what you write. In a paper, you can't say, "Well, do you know what I'm saying?" You have to have the evidence and how it's connected to something else, where you got the evidence from.

This is for us to know when we get out into the real world. . . . Habits of Mind stay in my mind whether inside of school or outside of school—so we'll continue to use this.

Because the work is theirs, because it is continuous, and because it is authentic, students are motivated: "That's what leads to the responsibility of the students you'll find in this school," says John.* "Where in every other high school in New York City, people skip classes every day, barely anybody at all skips school. The kids here just want to come to school—or maybe they don't want to, but they do." The sense of responsibility for oneself and one's work wins out in the tug of war with competing adolescent priorities.

Second, students gain confidence that they can achieve in the world outside of school because they have already had the opportunity to do so. Among the most important things students learn from their opportunities to test themselves in authentic situations are the perseverance and the self-confidence that eventually come from determined effort. Having been given the chance to engage in work on the world's terms through internships and college courses makes it easier to go out into the world with the expectations—matched with skills—for success.

There is outside validation for the views of students that they are prepared for what lies ahead. Joe Walters notes that colleges are increasingly willing, and sometimes excited, to review the students' nontraditional CPESS transcript and even portfolios. They are frequently impressed by what they see and even more impressed when they meet CPESS students, particularly "with the students' ability to speak and communicate in general, with the kinds of questions they ask, and the kinds of things they want to know about colleges. They see them as being much more prepared in that process than students from traditional high schools."

A recent report from the "SUNY 2000" task force of the State University of New York suggests that this acceptance of new modes of assessment is becoming more widespread. The report on college-level knowledge and skills explicitly encouraged performance-based assessment through portfolios, projects, and exhibitions as a tool for college admissions, freshman year counseling, and documentation of ongoing development throughout college. The Task Force urged that students engage in "a continuous authentic assessment experience throughout their high school years (and) create an assessment file that could be taken with them to college and used there for academic planning and advisement" (State University of New York [SUNY], 1993, xii–xiii). An increasing number of these campuses are engaging portfolio development and use with local high schools.

These encouraging developments were an unknown when CPESS launched its initial efforts, creating a great deal of uncertainty among the parents of the first graduates. As Darwin Davis recalls:

> The portfolio as assessment was a grand experiment. There was a point in time where the collective parent body hit the collective panic button. And that was at the time when their children were entering the 11th grade and were about to undergo that process known as applying to college. So PSATs, SATs, the variety of prep courses, the requirements by recruiters, and therefore schools, as to what students are supposed to display in order for them to enter colleges of their choice became very important. Parents were now having to confront their ideals with what I would call the political reality of entering the college of their choice. And the ideal was that "yes our students are these well-rounded, gifted individuals with multitalents displayed in these 14 portfolio items"; the real was that schools were asking for grade average, class rank, SAT score.
>
> That was a scary time for parents. It was a time in which we were tested. And several were ready to abandon the ideal for the so-called "real." There were a small group of parents and the then Senior Institute director, Haven [Henderson] in particular, who did a terrific job at convincing parents that if this school was going to succeed they had to stick by their guns. They had to stick by the 14 portfolio items. And perhaps in the first year every school would not be willing to change their guidelines to accept some of our students. But some would, and we needed to work with those that would. And when it was all said and done, there were several schools, I remember Syracuse being one in particular who was quite reluctant to do anything out of the ordinary, but in the end they did. They accepted something that was very different from what they were used to from CPESS, and I think that's paved the way for other colleges to broaden their own horizon and look at how do those class rankings actually lead to the kind of productive student that they say they want, but they've set up a different system for screening.

The evidence is that the CPESS system does lead to the kind of productive students colleges say they want. One recent CPESS graduate, now at Cornell, wrote in a letter to one of her teachers: "Those five CPESS 'Habits of

Mind' are proving very useful here." Another graduate wrote something similar: "They set us aside as special." People are "impressed," noted a third on his visit back to the school after graduation (Meier, 1992, p. 217).

Other outside assessments of students' work confirm this view of their readiness. In the course of a variety of exercises used to review and validate the portfolio assessments, CPESS invited university faculty to rate a range of papers. With respect to the Humanities portfolios, professors from local colleges were asked whether the papers as a group were comparable to freshmen papers and how they would be received as term papers. Even as they acknowledged the technical and structural problems exhibited by some of the papers, the professors' responses were positive about the comparability of CPESS students and freshmen entering city colleges. Bill Bernhardt of the College of Staten Island responded:

> My first impression was that most of these students would have passed the CUNY [City University of New York] writing assessment and been placed in regular composition classes. . . . It's refreshing to see the type of work these students are doing. The topics and books tackled here are pertinent to their lives and far more meaningful than usual.

His colleague, Peter Miller, commented: "I was struck that the problems are very much the problems of freshmen students in college. We are in the same area. . . . There are a lot of students who come into our college's English Department unable to do what these CPESS students are attempting to do." Nancy Barnes, from Lang College, agreed, noting that "these are the same problems we see in a moderately selective college."

A meeting of college and school faculty for a Math/Science portfolio review produced similar assessments. Gary Benenson, a professor at CUNY's Engineering School, noted that "this school has been successful in showing kids that knowledge is constructed. How do you do this?" Dave Feldman responded, "We throw back questions to the students. The teachers are only facilitators."

As facilitators, teachers help students take responsibility for becoming competent, resourceful learners, rather than dishing out answers in ways that maintain the teacher as powerful and the student as passive. The portfolio process supports this role. Regardless of the kind of life's work students decide they want to do, they are more able to organize themselves to do what is needed to get started and to succeed.

As it turns out, and totally against the conventional odds of secondary schooling in New York City, 96% of CPESS's first class of graduates in 1991 were accepted to college. Ninety-two percent were admitted to four-year colleges. The other two students from this class of 50 also achieved their goals: one was accepted to the Police Academy, and the other entered a computer training program. This is especially noteworthy in a big city school system that typically graduates only 60% of those who enter high school and sends only a small fraction on to postsecondary education or training.

CPESS provides a broader view of academic and vocational education than do most schools that focus on one in isolation from the other. Unlike most students going off to college, these graduates have had a chance to develop their interests and talents—to apply them in real-world situations, to know what they like to do and what they want to apply themselves to do. This is the first step toward a satisfying vocation and a satisfying intellectual life. A second important step is knowing that they can generate and meet their own standards for success while also meeting students' needs. Darwin Davis attributes the school's success to its willingness to take students on their own terms, find their strengths, and develop their talents.

> There should be more schools like CPESS, what I would call a child-centered school, where education needs are taken into account, the developmental stages of children and the variety of developmental stages—schools that accommodate that difference in a way that promotes educational goals and the development of that human being vs. pigeonholing that individual on the basis of rote seatwork. We need more schools that can take into account the development, the habits, the proclivities of children, rather than trying to force children to adapt to the habits and proclivities of institutions that pretty much everybody believes aren't working. Even our best and brightest aren't competing in the world arena. CPESS students can compete in the world arena. We need more schools like CPESS.

As one of the first graduates, Steve concurs that the CPESS approach has allowed him to develop his own evidence that he can and will succeed: "This environment gives us more standards. It makes us stand up straight. . . . It makes us look at ourselves in the mirror and feel proud of our accomplishments." His experience has given him a sense of self, an entitlement to be somebody, in contrast to the kids he describes feeling sorry for in his neighborhood, "who hang around wasting their lives." And he, like his classmates, has his work, tested against his own and the community's standards, to testify to the fact that his accomplishments are real and will stand up in the "court of the world."

NOTES

1. Some of the fieldwork for this chapter was conducted by Lynne Einbender and Fred Frelow of the staff for the National Center for Restructuring Education, Schools, and Teaching. Students' names have been changed and are denoted by an asterisk.

2. Teachers' real names are used throughout the case studies.

3. In the first class of 9th graders, 82% of those who stayed at CPESS (i.e., did not transfer or move) graduated within 4 years, and 97% graduated within 5 years. Statistics have been comparable in subsequent years.

4. Division I is the analog of traditional grades 7 and 8; Division II corresponds to grades 9 and 10; and the Senior Institute approximates grades 11 and 12. These divisional structures, however, bring with them highly personalized advisement and teaching arrangements that allow them to serve many student needs that traditional school arrangements ignore.

5. Co-director Paul Schwarz estimates that a minimum of 36 hours per year per graduate are spent in graduation committee meetings. Since the average graduation load is six students per teacher, Senior Institute teachers spend a minimum of 216 hours in graduation committees. It is not unusual for graduation meetings to occur after official school hours, in the evening, or on weekends to accommodate parents and other students.

6. This description draws substantially on the Senior Institute Handbook, supplemented by interviews and other school documents.

7. This requirement may be met through the New York State language proficiency exam or a College Board examination.

8. All students have already visited at least one college each year on advisory trips in Divisions I and II.

9. As a New York State Compact Partnership School, CPESS and other partnership schools are creating their own assessment and accountability systems to lead and inform state policy and practice.

APPENDIX: STUDENT'S SCIENCE PORTFOLIO

CENTRAL PARK EAST SECONDARY SCHOOL
1573 Madison Avenue, New York, NY 10029 Tel: 212 - 860 - 8935

Deborah Meier,
Co-Director

Paul Schwarz,
Co-Director

CENTRAL PARK EAST SECONDARY SCHOOL
PORTFOLIO ABSTRACT

Student Name _____

Advisor Name _____

Date Submitted ___3/12/93_____

                      A comparison of infrared rays and microwaves

Title of Project ___A comparison of hair straightners and hair removers___

Portfolio Category ___Science_____

Abstract: Write four to five sentences describing your portfolio item, including your purpose, main ideas, and themes.

My Science portfolio consists of two different parts; the first being an investigation of the effects of hair products on the scalp and hair, the second being a comparison of microwaves and infrared rays and the effect they have on eatable objects.

Be sure your portfolio item is complete. Include: organizations contacted, people interviewed, written materials, references, appendix, bibliography, audio-tape, video-tape, summary of presentation/demonstration, etc.

Science is a method of research in which a problem is identified, a hypothesis is formed and tested. Science is also the study of and knowledge of the physical and material world.

Physical science is the area in which I have focused my attention during my last couple of semesters at CPESS. The two labs I used for my portfolio deal with the physical aspects of science. The physical aspects are physics, chemistry and anatomy.

Material science is the study of a substance or substances of which an object is made or composed. One could say the difference between the physical and material studies is that in one, researching an existing object naturally formed is done while in the other, researching man-made items and substances is involved.

Researching the object is done through science application. An example of this would be the explosion at the World Trade Center. Science was applied during the investigation of what caused such a large and deadly explosion. The FBI found traces of nitrate near the area of the explosion; this led them to believe that the bomb was made of fuel and fertilizer. They pursued that theory and tested it.

The whole World Trade Center ordeal made it clear to me that both physical and material science work together. My two labs addressed the combination of the two studies, but I was researching another aspect.

For my first lab I went into the chemical formation of household products. I first studied the 103 elements of chemistry. Elements are substances that can't be broken down any further then they already are. When they are combined they form new products called compounds. These compounds are then placed in household products, food, etc.

I came up with a lab that could test the compounds in hair products and how they effect the scalp and hair. This was of interest to me because I often use the hair products tested in my lab.

For my second lab I investigated how we find physics in almost about anything we see and touch. I focused on the radiation aspect of physics; to be more specific, the effects of microwaves and infrared rays on eatable objects. This was of interest to me because I often use my microwave to warm up food and I wanted to know if there was a drastic difference between warming food in a microwave oven or warming in a conventional one.

Abstract

When you enter a beauty supply store do you look at what the substance contains? Well after reading this lab you might think twice about what you say helps your appearance. I was once naive to what type of chemicals manufacturers placed inside hair remover and relaxer products. And the chemicals to which I knew the products contained, I didn't believe had such a negative affect on the chemical make up of hair and skin.

Be prepared for what you are about to witness, because it might have a powerful affect on what you do to make yourself look beautiful.

Introduction

My lab deals with the chemical properties of relaxer and hair remover and how it effects the chemical properties and physical properties of hair and skin.

Hair and skin are made up of numerous cells, the cell that over shadows all other cells is keratin. Keratin is made up of two cross-link bonds, disulfide and hydrogen. A break down of these bonds can cause a difference in the physical characteristics and chemical reaction.

Relaxer and hair remover are two substances that can breakdown the disulfide and the hydrogen bonds. Substances that can cause a break down are called kerantinase. It dissolves the protein in the hair shaft, turning it into a gelatinous mass that can be wiped away, this is what happens when hair remover is applied. Being that the substance doesn't affect the hair root, regrowth of hair occurs.

When relaxer is applied to the hair on top of a person's hairs, it too, dissolves the hair. But before the relaxer causes the hair to fall out, he/she is to rinse the relaxer out. When a perm is not applied properly the loss of hair will sometimes occur.

Since relaxer and hair remover have similar ingredients, in their chemical make up, similar reactions will occur (like hair loss). The relaxer used for this experiment doesn't have lye in it but it does contain hydroxide (as does the hair remover). Hydroxide, no matter what it's mixed with, will have a high base content. As a result when either hair remover or relaxer is placed on or near the skin, skin irritation and extensive burning may result.

When people came up with the "conk", numerous people experienced hair loss, and skin irritations. This was due to the high level of base contained in lye. As a result of the injuries, manufacturers added other ingredients that would neutralize the Ph in relaxers. If I were to compare the most recent relaxer to the "conk", I'm sure there would be a drastic difference in the level of bascity or alkalinity in the substance.

My experiment consists of taking two substances that are used for different purposes, (but similar ingredients) and comparing how they affect the make up of hair and skin[+]. I will then test and compare the pH levels of both substances.

Focus Question
How do the active ingredients in hair remover and relaxer compare when applied to hair and skin? How do they compare when tested for pH level?

Materials
Revelon Relaxer w/o lye
ACTIVE INGREDIENTS:
* water
* mineral oil
* calcium hydroxide
* cetearyl alcohol & ceteareth-20
* propylene glycol
* PPG-12 PEG-65 lanolin oil
* cetyl alcohol
* dea-lauryl sulfate & sodium laurominopropionate & dea-lauromino propionate

Nair lotion hair remover
ACTIVE INGREDIENTS:
* water
* mineral oil
* calcium hydroxide
* sodium thioglycolate
* cetearyl alcohol
* calcium thioglycolate
* ceteareth-20

+ Instead of using actual skin for this experient, slice of ham will be used in its place.

* cocoa butter
* fragrance
* tocopherol (vitamin E)
* D & C yellow #8

Human Hair
ACTIVE INGREDIENTS:
* keratin

Comb	*Rubber Gloves*	*Ham*
Mannequin	*Microscope*	*pH Paper*

Procedure
step #1—rinse hair with hot water

#2—blow dry hair, till no longer damp

#3—cut hair into 4 pieces, label the pieces A, B, C, and D (consecutively)

#4—place hair pieces on mannequin, and put on rubber gloves

#5—take one strand of hair from each hair piece

#6—look at hair strands under microscope (record observations)

#7—apply Revelon relaxer to hair pieces A and B

#8—comb relaxer through hair till all of the hair is covered

#9—apply Nair hair remover to pieces C and D

#10—comb hair remover through hair till all of the hair is covered

#11—record observations

#12—after 15 minutes, rinse out hair pieces A and C (let pieces B and D sit for another 15 minutes)

#13—blow dry hair till it is no longer damp

#14—record observations (for all 4 hair pieces)

#15—take strand of hair from pieces A and C

#16—place the hair under the microscope and record all observations

#17—repeat steps #12–#16 using hair pieces B and D (opposed to using A and C)

#18—record all similarities and differences between hair pieces A, B, C, and D

#19—place a piece of ham under the microscope and record observations

#20—label two pieces of ham X and Y

#21—apply a sample of relaxer on piece X

#22—record observations

#23—rinse substance off of piece X

#24—place piece X under microscope and record observations

#25—repeat steps #21–#24 using piece Y and hair remover

#26—take three pieces of pH paper and place them on a clean surface

#27—label the pieces of paper M, N and O

#28—place a sample of relaxer on piece M

#29—place a sample of hair remover on piece N

#30—place a sample of hydroxide on piece O

#31—record observations

#32—take off the rubber gloves and dispose of them in the garbage

Results and Observations

Piece	Color Change	Coarse/ Straight	Stable/ Removed	pH level
A	N	C	S	10
B	N	S	S	10
C	N	S	S	11
D	N	C	R	11
X	N	-	R	10
y	N	-	R	11

Fig. 1   Fig. 2

Hair Remover

Fig. 1   Fig. 2

Relaxer

1. *What kind of texture was hair/skin originally?*
   The hair, was coarse and very wire like (I used dreadlocks) while the ham was moist with small pores.

2. *Did the texture change after substance was applied?*
   A no there was no change in texture
   B yes there was a change, the texture was thinner
   C yes there was a change, the texture was rough and the hair was begining to split
   D yes there was a change, the texture was rough and was breaking apart
   X a slight change occurred, the ham began to peel
   Y yes there was a change, the ham began to fall apart

3. *How did the two substances differ?*
   The hair remover was a yellow lotion with a strong odor before and after it was applied, while the relaxer was a white cream like substance that smelled after it was applied.

4. *How did the two substances compare?*
   Both the hair remover and relaxer had a reasonably high pH level and both were easy to apply to hair and the ham.

5. *What did you see under the microscope prior to applying the substance?*
   The hair was coarse and looked like wire when placed under the microscope. The hair was also a deep black. The ham resembled skin under the microscope because it had pores similar to that of human skin. The ham was also a dull pink.

6. *What did you see after you applied the substance?*
There were certain parts of the hair where it looked as if it fell apart, and other spots where you could tell the fiber of the hair was splitting. The ham stayed the same color but you could see that it lost some of it's moisture, and the pores were slightly bigger than before.

7. *Do the relaxer and hair remover have the same affect on hair?*
No, the hair remover had a stronger affect on the hair. It caused it to split after being applied after only, 15 minutes. I believe this was a result of it having a stronger pH level.

8. *Do the relaxer and hair remover have the same affect on skin (ham)?*
Yes, both substances caused the ham to loose moisture and peel. The only difference was to what extent the ham peeled. Once again the hair remover demonstrated its strength over relaxer.

9. *What happened after the extra 15 minutes (pieces B and D)? Why?*
Piece B, was of a thinner texture than piece A. This was a result of the relaxer needing time to take affect, but piece D wasn't as stable as piece C. When touched the hair broke causing a split of the fiber. This is an example of what can happen when hair remover is left on for a long period of time.

10. *Did a break down of the disulfide or hydrogen bonds occur? If yes, what happened?*
The break down occurred when the hair lost its strength, and when the ham lost its form and moisture. I believe the two bonds in fact have a lot to do with the object staying intact, and after this experiment its easy to see that this wasn't the case.

11. *Is there a drastic difference in the alkalinity of the relaxer, hair remover and sodium hydroxide? If yes, why?*

Hair remover—11   Relaxer—10   NaOH—11

The substances contain hydroxide. Hydroxide has a very high pH level, and to neutralize it would take numerous chemicals that have a very low pH level. Even then the pH level of hair remover and relaxer might not decrease.

Conclusion
The idea of both substances sharing numerous chemicals is a scary one. Since relaxer is used to make one's hair more manageable . . . but just think about it, relaxer is strong enough to remove hair from the scalp, and expand ones pores.
Before I actually tried the experiment I thought the mineral oil and water would somehow neutralize the substance but I've come to realize that both are probably used to soothe the scalp after such a harsh substance. My original idea is kind of a silly one because as a scientist I should have known that hydroxide is a powerful substance no matter what it is combined with.

Knowing what relaxer can do to the hair and skin, can turn one away from applying it to one's scalp. It's no wonder more African-American women are allowing their hair to grow naturally, and are using more natural herbs and oils for their hair. After repeatedly applying powerful substances the breakdown of the disulfide and hydrogen bonds is obvious to a beautician, but not the ordinary person who looks at the hair.

Overall, we as consumers need to pay closer attention to the chemical make-up of the products we purchase, because one would never think that the hair remover and relaxer contain the same chemicals.

Bibliography

Tortora, Gerard J. and Anagnostabos, Nicholas P.
Principles of Anatomy and Physiology: sixth edition
New York
Harper & Row Publishers
©1989

Oelerich, Randall
Case Studies in Anatomy and Physiology
Missouri
Mosby-Year Book Inc.
©1992

Hair
Colliers-Encyclopedia
MacMillan Educational Co.
©1990
Volume 11, pp. 579–580

"Black Like . . . Shirley Temple"
Harpers
February 1992
pp. 102–105

"Hair Problems Solved"
Essence
January 1993 (Volume 23, #9)
pp. 8–10

"Hair Trend Watch"
Essence
January 1993 (Volume 23, #9)
pp. 20

Keratin
The Merck Index: an Encyclopedia of Chemicals and Drugs
Merck and Company, Inc.
©1976
pp. 694

Kerantinase
The Merck Index: an Encyclopedia of Chemicals and Drugs
Merck and Company, Inc.
©1976
pp. 694

3

THE SENIOR PROJECT AT HODGSON
VOCATIONAL TECHNICAL HIGH SCHOOL

"When Jake[1] was in first grade for only three days," recalls his mother, "I got an unexpected call from his school to come and take him home because he refused to come out from under a table where he'd been hiding for two hours." She hesitated, as though freshly stung by the pain of an event that occurred eleven years earlier: "You don't know how it feels to have something like that happen to you. What do you do when the school calls and tells you they don't want your child?" Jake Lott was later found to be dyslexic. He is still withdrawn. Now, however, as a Hodgson Vocational Technical high school senior, he shyly explains the geometry he used to construct the blonde mahogany, 18th century pencil-post bed that he is exhibiting, and his mother beams proudly.

Jake is engaged in the formal public presentation component of the three-part Hodgson Senior Project. His project committee, consisting of three teachers—his carpentry teacher, his English teacher, and another vocational teacher—is in the process of evaluating his presentation. They watch and listen intently, barely able to contain their delight. Jake has already completed the two other project components: the product, which is the actual bed (valued at $2,500.00), and a typed, properly annotated, multisource, 20-page research paper on the craft of bed making.

In the public presentation, Jake demonstrates his knowledge and skills by integrating the academic and vocational components of his course of study in carpentry and language arts. Guided by note cards, he takes his audience through the history and process of bed making, with carefully planned narration and demonstrations that make the craft he has learned visible and accessible. Jake demonstrates a lambstongue cut—a cut typically used by 18th century craftsmen. He passes around a template he designed and a sample of the wood he used to construct the bed. While displaying various tools, he explains their uses. He discusses the factors that influenced his choice of materials: cost, aesthetics, appropriateness, and effect. He instructs his audience in related linguistic phenomena—such as the derivation of the well-known phrase, "sleep tight"—as well as the history of the antique hardware he used.

Jake's committee questions him to assess the depth of both his academic and his vocational knowledge: "What tools did you have that an 18th century craftsman would not have had?" "How does a crafted bed differ from a mass-produced one?" "What different types of finishes did you use?" "What was the hardest thing about making the bed?" "Why did you choose this project?"

Jake's answers to the last two questions reveal the power of the Senior Project to act simultaneously as an assessment of and a catalyst for deep learning. He explains: "The hardest thing about the project was the time required to do high-quality work. Exact work. Not sloppy work." (Jake's mother later confides that he worked on the bed over spring vacation when school was closed: "He got up at 6 a.m. and went to his co-op furniture shop to work on his bed.")

Jake explains that he chose the bed project for aesthetic reasons and to challenge himself: "I wanted to see if I could do it. I liked the simple, clean design." His mother reveals how his trepidation turned to new-found self-confidence. "He picked something he didn't think he could do, something he didn't want to do, and found out something he can do." Carpentry teacher Dave Lutz explains Jake's initial resistance: "Jake didn't want to do this at all. He almost walked out!" Jake agrees: "I doubt my skills all the time. This proved I could do anything if I put my mind to it. Now I know I *have* skills. I learned that I like making furniture."

The authentic performance that constitutes the Senior Project has taught Jake a personal work ethic: perseverance, self-motivation, high standards, pride in his craft, and self-confidence. The gathering of family, teachers, and the school principal at Jake's exhibition is this assessment's ritual for evaluating and celebrating students' skills and knowledge in the school's integrated career and academic program. In its second year when we visited during 1991–92, the exhibition already had begun to serve as both a celebration of students' personal achievement and as a symbol of the school's achievement as a community organized for success.

Paul M. Hodgson Vocational Technical High School is one of three vocational-technical high schools in New Castle County, Delaware. The Hodgson Senior Project was the school's first of many education reform initiatives in response to the school's recent conversion from a shared-time vocational center to a full-time academic-vocational-technical school. Located in suburbs 20 miles southwest of Wilmington, Hodgson's 17-year-old, modern style building sits comfortably on a grassy, 30-acre campus directly off a local highway. Over 800 students from New Castle County choose to attend Hodgson full-time, in grades 9 through 12. They participate in one of 22 career programs that the school offers in conjunction with a comprehensive academic instructional program. The student body is about 30% minority; most students come from working-class families. The students reflect the full range of achievement levels, from a substantial proportion identified for special education services (roughly 15%) to a minority aiming at 4-year colleges. Approximately 25% continue on after graduation to postsecondary schools.

THE RATIONALE FOR THE SENIOR PROJECT

Under the 3-year-old administration of Hodgson's principal, Dr. Steven Godowsky, the Senior Project was launched in conjunction with several other initiatives that focused on rethinking school goals and practices. Hodgson was eager to incorporate the goals of the Southern Regional Educational Board for higher expectations of vocational students in the areas of communication, mathematics, and science. Hodgson staff became acquainted with Theodore Sizer's set of ideas about schooling through Delaware's participation in "Re:Learning," a joint effort of the Coalition of Essential Schools and the Education Commission of the States, aimed at restructuring secondary schools to better meet the needs of students. In order to generate interest in reform and to allow staff to examine Sizer's principles, Godowsky sponsored morning and afternoon faculty "conversations" over the period of one year. These conversations became the forum for educational debate among Hodgson staff, and the wellspring for the school's restructuring efforts.

Starting with the concept of "diploma by exhibition," and manifesting their commitment to the idea of "student as worker," the staff settled on the idea of a senior project as the first initiative toward a more ambitious goal of awarding diplomas based on student performance. As activities that enable students to demonstrate expertise, exhibitions gave them a familiar starting point. Hodgson could draw on its history and expertise as a vocational-technical school with a variety of traditional vocational approaches to competency-based education, exhibitions, and performance-based assessment. The school had long participated in such exhibition-based events as the annual VICA competitions; consequently, many students and teachers understood the concept and value of performance-based evaluations of competence. Students also undertake a number of projects that engage them in real work producing real products for their use and that of others. For example, Hodgson students recently built dugouts for their baseball field and have completed two portable houses for the county's low-income housing program.

The Hodgson English Department has always required seniors to do a research paper that integrates the vocational and academic components of their course of study, and another outcome of staff conversations was the formation of a staff committee whose mission was "to investigate the possibility of expanding this [English] paper to create a multicomponent senior project that would require students to demonstrate skills mastered in career and academic programs" (Godowsky, Scarbrough, & Steinwedel, 1991, p. 1).

The English department's career-based senior research paper, which had recently replaced the traditionally required literature-based research paper, was an ideal starting point. It was popular with vocational teachers and successful with Hodgson's full range of students, most notably with those special education students who were mainstreamed into regular classes. Although the content of the paper had been changed from literature to shop, the rigor required by a thorough research process was uncompromised. Students still had to learn and demonstrate appropriate understanding of research conventions, such as compiling a bibliography, using multiple formats (such as charts and photographs in addition to text to represent their findings), gathering their information from a variety of sources, and then typing the paper. English Chair Mary An Scarbrough also asked the students to "do some kind of application in the paper. They weren't asked to do a physical project per se, but many of them did, just because they wanted to find out how [what they had researched] worked, and they wanted to write up their analysis, or their results, in the paper."

The Senior Project: An Exhibition of Achievement was, as Scarbrough says, "the next logical step." In 1990, at a summer institute sponsored by the Coalition of Essential Schools, a four-teacher team composed the first draft of the Senior Project: a three-part plan that consisted of:

- A shop-based research paper that requires students to expand their knowledge
- A shop product, designed, constructed, and related to the student's vocational program and research paper, which requires students to expand their abilities
- A public, formal, oral presentation.

At in-service days prior to the opening of the 1990 school year, the entire staff responded to the plan. As a result, the Senior Project Evaluation Committee (SPEC) was formed to make the revisions suggested by the staff's critique. The pilot Senior Project, implemented that year, built upon the school's knowledge base of successful practice, was rooted in the school culture, and emerged not from an external directive but from an internal process of inquiry. Thus, the staff had substantial ownership and investment in the project's success.

It was hoped that the conception of the Senior Project as a final exhibition of knowledge—an accumulation of 3 years of achievement and skill in one shop area—would encourage students to demonstrate a level of mastery in both vocational and academic domains. The project provided the school with the opportunity to reinvigorate and challenge students who were convinced, as Scarbrough states, that they "were at Hodgson because they couldn't make it in the academic world."

THE ASSESSMENT IN OPERATION

The Senior Project process has five steps, as described in Hodgson's "Senior Project Manual":

1. Selecting an advisor and Project Committee members
2. Selecting a topic
3. Researching the topic and preparing the research paper, the product, and the oral presentation
4. Making a formal public presentation before the Project Committee
5. Evaluation

Following is a description of each of the five steps.

Selecting an Advisor and Project Committee Members

At the end of their junior year, or the beginning of their senior year, students select a faculty advisor from either the academic or vocational-technical faculty. Together, students and their advisor work to orchestrate the student's progress through the senior project in a fashion similar to the doctoral dissertation process. In consultation with their advisor, students select a Project Committee, which serves as a resource during the entire project and evaluates the student's research paper, product, and presentation at its conclusion. The Project Committee must consist of at least three adults, including the advisor, an English teacher, and a teacher from the student's vocational program. Students have the option of adding other individuals to their committee, and some have included representatives from industry and business, ministers, the employers with whom they have co-op work study placements, former students, and other faculty. After students have formed their committee, they must submit the members' names to the Senior Project Evaluation Committee, which plans and coordinates the Senior Project process.

Selecting the Topic

The next step in the process is the selection of a topic. Since one of the project's goals is to increase opportunities for students to challenge themselves, students are encouraged to select topics that are of authentic interest to them, that pique their curiosity. In order to discover their interests, students must begin to engage in a process of self-inquiry. Through this process they learn about their talents as well as their interests, and about the power of their talents and interests to generate initiative, hard work, and satisfaction: the cornerstones of a life-long work ethic.

Allan Angel, Dental Lab teacher, explains the process he uses to help students select a topic:

In their senior year, students pick an area that they're going to special-
ize in, like dentures, orthodonture, crown and bridge. From that specialty they have to pick their senior project, because they'll be able to
use a higher skill level and higher order thinking skills. The students
and I will brainstorm together for a senior project topic. It may take
two periods, but it's basically what they want to do. If they don't know
what they want to do, I will sit with them and review what their talents
have been and what they did best in. This helps them make a decision.

Angel's theory about the engagement and sustained efforts of students
in their projects certainly appears to prove true. Dental lab projects on topics ranging from "Glass Teeth" and "Porcelain Crowns" to "Obturators" exhibit both careful lab work and painstakingly clear descriptions of procedures,
advantages, and disadvantages of different types of dental materials and
options, and discussions of related physiology, complete with graphics and
extensive references. The following excerpt from Angela's* paper on porcelain crowns illustrates how carefully students describe their procedures,
defining terms and explaining why each step is important along the way.

Begin with forming the lingual collar. This is a collar around the tooth
on the surface facing the tongue. It runs from contact point to contact
point. The contact point is where the teeth touch on each side (see
figure 2). The function of the lingual collar is to give strength and sta-
bility to the porcelain as it rests on the framework. Enough support
should be given to the framework in order to allow the porcelain to
be applied without causing problems. It should be designed to support all functioning areas of porcelain. There are a variety of designs
for anterior frameworks (see figure 3). . . .
    The supporting structures of a wax-up, which is the lingual collar
in the construction of an anterior crown, should be smooth to avoid
being fractured while being fired. It should have extensions far
enough into porcelain to protect the porcelain from damage as seen in
figure 4. This shows a metal island in the center of a posterior tooth.
For porcelain bridges, if the metal is extended to the marginal ridge,
this will provide an island of alloy thickness. This will increase bridge
rigidit. (see figure 5.) A marginal ridge is an elevation of enamel that
forms the boundary of a surface of a tooth. (Boucher 346)

By the time Angela reaches the end of her carefully written and illustrated paper—which is accompanied by the porcelain crowns she built as her
product—even the totally uninitiated reader knows a great deal about the
creation of porcelain crowns. She concludes her paper with this statement:

As you can see there is a great deal of time and artistic skill put into the
fabrication of a porcelain crown; however, it is well worth it for a nice

smile. By doing this research paper, I have learned many new things that will benefit me in my dental career. Hopefully I have successfully explained to you the step by step procedures in fabricating a porcelain crown. Perhaps you have a porcelain crown or maybe someday you will. Now you have an idea of how one is made.

Like Angela, students often relate their own career intentions to the topic they examine. For example, in "Diabetes and the Medical Secretary," Melodie* starts out:

If you were a diabetic, would you want yourself in the hands of a health care professional who knows nothing about your disease? It is very important for a medical secretary to inform her employer of new technologies on the market, to let the doctor know if the diabetic patient is experiencing problems coping with the disease, to offer any services she can, and to help the patient further understand this disease, and to be a friend who listens and cares.

Melodie's paper goes on to review the types of diabetes, the risk factors, symptoms, complications, effects, and treatment. Then she outlines the responsibilities of a medical secretary in ensuring proper communication with the patient, providing instruction, and managing emergency situations. This and other projects illustrate students' capacities and their commitment to their future professions.

Because the project topics emerge from the interests, talents, and strengths of the students, and because they elicit their curiosity, they have the potential to be intrinsically motivating and to deflect students' initial and lingering resistance to the hard work that the project demands. Both Dave Lutz and Carolyn Steinwedel, Special Education English teacher, delight in telling stories of students who, upon learning that the project would be required, threatened to transfer to other schools or asserted that the staff had gone crazy to think that they and their classmates would actually take such a hard project seriously, do it, and complete it. Joshua,* a Hodgson senior, recalls: "Everybody, like, had a problem with the Senior Project at first, because nobody wants to do the work. Because you're seniors, you want to lay back and just cruise through."

Students select their topic in consultation with their Project Committee. Both the shop teacher and English teacher, along with the advisor (if the advisor is not one of these), must sign their approval of the project topic. If any of the teachers is dissatisfied with the topic, they confer with one another and the student until a consensus is reached. The English teacher then submits the approved topic to the Senior Project Evaluation Committee, which formalizes the agreement by publishing the student's name, topic, advisor, and committee. The commitment is now public.

Although the procedure for topic selection is streamlined and smooth, the process of decision making about the topic is more complex, and captures the untidiness and complexity of "pathfinding" inherent to the project as a whole. While a student's interest and curiosity about a topic can ignite and sustain self-motivation and perseverance during periods of frustration, student interest and curiosity do not by themselves assure topics of substance and appropriate challenge—topics that will, as required by the Senior Project guidelines, extend students' knowledge. Lutz explains that evaluation criteria drive substance, focus the staff on the rigor of project topics, and direct the staff's discourse about the project back to its goals. Criteria such as the demonstration of higher order thinking skills, originality, and creativity set a framework for both the senior project topics and the committee's discussion about the suitability of individual student's topics.

During the first year of the project, mundane topics were not unusual. Lutz describes them as "topics that were in-shop practices and had very little to do with higher order thinking and challenging and pushing the student." Lutz cites "The Alphabet Line" as an example of a first-year topic that was basic to a drafting course, and compares it to a second-year topic from the same shop, "Cochran's Grange: A Study." Where "The Alphabet Line" project required the student merely to demonstrate knowledge of definitions of various lines, the "Cochran's Grange" project demanded that the student study an historically significant architectural structure from an interdisciplinary perspective.

To extend the scope of projects in the second year, the Evaluation Committee encouraged increased collaboration between the English and shop teachers, and involved the librarian as well. The second-year and third-year projects reveal more challenging topics, which reflect a sophisticated notion of integrating multiple disciplines, not only English and shop. Projects on "Satellite Communications" and "Brain Tumors," for example, rely on extensive library research in scientific and medical journals, as well as on interviews and other sources of information. Many projects include historical research on the topic as well. For example, this excerpt from a senior project on obturators ("a dental prosthesis designed to close a hole in the palate") starts by noting:

> The first obturators were constructed in the early fifteen hundreds by Ambroise Pare. He was from France. These were made with a large piece of gold to cover the defect. On top of this gold was a small clip. A sponge was put into this clip. The sponge was put in the nasal cavity to absorb fluid. Obturators were first brought to public attention in 1563 in Pare's *Ten Books of Surgery.*
>
> Pierre Fuchard also made some of the early obturators. This is a picture of an obturator made by Fuchard. This type of obturator was not practical or comfortable but it was used for many years. [Figure follows here.]

The paper goes on to describe how these devices are currently made, in exceedingly thorough detail, defining terms and reasons for particular procedures, and discussing aspects of mouth physiology that are important to understand for those designing and fitting the devices.

The range of student interests and talents is quite wide. Other project topics have included: "History of War Propaganda Poster Design," "AIDS and the Dental Office," "Drainage Systems," "Malpractice Insurance," "Fiber Optics," "Using Information Systems and Service Skills in Sports Journalism," "The Effects of Stress on Children," "Cajun Style Cooking," "Nail Disorders," and "The Architecture of the Sistine Chapel and Its Effect on Other Churches."

Scarbrough discusses the significance of ongoing communication, negotiation, and shared decision making between academic and vocational faculty to assure that students select self-challenging topics:

> I say to the shop teachers: "Nobody knows this kid better than you. You have them three periods a day and you've known some of them for over three years. You know what this kid can do better than I know what this kid can do. When you have to sign that paper [i.e., approval for the topic], when he has picked a topic, don't sign that paper unless you're sure that the topic is something challenging to that student." Shop teachers reject topics left and right based on that.
>
> I have a kid right now who wants to do screw threads in machine shop. He and I and the shop teacher sat down and I said, "Okay, now you tell him—the shop teacher—what you're going to do for your product in shop. What are you going to make?" Because we had talked about what he was going to research. And he said, "This is what I want to do." And the shop teacher said, "Too easy." And the kid said, "Well, okay, *this* is what I'll do." And the shop teacher said, "Nope. Too easy." So the kid said, "What would you like me to do?" The shop teacher said, "This is what I'd like you to do." And the kid said, "Well, that's hard." And both the shop teacher and I said, "Yes. But it's do-able, isn't it?" The kid said, "Yeah. I could do it if I really put my mind to it." That's what we want.
>
> Sometimes, the shop teacher will approve a topic that sounds fine to me, but the librarian will say, "We can't get those materials," or "It's not narrow enough." Then the shop teacher and the librarian have to come to an accord.

In order to increase the active participation and support of the staff for the project, Hodgson provides regular opportunities at inservice meetings to elicit teacher feedback. This input is promptly followed up on. When shop teachers wanted to be regularly rather than intermittently informed about their students' progress, the English teachers, who were keeping the forms and records of students' progress on the projects, quickly put together folders with a checklist attached to their inside flap. Such responsiveness builds credibility among the staff and increases the level of ownership teachers feel for the project.

Preparing the Research Paper, the Product, and the Oral Presentation

Once the topic is selected, students begin both their research and product. Malik,* one of Hodgson's star athletes, explains how the countervailing forces of resistance and authentic curiosity, coupled with relentless teacher encouragement, propelled his project (a 3/4" to scale, basic residential house) toward completion:

> When I first started, I was like, "Man, forget this! I don't want to do it." And my teacher, Mr. Sarro, he's like, "What are you talking about? You're going to get this thing done." So I said, "All right. I'm going to do it." At first it seemed like it was too hard, like it was going to be a whole lot of work, and I had a whole lot of things going on. I was training sports around the clock, and I didn't think I had time to do a project that big. But I just made time, stayed after school. I used to come in after games and come in at night—they had night school—and work on it, because *I wanted to see it get done. I wanted to see what it looked like. I mean, after you draw up all the plans and you looked at it, I said, "I wonder what it's going to look like when it's sitting right in front of me."* [Italics added.]

As students get underway, they are spurred on by their teachers as well as by their innate drive and curiosity. Both their English and shop teachers give them class time to do the work on their papers, products, and to practice for their public presentation. Faculty members systematically teach students the skills necessary to successfully engage the tasks. For example, the English teachers teach a step-by-step process for conducting research and for writing a research paper. They show students how to design and use visuals in their public presentation, as well as how to use note cards as cues.

Most papers written during the second and third years of the project (1992 and 1993) contain all of the structural features of a carefully constructed research paper: an outline and table of contents; introduction, topically organized body, and conclusion; charts and figures to illustrate key points; definitions of key terms; and a substantial bibliography with appropriate citations to literature and personal interviews. They also include a clear, logical exposition of ideas, accompanied by useful graphic illustrations. The consistency with which the papers include these elements of expository writing makes it clear that students are not left on their own to magically uncover the secrets of writing a research paper. They are carefully taught.

Shop teachers guide the design and construction of the product, directing students to useful books, suggesting materials, participating in students' decisions, and helping them to solve problems as they arise. Among the products constructed in 1992, in addition to Jake's bed and Malik's residential house, were an irrigation system for Malik's residential house, a full set of dentures, a course and kit for dressing for success, a catered school dinner, and a cut-stone fireplace.

Students schedule regular meetings with their advisor and committee as doctoral students would when working on their dissertations. Their committee members act as mentors and coaches, guiding them to resources, encouraging them during setbacks, and correcting the many drafts of the research paper they must submit prior to its completion. The shop teacher critiques the content while the English teacher evaluates usage and style, and both make suggestions for substantive revisions. Students are responsible for keeping a log of the meetings and must adhere to deadlines set by the SPEC and by their individual teachers.

Because the Senior Project is designed for students to extend knowledge, their research must take them beyond the confines of the school library. Hodgson's library is linked by computer to public libraries around the state, which gives the librarian access to much material needed for student research. Students' research often takes them beyond the confines of the school. They conduct research the way social science researchers do, and the authenticity and nonroutine quality of the process impresses and excites them. Frank,* a special education student, explains how he researched his project on domestic water well systems.

When I first started, Ms. Steinwedel told me to call around, to ask for information on the phone. I thought, "I'm not gonna get an answer. Nobody's gonna help me." But I got on the phone and started calling people in the phone book. And they're like, "Come on over. We got all kinds of information on well systems. You can take pictures. Bring your camera." I had all kinds of information for my paper. Got all kinds of packets and rock samples. I wrote to Gould's Pump—it's like the biggest well pump company around—and told them what I was doing a senior project on. I told them anything that they could donate to me for my project would be a good help for me. And they sent me information. They sent me switches, electronic switches, you know, when the water cuts off.

I went to the University of Delaware—to the center where they study the earth by digging wells. They dig down and test the different levels of the rock, different types of rock, granite and other kinds. They study the earth, test the water, and drill wells. I have a picture of the drill. They had a drilling truck there—had everything. *They had different definitions for a well, like three definitions for a well, instead of the one definition in the dictionary* [italics added]. I went to the University and spoke to the professors in the department. They just get paid to study and write little pamphlets all about wells, ground water, statistics on wells in Delaware. Everything, everything you'd want to know about wells, they had it there. They knew about it. I just sat down and had a meeting with them. I came in, signed in on a little paper, was talking to them for about an hour. They let me leave school! I had permission to go there! Came back to school.

Took pictures down there and everything. Even let me operate the drill truck. I was in there driving it!

The impact of Frank's experience is best captured by his awareness of Hodgson's departure from school conventions, such as permitting him to leave the school and trusting him to negotiate his own learning. Predictably, Frank's self-initiated field experience expanded his knowledge of wells, but this new-found independence also released him to critically evaluate sources of information (i.e., his discovery of the dictionary's limits). He became a more knowledgeable and critical researcher.

Other students have used their co-op employers in the development of their project. Employers have provided technical support as well as information. Some students have integrated their co-op work experiences into their project. They have had themselves video-taped working at their job, and then included the tape in the project.

The Formal, Public Presentation Before the Project Committee

The culmination of the Senior Project is the formal public presentation, during which students synthesize what they have learned from their research and product. The presentation cannot be less than 10 minutes or more than 30 minutes. This is the most intimidating component of the project for the students. Erica* explains: "People were worried about talking in front of people, like getting in front of the committee, as we have three or four people that you have to get up in front of and talk to. People didn't want to do that because they figured they'd all start laughing, or choke up and start stuttering. They have to do it to get over it."

Malik's presentation lasted an hour. He presented for half an hour and was questioned for another half hour. As at Jake's presentation, the questions asked were both technical and general. When the state superintendent, who attended Malik's presentation, asked how he determined the pitch of the roof on his model residential house, Malik explained, step by step, how he used the Pythagorean theorem. He continued to explain how all of his subjects related to his project (Figure 3.1). His initial fear gave way to exhaustion because, each time he thought he was finished, someone else would ask a question. "But," he said, "I learned how to speak in front of people. I had never done that."

Dave Lutz says: "We're looking to see if kids can think on their feet. We're looking for higher order thinking: Is this something they're repeating from a book they read, or do they really know it? Can they think? Can they synthesize this information? Can they apply it to another situation?" The students' and teachers' responses to the public presentation reveal how it takes the research paper one step further: it tests the depth and degree of students' personal integration of knowledge. The public presentation calls for their voice—the unique way in which they have constructed this knowledge, how they have made it their own, and how, in a public forum, in response

Figure 3.1. Malik's presentation

to spontaneous questions, they reconstruct it and enrich it as their own. A comparison between students' preparation for the public presentation and for traditional tests illuminates a fundamental difference in the potential for lasting learning. In preparation for the public presentation, students review their subject matter for deepened understanding, whereas for conventional test situations, they would have to memorize for short-term recall.

The presentation turns out to be both the most powerful and the most threatening learning task for many students. It is the only component that a few students have refused to do and that some parents have objected to as being too difficult. Scarbrough recalls students telling her, "I'll do that paper. I'll do that product. But I'm not doing the oral presentation!"

But the old saw about the greatest risk bringing the greatest reward holds true. The public presentation teaches students about learning and knowing in the most profound of ways. They learn that knowing means internalizing and owning knowledge; that this ownership can occur only through the individual struggle of having to make personal sense and meaning of information and experience. The public presentation is the kind of incentive necessary to induce the struggle required for the construction of authentic knowledge, because it is an act of public accountability. Students come face to face with their judges and with their work—not a proxy test of their ability to recall a test-designer's definition of knowledge, but their *actual* work. They define their own knowledge by making the decisions as to what to present and how to present it.

The oral presentation provides students with the opportunity to construct and express their knowledge in their own voice. But then it demands that they locate their voice. This is both a liberating and a terrifying responsibility. Anthony* explains: "I think people are scared about talking in front of a lot of people, because they really don't know anything about the subject when they start. But once they get all this input into their brains, it comes out once they start talking about it. It makes it a lot easier on you after you do all your research." Similarly, Erica reports: "At first I was embarrassed to get up in front of a whole lot of people. But I'm not nervous anymore because I think I know what I'm talking about." The presentation persuades students, as well as their assessors, that they truly understand.

Evaluation

Although the Senior Project creates the opportunity for authentic interdisciplinary learning, evaluation for the project was still departmentalized when we were conducting our research, reflecting the school's struggle toward vocational and academic integration. Each of the three components—research paper, product, and public presentation—constitutes a grade for either shop or English. Although the English teachers have agreed to a uniform departmental credit policy, each of the shop teachers retains individual credit policies. The research paper fulfills the English requirement for a research paper and the formal public presentation constitutes the final English examination. If students choose not to do the Senior Project, there is a strong likelihood that they will not pass English. The product is integrated into the shop final, which constitutes 10% of the students' vocational grade. However, some shop teachers assign the full 10% credit to the senior project product, while others assign less.

This variation in credit policies reflects the yet-to-be conquered resistance to collective decision making. Steinwedel believes this inconsistency is related to ownership of the project. As feelings of ownership increase among the faculty, she says, so will their capacity for the consensus necessary to formulate a consistent credit and grading policy. Lutz's analysis reveals some of the instructional dilemmas a school confronts when it undertakes assessment reform. Old habits don't die easily, responsible curriculum reorganization is complex, and a balance between consistency and respect for individual course integrity is not struck quickly. He explains:

Some shop teachers have other things that are legitimate that they
need to incorporate into the final exam. For example, in cosmetology.
To become a cosmetologist, students must pass the state boards, so
the cosmetology teacher wants the students to demonstrate a readiness to pass the state boards. Some shop teachers have used written
exams for ten and twenty years, and they don't want to give them up.

They're uncomfortable with performance assessment as opposed to a written assessment. You work toward consistency, yet you also have to work towards the individualization of each shop, which is trying to prepare students for specific vocations.

The potential for collaboration between the academic and vocational faculties is evident in the evaluation system and grading rubric for the public presentation. Members of both faculties created this assessment, which integrates judgment criteria used in both domains. As used during the 1991–92 school year (though since revised), the grid for evaluating the public presentation relies on four performance indicators: content (30 points), organization and plan of work (30 points), communication skills (30 points), and personal appearance (10 points). (See Table 3.1.) Individually, each member of the Project Committee scores the presentations on the grid.

The criteria for evaluating content require students to exhibit understanding, knowledge, creativity, originality, higher order thinking skills, proper procedures for demonstrations, and appropriate responses to questions. For the organization and plan of work, students must demonstrate the use and understanding of conventions, show evidence of preparation, use appropriate aids and equipment, and finish within time limits. In their exhibition of communication skills, students must communicate clearly using proper grammar, posture, and eye contact. Their personal appearance must exhibit dress that is appropriate to their project. In each category, numerical ratings correspond to judgments of excellent, good, satisfactory, and unacceptable.

Immediately after the presentation, the committee members individually complete their grid and briefly meet to total their scores for a combined score. The committee then conveys the score to the student. If serious discrepancies occur, the committee will discuss them. Simultaneously, students complete the Student Survey regarding their own experience of and views about the Senior Project, which the staff uses to review, evaluate, and continually revise the project and how it operates. A staff committee meets one afternoon per week to discuss and develop project changes.

In the first year, although none of the 85 students failed to complete the senior project entirely, 3 students refused to do the presentation (all of them had sufficiently high grades that they did not need to do so in order to pass at a high enough level to satisfy themselves). A few students did not complete the paper, although they did prepare and present a product. With the increased preparation and support in place for year two, along with the strengthened expectations of full participation born of experience and prior success, staff members felt confident that an even greater number of students would attempt and complete a full project in year two. In fact, in 1992, 144 of the 150 students enrolled in senior English successfully completed all aspects of the Senior Project.

Table 3.1. Senior Project: An Exhibition of Achievement—Public Presentation Evaluation Form

Name: Date:
Shop: Advisor:
Topic:

Evaluation Components	Excellent	Good	Satisfactory	Unacceptable
Content/Total pts. 30	28–30	25–27	20–33	0–19
Demonstrates thorough understanding of knowledge				
Demonstrates creativity and originality				
Exhibits a higher order of thinking				
Uses proper procedures for demonstrations				
Responds appropriately to questions				
Organization and Plan of Work/Total pts. 30	28–30	25–27	20–23	0–19
Follows guidelines				
Uses introduction and closing				
Shows evidence of preparation				
Uses appropriate aids, equipment, etc.				
Stays within time limits				
Communication Skills/Total pts. 30	28–30	25–27	20–23	0–19
Communicates clearly				
Uses proper posture, eye contact, etc.				
Uses proper grammar				
Personal Appearance/Total pts. 10	9–10	8	7	0–6
Wears appropriate dress, uniform, or costume				
Total Points				

Although the Senior Project is quite sophisticated instructionally, as the conflicts surrounding grading and credits reveal, its full impact on instruction that integrates academic and vocational learning will be known only when more of the tensions articulated by Steinwedel and Lutz are resolved. This process is aided by the sensitive and steadfast leadership of Godowsky, who respects and manages the tensions created by his vision for reform and the staff's needs to develop their own vision. In addition, the energetic commitment of a core of academic and vocational teachers has been critical in enabling the Hodgson staff to tolerate the contradictions, conflicts, and ambiguities inherent in any change initiative. As the Senior Project increasingly penetrates the culture of the school with new rituals each year, Godowsky and the staff Steering Committee become increasingly confident about setting a deadline for converting the school from a system of graduation by credit to a system of graduation by exhibition that fully integrates the academic and vocational programs.

INFLUENCES OF THE SENIOR PROJECT ON TEACHING, LEARNING, AND STUDENT SUCCESS

As the Senior Project has begun to take hold at Hodgson, faculty and students note differences in the nature of teaching and learning opportunities that occur. These result from the focused energy students apply to their in-depth inquiry and from the ownership and pride they develop in their work; from the collaboration and increasingly shared norms among teachers in discussing and shaping teaching and learning; and from the opportunities for interdisciplinary study that allow students and teachers to look at ideas and problems in new ways.

The Kinds of Learning Reflected in Students' Projects

One of the things that stands out in reviewing students' senior projects is how consistently students take integrative approaches to their topics, looking at them through several disciplinary lenses and from a number of vantage points. For example, Tricia's* paper on "Medical Malpractice" includes actual case studies of malpractice cases, while also covering legal considerations of relevance to a medical assistant ("breach of duty," "contributory negligence," "comparative negligence," and "assumption of risk," among others). Using mathematical tools in a series of graphs and charts to show the dramatic annual increases in malpractice claims and insurance premiums, she then turns to a scientific and medical explanation of one area of frequent malpractice complaints, laparoscopic surgery.

Another common characteristic of the papers is how consistently they weigh and balance the pros and cons of different technologies or approaches to a problem. Paul's* paper on "Roofing in America" traces the history of roofing materials, recounting reasons for the use (and disappearance) of thatch in the British Isles and in America through the mid-seventeenth century, the use of ceramic tile through the mid-nineteenth century, and the use of slate, metal roofing, asphalt, tar, and wood shingles. The paper also includes a careful analysis of the advantages and disadvantages of each type of roofing. For example:

> Records show that slate roofing was used before the American Revolution. During the Revolutionary period, only elegant homes such as the Carpenter House in Philadelphia and the Thomas Hancock House in Boston were covered with slate. After the Revolutionary War, slate usage became more common. In fact by 1830 it was reported that nearly "half of the roofs in New York City were covered with slate." Slate was one of the popular roof coverings of the time (Waite 138).
>
> Slate was a valued roofing material. It was favored for a number of reasons. One was that slate was a maintenance-free roofing material, unlike other roof coverings such as metal. Slate was also regard [sic] because of its "handsome appearance" (Waite 138–39). See figure 2.
>
> Like other roofing materials slate did have its drawbacks. One was the cost. Also slate was a heavy material that put excess stress on the roofing system. For a time there was a decline in slate until the population explosion during the middle of the nineteenth [sic] century (Waite 139–40). . . .

Diandra's* paper, entitled "Glass Teeth," describes the advantages and disadvantages of cerestore, ceramo-metal, and dicor crowns, along with such dimensions as costs, aesthetics, strength, and X-rayability, as well as describing how they are made and used. Greg's* paper on "trusses" compares the different kinds of trusses and the relative advantages of trusses versus rafters in houses and other structures. His product was a series of trusses produced in different styles built to scale.

While these three papers, which were completed in the first year of the Senior Project (1991), exhibit evidence of analytic thinking, they are not nearly as sophisticated as the papers and projects completed by the graduating class of 1993. These later papers exhibit more analytic depth in their treatment of concepts and ideas; they are also more clearly written, with more complete and informative discussions and bibliographies.

In these later projects, more sophisticated treatment of science topics and more extensive use of mathematics are evident. Laura's* paper on the "Diagnosis, Treatment and Nursing Care of Patients with Frontal Brain Tumors" explains at length the structures and functions of the brain, the types of brain tumors, the causes, incidence, symptoms, and treatment of tumors, as well as nursing care for a patient following surgery. An array of standard medical texts on oncology, along with basic and specialized nursing texts (e.g., *A Guide to Neurological and Neurosurgical Nursing*), are referenced throughout. She also cites an interview she conducted with an expert. The clarity of the discussion of brain tumors is impressive.

> Tumors can be benign or malignant. A benign tumor is non-cancerous and a malignant tumor is cancerous. A doctor is able to determine whether a tumor is benign or malignant from looking at x-rays. The benign tumor is usually oblique and has a smooth surface. A malignant tumor has projections and is somewhat star shaped. (See Figure 3.) (Weigand). . . . Malignant tumors grow and metastasize. "Metastasize" means the tumor can spread through the circulatory system to any part of the body (brain). For example, tumors can metastasize from the lungs, breasts, ovaries, kidneys, and GI tract. Most brain tumors metastasize from the lungs. Brain tumors can originate in the brain, but once they develop there, the tumors usually don't metastasize (Leslie 82).

Laura continues with a thorough discussion of causes, symptoms, and treatments of different types of brain tumors, before concluding with a section on nursing care. This excerpt illustrates that she has a creditable grasp of the goals of nursing care, especially for a young high school student who has not yet even entered nursing education.

> Following surgery, the patient must maintain reduced intracranial pressure (ICP). To reduce intracranial pressure, the head must always be in an upright position. Neurological checks are another way to take precautions. Neuro checks are check-ups done by the nurse or doctor to be sure the patient is still stable. Neuro checks are done every hour. Vital signs are checked, medication is given, and the nurse checks to see if there are any signs of ICP. Some signs are headache, disorientation, dilated pupils, and restlessness. The most important assessment is to make sure there is no pressure on the brain (Weigand: Leslie 85).
>
> Positioning the patient is very important after surgery. Do not lay the patient on his operative side because it puts pressure right on the brain and could displace brain structures (Weigand: Leslie 85). Know whether the patient has had supratentorial or infratentorial surgery. That lets the nurse know what position to put him in. Elevate the patient's head 30 degrees if he's had supratentorial surgery. Elevation of the head is very important to increase the flow of blood to the heart from the peripheral vessels. Peripheral vessels are vessels in the limbs. If the patient had infratentorial surgery, he may have to stay off his back for 48 hours (Long and Phills 507). [Here follows a discussion of infratentorial and supratentorial surgery.] . . . If there are changes in the patient's vital signs, intracranial pressure, or level of consciousness, report them immediately to the doctor. . . .

Like Laura's paper, Mike's* research on Satellite Communications Systems demonstrates a clear understanding of the functioning of the satellite systems he set out to examine. His project was a satellite dish he constructed for the school, which is currently in use. His paper includes an overview of the history of satellite communications; a discussion of satellite positioning in space, drawing on earth science and physics principles; and a technical description of how satellite systems operate. These are supplemented by carefully chosen graphics to explain and illustrate key concepts. This excerpt demonstrates how clearly Mike is able to explicate what he has learned. Following a definition of elliptical and circular orbits supplemented by graphic illustrations, Mike explains:

> Due to the fact that a satellite must be in direct sight in order to send or receive to or from a given point on earth, it is important to know the amount of time a satellite is in view. The longer the satellite is in view, the more data that is able to be sent and received. A satellite in an elliptical orbit will be in sight for varying amounts of time during its orbit. This makes it hard to predict and follow. Satellites in circular orbits, however, are visible for the same amount of time every time they appear. Because they are predictable, they are much easier to follow. This made circular orbits the best choice for communication satellites.
>
> By changing the altitude of a satellite in circular orbit, it is possible to change the speed of a satellite. The higher a satellite is, the slower its rotation. This makes it possible to calculate the exact height needed to place a satellite so that its speed gives it a rotation period of 24 hours, the same as earth's. (See Figure 3.) This is known as a geostationary orbit. The plane of the satellite's orbit must contain the equator ("Satellite Communications," *Encyclopedia of Electronics*). The height needed is 35,803 kilometers.

Mike's paper goes on to describe how the satellite receives and transmits signals until it makes its way into your home television. The clarity with which Mike explains concepts like uplinks, transmitters, receivers, downlinks, signal bands, modulation, frequency deviations, and transponders turns a topic that might be mystifying into one that can be readily understood, and illustrates that Mike understands this technology well.

The changes in the quality of papers over just two years of the project's development illustrate that the project has effects on teaching—and consequently, learning—beyond the effects it has on students' motivation and personal development. Below we examine how the faculty's work over these initial years created new learning opportunities for students.

Changes in Curriculum and Teaching

As teachers have experienced first-hand the salutary effects of the Senior Project on students, they are increasingly willing to consider changes in their curriculum and teaching practices in order to increase students' opportunities to succeed in the project. Godowsky explains how the staff has engaged in "backward planning" (McDonald, 1993) to determine changes needed: They observe and analyze the skills and knowledge students need to successfully meet the demands of the project and then design changes based on that information. Although initial resistance and conflict are common, ultimately most of the staff and students embrace the changes because they are persuaded by both the results of the project—including the hard work and motivation of the students—and the critical core of teachers vigorously encouraging their involvement. The project is a constant catalyst for whole-school inquiry on the issues of teaching and learning.

Reshaping Curriculum

One initial, direct curricular change was the revision of the 12th grade English curriculum to include one semester of technical writing so that English teachers could teach students the skills necessary to write the research paper. In order to prepare lower grade students for the research they will do as seniors, both academic and vocational teachers in grades 9 through 11 have added research components to their courses, and are increasingly developing project-based curricular units. Ninth grade teams introduce both research papers and oral presentations in both English and shop classes.

Two 11th grade teachers, Jim Lacey and Kay Bach, formed an interdisciplinary core team for the required American History and American Literature courses, combining them into one course called "The American Experience." One of the units, which requires students to do a video-taped oral biography, is a direct outgrowth of the Senior Project's public presentation component and one of the school's efforts to provide students with the skills necessary for it.

In addition, The American Experience engages students in both individual and group projects and in activities ranging from mock trials, simulations, and role-playing of important historical events and persons to oral histories, journals, and research papers. The course is organized around four major themes of American life—frontiers, war, diversity of people, and core values, such as equality—and around authentic questions that allow for many modes of exploration. The students develop many hands-on, experiential, as well as research-based, inquiries into such questions as "How does diversity make America a stronger place?" "What values are constants in American life?" and "What qualities do Americans develop from crossing frontiers?"

The American Experience is one of several interdisciplinary courses that have been developed with the encouragement of block scheduling created by Godowsky at the request of any teacher team with a strong curricular idea and a willingness to experiment. A Biology/English block has just been started in the 10th grade, while 9th grade English, Science, and Social Studies are taught in a block schedule in which a group of teachers works with the same group of students. All of these provide opportunities for integrating disciplines, developing more authentic learning tasks, and coming to know students' minds and talents better.

Similarly, each mathematics teacher has been released from the usual course load for one period daily to work with a cluster of shops, teaching strands of theory in application. For example, the Pythagorean theorem and other aspects of geometry and algebra find a comfortable home in carpentry class. In a Principles of Technology course, technology and mathematics teachers teach scientific notation together. Over time, the integration of academic and vocational learning grows, as traditional academics are used to enable more powerful, hands-on work, and vocational applications bring practical power and relevance to traditional academics.

Hodgson has also experimented with integrating other vocational and academic courses, such as horticulture and biology. Increasingly, academic and vocational teachers visit one another's classes to learn about one another's fields with an eye toward future collaboration. As ideas emerge, Godowsky remains committed to working through the scheduling changes required for block scheduling that allows interdisciplinary work.

These initiatives—along with the move toward more authentic assessment—also enhance the success of ongoing efforts to reduce tracking in the school. Hodgson has moved from the five-track curriculum that existed several years ago—Advanced Placement, college preparatory, general, career, and special education—to a curriculum that is increasingly non-tracked, with heterogeneous classrooms and interdisciplinary/interprogrammatic courses of study replacing the old, highly programmed single-track models. Advanced Placement courses no longer exist, and students with college and employment intentions take an increasing number of courses in common. Special education students participate in regular shop classes, and more are being mainstreamed into other regular classes as teachers with both special education and disciplinary backgrounds become part of teams in which they feel comfortable working with more special education students. The authentic assessment strategies often enable these students to experience greater success because students are allowed a wider range of options for demonstrating competence and understanding, and performance tasks (in contrast to timed classroom tests, for example) can be structured to provide them with the time they need to complete a job well.

Redesigning Instruction

To the satisfaction of both staff and students, the senior project has helped to personalize instruction. It has demanded increased student-teacher interaction, casting teachers into the roles of mentor, coach, cheerleader, tutor, and mediator, as well as advisor. Anthony comments: "The Senior Project involves teachers a lot more than when they would be teaching just regular stuff." Al Angel concurs: "The Senior Project has really brought us [students and teachers] closer. [The students] rebel all the way until they get almost through it; and then something clicks in their head and they say, 'This is kind of neat.' "

It is the power of relationships—between students and staff and between staff and staff—that helps to bring about change. The elixir of student success in the Senior Project propels the student-teacher relationship. Teachers are relentless in their determination that students will succeed. Students eventually acquiesce, applying more effort than they ever thought they would or could exert to ensure their own success.

Staff relationships and increased collegiality sustain and strengthen the project as teachers encourage one another to persevere through student resistance, and as they encourage one another to surmount their own resistance, to forsake old habits and practices for new ones, to open their doors and relax the age-old boundaries that traditionally have kept vocational and academic faculties isolated from one another. This building of community does not go unnoticed by the students. As Frank reflects: "The Senior Project makes everybody come together a little bit more. It makes you feel like getting involved with the school a little bit more."

The school administration has changed the instructional schedule to accommodate the Senior Project, and individual teachers have used flexible scheduling for innovative instructional activities. In order to provide the necessary research and oral presentation skills to co-op students, who spend much of each day in on-the-job employment situations, a double period of English was added to their program. In their American Experience course, Lacey and his new partner, Carol Adams, regularly rearrange their classes and schedule based on their instructional goals.

Innovative practices include the English department's use of student-produced materials that provide concrete models of research papers for beginning researchers. The research papers of former students give current students an understanding of the criteria that will be used to grade their papers. Math teacher Robert Riehs has replaced what he calls his "chalk and talk" method of teaching with projects and math manipulatives. Faculty note that the Senior Project has helped a lot of teachers look differently at the way they teach and the way they measure what students do.

Because teachers experience the public presentation component as a personal assessment of their teaching—a form of public accountability—it has prompted some to reflect on their teaching practice. Although teaching practice at Hodgson is still predominantly traditional, teachers are increasingly likely to direct students to find their own answers to questions rather than to provide the answers themselves. They are increasingly likely to ask probing questions and create inquiry-oriented classroom activities rather than simply to lecture. Teacher collaboration has increased. On some of the core teams, teachers give students a joint grade for their courses. They plan together, and they review students' work together.

As discussed earlier, the learning tasks that characterize the Senior Project have begun to find their way into classrooms before 12th grade, increasing students' opportunities throughout their high school years to engage in public presentations, active learning, interdisciplinary studies, and the integration of academic and vocational curriculum. In the 11th grade American Experience course, for example, students formulate research questions and subsets of questions that will shape their research, often connecting these to their vocational studies. For example, students majoring in culinary arts did a project on ethnic foods.

Bach and Lacey believe that the juniors who went through this course will be much better prepared for the Senior Project. Confronted with a change from the passive modes of teaching and learning they have grown used to, the students often ask initially, "Can't we just learn out of the book?" By the end of the course, these students have had experience speaking before a group, doing research, and taking responsibility for much of their own learning. Bach observes that, although the students had to produce much more work for each grade they attained in this class, they also experienced lower rates of failure. The opportunity to take responsibility and to help fashion their own learning experiences stimulated greater effort and a sense of efficacy on the part of students.

In Riehs' math class, students spend increasing amounts of time developing problem-solving strategies and engaging in inductive reasoning to formulate mathematical theories. In carpentry shop, students are also asked to do research, to write their own tests, and to develop their own vocabulary lists from their work. Lutz notes that students who have had the 9th grade core team experience have a different initial response to this kind of work than do students who have been accustomed to asking the teacher to "tell us the answer." Rather than responding with fear, and claiming they can't do the work, these students seem to know how to get started, how to tackle a task, and how to ask questions that will give them the information they need to make progress. They seem more verbal, more involved, and more willing to work with one another. They also respond differently to lectures, he feels, being more apt to ask thought-provoking questions about how things work and why, probing for theory and for depth rather than simply writing down information. In short, they are again becoming the inquiring learners they were when they entered kindergarten years ago, before they learned how to behave in school.

Creating New Opportunities for Students

The most dramatic changes brought about by the Senior Project have been in the kinds of learning activities students have the opportunity to engage in. The research paper, the product, and the presentation are characterized by authentic learning: Students research something they do not know in order to increase their knowledge, not to obtain preconceived "correct" answers. Their research takes them into the world of work where they encounter what they are studying in practice. Neither the experiences nor the outcomes of the research strategy have been preplanned. Instead, students design their own research plan so that the projects develop organically, with individual needs and interests dictating the course of learning, and with space for the intervention of serendipity.

The organic development of projects is illustrated by Frank's research activities on wells and Terrance's* activities for his sports journalism project, "Using Information Systems and Service Skills in Sports Journalism." Terrance, an autistic student whose passion for sports statistics became the basis for his project, initiated and established contacts with local sports journalists, interviewed them, attended sports events with them, visited their offices, and interviewed coaches and student athletes at a local university. Terrance's "networking" landed him a summer job in the computer department of the University of Delaware.

The active learning required by the tasks changes students' attitudes toward learning and school. Frank observes that students are no longer simply "opening a book and writing questions and answering them." He says the project "makes school cool. It's fun to be researching and working with other people. You're drafting the research paper, you're drawing up the blueprints on the well and putting it to scale, you're setting dates to interview people and meet with your teachers."

Academic and vocational experiences are naturally integrated. Because students must incorporate primary sources in their research, the project's academic component promotes its vocational component. Invariably, students visit job sites, conduct interviews, and interact with adults in local institutions: contractors, union officials, workers, craftspersons, and staff from museums, hospitals, and research and development labs. Students gain a better understanding of the expectations, values, and conventions of the workplace. They learn how to take the initiative and access resources. As Anthony says: "The students have to do the whole thing themselves. You learn how to get hold of people, to get people who know stuff to help you. You use people that might know something about what you need to know, or know where you could find whatever you're looking for." Students mature and, despite their resistance, their grades, as Al Angel points out, almost always go up, with the biggest leap occurring for the most marginal students.

Interestingly, some of the greatest success stories in the Senior Project are Hodgson's special education students. Special education teacher Carolyn Steinwedel reports that out of a total school population of 800, about 100 are identified for special education, mostly as learning disabled. These students—many of whom have been with Steinwedel for 4 years—do only the Senior Project in their senior year, creating more time for them to undertake this major piece of work. They do the same paper, presentation, and product as do all other students and are similarly evaluated by a committee of teachers, but their project is structured with more checkpoints at which adults touch base to see that the work is progressing. While these students initially show more resistance to the project because they have more anxiety about change, they ultimately achieve higher grades and more solid learning than under the traditional system. Their self-esteem and skills increase, enhancing their ability to find jobs and succeed at them after high school. According to Steinwedel, the benefits for her students produce benefits for her as well: "I've taught school for 17 years and [the Senior Project] is probably the most rewarding thing I've ever done."

Faculty and students cite increases in homework completion, increased competence in writing and research ability, improvement in academic and vocational knowledge and skills, greater motivation, better attendance, and increased task commitment as additional benefits of the Senior Project. These results are corroborated by the Student Survey, which each student completes at the conclusion of the public presentation. Students also report that they have improved their time management capacity and organizational skills as a consequence of taking more initiative and becoming more engaged in their learning. Teachers report that their students are better able to follow through with long-term goals and to develop practical applications from technical information.

The project has even penetrated the student culture. Lunch-time conversations now include talk about the project: When one student asked another about his weekend plans, the answer was, "I'm going to be working on my Senior Project." At the conclusion of the project, the vast majority of students report that they would prefer assessments such as the Senior Project to the traditional paper-and-pencil, multiple choice tests, even though the Senior Project is more difficult, more demanding, and more time consuming. The rewards for such authentic assessments are greater; they bring more personal satisfaction and an increased sense of accomplishment.

Given the differences in the nature of the abilities being assessed, it would be unreasonable to expect the Senior Project to significantly influence Hodgson's standardized test scores. However, it is possible that the companion efforts to integrate mathematics into the vocational curriculum had some bearing on the increase in the school's Stanford Achievement Test scores in math between 1991 and 1992. Other indicators of the success of the range of curriculum, teaching, and assessment changes at Hodgson may be gleaned from the fact that between 1990 and 1992, student attendance increased, infractions of school rules declined, and honor roll participation increased by almost 50%.

More important than looking for any direct effect of Hodgson's initiatives on such a disparate measure as standardized test scores is the fact that the Senior Project has challenged the narrowness of such assessments by highlighting the contrasts in what is measured and what it means. In the presentation of his 3/4-inch scale residential house, with frame, rafters, joists, jambs, and beams complete and in place, Malik was able to recount, step by step, how he used the Pythagorean theorem to determine the pitch of the roof. On his SATs, however, he has been unable to achieve a cumulative score of 700, with the result that he will be denied an athletic scholarship for college.

With the increased use of authentic assessment, teachers have growing certainty that what they can see students actually doing is a stronger measure of their capabilities and potentials than are students' scores on more abstract multiple choice tests. Consequently, they are more willing to challenge traditional assessments of students' abilities and to push them to greater achievements. Students are beginning to believe that they can and will accomplish complex tasks their test scores once persuaded them were out of their league. It is possible that at some point, the constraints on teaching and learning occasioned by the influence of less authentic assessments will be reevaluated as the value of performance assessment is recognized by teachers, students, and their parents. As we describe below, this is already beginning to happen in Delaware.

CHALLENGES AND POSSIBILITIES

In all schools engaged in change, new initiatives pose new problems and new possibilities. Issues that have emerged as the Senior Project has been implemented are typical of those encountered in other schools attempting change:

- Initial student and teacher resistance to the proposed changes.
- Need for technical knowledge to support the reform: for example, development of new instructional strategies for courses integrating academic and vocational curriculum.
- Conflicts between the traditional school regularities and the reform's new requirements, such as finding time for students to do their Senior Project research without stealing time from the regularly scheduled classes, dealing with the logistics of managing projects for increasing numbers of seniors, and reinventing the schedule to allow for more interdisciplinary courses.
- Conflicts with district and state curriculum and assessment mandates: the district senior English course curriculum in British Literature vs. Hodgson's technical writing course, for example, and new state certification exams in vocational areas that require traditional configurations of courses that undermine a more integrated approach.

- Institutionalization of the reform: strategies for building teacher and school capacity to achieve the goal of diploma by exhibition.

Any substantive change attempted in a complex organization will inevitably bring about other changes that the institution may or may not have the will and capacity to respond to. In some respects, Hodgson has had unique advantages in confronting these challenges. Because it was recently "re-created" as a merged academic and vocational-technical school, it has had some of the characteristics of a new school, one in which new norms and ways of working could be fashioned in the breach of discontinuities created by this unsought, district-level initiative. As Godowsky put it: "We're young as an academic school. We're building our future here. . . . The old approach [of having vocational courses only] is dying out. If we don't bring reading, writing, and thinking into vocational programs we're missing the boat." At the same time, Hodgson had the advantage of having been a vocational school in which the concepts of "student as worker" and performance-based assessment were natural rather than alien ideas. As Dave Lutz observed: "Our kids demonstrate their knowledge every day in vocational work."

A new mix of staff, some early retirements, and a changed mission allowed new thinking to begin to find a foothold. Careful, respectful change processes allowed it to expand. From the very beginning, when "conversations" were first held before school and over dinners, the priority was inclusiveness of interested staff and widespread sharing of information. When the Senior Project committee was formed, copies of all committee meeting minutes were sent to all school staff. The committee members used their personal relationships as a basis for reaching out, and all ideas and documents were developed by faculty members working in various committees and teams, rather than "brought in" by outside experts—though a number of outsiders with ideas that proved useful were part of the process at various points. Echoing the constructivist reality of all change efforts, one teacher observed that "The best things we've done are those we've done ourselves . . . for example, working through our mission statement."

Another helpful factor is the district superintendent, Dr. Dennis Loftus, who supports change and is willing to seriously consider new ideas. Godowsky, who describes Loftus as an innovator and a mentor, noted wryly that "Another good thing is that we fight the district on issues of importance, and sometimes we even win." The school has proposed curriculum and scheduling revisions that have met with approval, thereby enabling interdisciplinary initiatives and time for team planning for teachers. The conflict between the school's senior writing course and the district's British Literature curriculum was ultimately resolved in favor of the school's program, allowing the continued integration of the curriculum necessary for the interdisciplinary Senior Project. With school site control over staffing and budgeting, Godowsky has also been able to begin to reduce the teachers' course loads by rethinking programs and staffing, eliminating some pullout remedial classes and staff in order to invest in the core program.

Finally, starting in 1993, support for authentic assessment is beginning to come from the state level as well. Delaware took the decisive step of dropping its norm-referenced, multiple choice, standardized testing program at the state level and introducing instead a performance-based test in reading, writing, and mathematics that is an interim step en route to a more full-blown system of portfolios and performance assessments. This step may give greater support to schools that are attempting to move "beyond the bubble" in their own assessment efforts, and may legitimize and strengthen the commitments of time, energy, and inventiveness that faculties, students, and parents are willing and able to expend.

Still, no major change is ever easy. Time was, and continues to be, a problem. Initially, teachers volunteered all of the time necessary to begin the project: conversations, individual meeting time with students, committee participation time, and coverage time to release teachers for participation at public presentations. Since teachers would not be compensated for the extra time they had to devote to the project, Godowsky requested—and was granted—permission to change the daily class and bus schedule in order to provide teachers with one daily period for professional development activities. This was done without any reduction in instructional time. But other issues remain: The class time required for teachers to participate at public presentations disrupts the instructional continuity of the classes that need coverage, and students sometimes complain that they miss their teachers.

The Senior Project has expanded the narrow and conventional conception of teaching work as that which occurs with one teacher in a classroom with a full class. Teaching work for the Senior Project is more collaborative and calls for more diverse teacher roles. In fact, if teachers had not been willing to diversify their roles and their work, the Senior Project would not have made it to the drawing board. Teachers participating in the Senior Project work on governance and design committees. At formal and informal meetings, they work to inform, encourage, and persuade their colleagues to participate in the project. In many one-to-one interactions, they work at advising, facilitating, encouraging, tutoring, mentoring, and critiquing and rereading the research papers of their advisees (who may or may not be in their classes). They work at evaluation on the Project committees of their advisees. The new kinds of learning that result from the Senior Project can occur only if teachers adopt new and diverse roles that fundamentally reconceptualize their work. Learning cannot change if teaching work doesn't change.

The new notions of teaching work at Hodgson also include inventing and managing the school's change process. Hodgson could have adopted any of the fashionable models for site-based management or shared decision making, or invited any of a number of "experts" to design and plan a new assessment. Instead they chose to engage in a process of inquiry and to invent their own grassroots process for community-building and change. That process is characterized by an ethos of inclusion, which depends on interpersonal relations, frequent, regularized communication, and whole school inquiry and reflection.

As just one example of the fruits of the many staff-led activities and committees, faculty recently planned an inservice day in which they developed and ran their own series of workshops based on some of the core issues at the school: integrating mathematics into other curriculum areas; creating vocational subject clusters; core team planning; inclusion of special education students in courses; school-wide reward and incentive plans; and a survey of all students, parents, and teachers.

Perhaps even more interesting, and certainly more unusual, was a two-period-long "inservice" experience for students and teachers in which they jointly discussed the school's mission statement and two of the Coalition's key principles: establishing a "tone of decency," and viewing the "student as worker." Together, students and teachers discussed what they felt these ideas should mean and how well they felt the school was pursuing these goals. In these and other events, the school community simultaneously creates, achieves, and revises its collective work, which evolves as the staff and students grow and change together.

Increasingly, Hodgson is able to see itself as a dynamic educational community continuously creating itself based on its assessment of its goals and needs. As the staff's confidence as agents of their own change increases, they are ever more able to forsake their dependence on time-worn rituals that have outlived their effectiveness. This is demonstrated by the growing support for the project. As increasing numbers of teachers observe first-hand the project's effects on students, their resistance diminishes and they become more receptive, not only to the project but to its underlying educational principles. This conversion is necessary if the reform is to last and if its implications for teaching and learning are to be fully realized. Hodgson's grassroots change process has enabled the school to put the needs of its students at the center of its reform efforts.

CONCLUSION

Hodgson's Senior Project supports a growing number of authentic teaching and learning opportunities throughout the school, both before and during senior year. It also encourages integrated vocational and academic learning. The assessment adds an intellectual component to the traditional competency and performance-based vocational assessment. It evaluates students' intellectual knowledge of their vocational specialty, along with the traditionally academic skills of research, writing, and communication. Criteria for the public presentation are drawn from the traditions of both academic and vocational education: The use of research conventions and a press for higher order thinking skills are normally thought to be the domain of the academic tradition, and the use of demonstrations and products to assess competency emerges out of what is normally considered the vocational tradition.

The assessment creates an interdependency between learning that is "hands-on" and learning that is "minds-on." This interdependency connects the academic and vocational domains, but it also extends students' knowledge and skills in both of the domains as each type of learning plays off the other. The Senior Project diminishes the traditional division between those who work with their hands and those who work with their heads, along with the pernicious social class and status distinctions associated with this view. As Scarbrough comments: "If they're going to be plumbers, carpenters, masons, cosmetologists, why can't they also be educated plumbers, educated carpenters, educated masons, educated cosmetologists? Why do they have to choose between labor and intellect? Why can't they have both?" The assessment provokes teachers to think more deeply about the possibilities of academic and vocational integration in their shop and academic subject curricula, just as Al Angel considers how he would like to integrate both math and physics into his dental lab.

The new assessments, even in their early stages, have impressive potential for bringing about a closer correspondence between the tasks and values of school and the workplace. The tasks of the Senior Project are authentic, as are workplace tasks. Students are held accountable for their work and assume responsibility for their project as they would in the workplace. Workplace values, such as cooperation, initiative, and standards of quality, are emphasized both in the process of the assessment and in the evaluation component. Scarbrough explains that "The project enhances students' capacities to do their job, because they're better communicators on the job. They can read, write, speak, and listen better as auto technicians than they did before." She continues: "Students are learning life skills: problem solving, how to be a good worker, how to give and follow directions, how to pose and find answers to questions." The Project teaches students to challenge themselves. It gives them experience coping with the pressure of deadlines, with resistance and frustration, and with the anxiety of risk-taking inherent to self-challenging work—and it rewards those who challenge themselves most.

Perhaps the most powerful lesson is that work should be meaningful rather than perfunctory, that work should bring pleasure rather than boredom. And the Project teaches both students and teachers to be conscious of these distinctions in school and in the workplace. Unfortunately, the traditional lessons of school and, for many, of the workplace are the reverse. Hodgson's Senior Project endows school-work with a dignity of which it is often deprived, especially non-college preparatory work. It teaches, as Al Angel says, that vocational work is about "using your hands and your mind well together." It enables students to develop a sense of professionalism about their field as they acquire a level of specialized knowledge and expertise. It raises not only their competence but their expectations as well, thus opening new doors to a future full of promise these young people feel capable of reaching for.

NOTE

1. In general, students' names have been changed and are marked with an asterisk. In this case, by request of student Jake Lott, and his mother, the name has not been changed. The names of faculty members have not been changed.

4

COLLABORATIVE LEARNING AND ASSESSMENT AT INTERNATIONAL HIGH SCHOOL

In a July 4, 1988, editorial, *The New York Times* asked the $64-million school reform question about a school that, under normal circumstances, many might think doomed to fail:

> International High School is one of the more exclusive secondary schools in New York City. Only students who have been in the United States less than four years and who score below the 20th percentile on an English language proficiency exam are admitted. The 310 students come from 37 nations and speak 32 languages.
>
> . . . All students are considered "high risk," likely to drop out. Yet the daily attendance rate is 90%, compared with a citywide average of 80%. And the dropout rate of the three-year-old school is 3.9%, compared with nearly 30% citywide. The first senior class is graduating this year; every one of the 54 seniors will start college in the fall.
>
> Why does International succeed where so many city high schools fail? (Sturz, 1988)

The answer to this question lies in International High School's commitment to a collaborative, experiential approach to teaching and learning, married to school-wide processes of reflection and authentic assessment deeply embedded in all the activities of the school. International is committed to viewing teachers and students—along with community agencies and workplaces—as resources for each other, using participation in decision making and collective action as the basis for growth and development. The school's policies and classroom practices foster self-assessment and responsibility as the foundations for lifelong learning. These commitments are reflected in the educational principles that underlie the school's approach to instruction, enumerated in its *Educational Philosophy* document:

1. Limited English-proficient students require the ability to understand, speak, read, and write English with near-native fluency to realize their full potential in an English-speaking society.

2. Fluency in a language other than English must be viewed as a resource for the student, the school, and the society.
3. Language skills are most effectively learned in context and when embedded in a content area.
4. The most successful educational programs are those which emphasize rigorous standards coupled with effective support systems.
5. Attempts to group students homogeneously in an effort to make instruction more manageable preclude the way in which adolescents learn best, i.e., from each other.
6. The carefully planned use of multiple learning contexts in addition to the classroom (e.g., learning centers, career internship sites, field trips) facilitates language acquisition and content area mastery.
7. Career education is a significant motivational factor for adolescent learners.
8. The most effective instruction takes place when teachers actively participate in the school decision-making process, including instructional program design, curriculum development, materials selection, faculty hiring, staff training, and peer evaluation. (IHS at LaGuardia Community College, n.d.-a)

This philosophy was much in evidence in the observations we conducted during the 1991–92 school year in classrooms and at portfolio committee conferences, and through interviews with faculty and students and reviews of school documents, curriculum, and student portfolios.

THE SCHOOL'S STUDENTS AND SUCCESSES

In 1992 International High School, representing a 7-year-old collaboration between the New York City Board of Education and the City University of New York, served 459 students from 54 countries. These included native speakers of a total of 39 different languages, with the students representing a wide range of language and literacy proficiencies both in their native languages and in English. Students in this citywide magnet school are placed in grades 9–12 and range in age from 14–21. The ethnic composition is 45% Latino, 30% Asian, 22% European, and 3% Caribbean or African American. Three-quarters of the students qualify for free or reduced-price lunch.

With this kind of highly diverse student body, International has achieved outcomes that far surpass those accomplished by schools with much more affluent and traditionally advantaged students. It continues to have a graduation rate of over 95%, while more than 90% of its students are accepted each year at postsecondary schools. As Table 4.1 indicates, virtually all of the students pass the New York Regents Competency Tests, an unusual accomplishment for students whose first language is not English and who

Table 4.1. International High School Regents Competency Test Results (Number and Percent Passing by Year)

Examination	1990 (n = 94)		1991 (n = 64)		1992 (n = 92)	
	No. Passing	%	No.	%	No.	%
Reading	89	95	63	98	91	99
Writing	87	93	64	100	90	98
Mathematics	94	100	64	100	92	100
American Studies	84	89	63	98	89	97
Global Studies	—	—	64	100	92	100
Science	—	—	64	100	92	100
Occupational Education	—	—	—	—	92	100

have been in this country for only a short time. More important, students accomplish much more intellectually challenging tasks than the state tests require as they work through the demanding performances posed in their classroom and internship assessments.

The school's accomplishments have received repeated national recognition. In 1986, the Council for Advancement and Support of Education gave International and its partner, the City University of New York, its award for the Best New High School/ College Collaboration in the nation. In 1989, the school received the National Council of Teachers of English (NCTE) award for Excellence in English/Language Arts Instruction, and in 1990 NCTE named it a Center of Excellence for At-Risk Students. The American Association of Higher Education gave its 1991 award for Outstanding High School/College Collaboration to International. In 1992, the school received both a Democracy '92 grant from RJR Nabisco and a National Academic Excellence award from the U.S. Department of Education.

Commitments and Practices at International

International High School describes its mission as fostering the "linguistic, cognitive, and cultural skills necessary for [students'] success in high school, college, and beyond" (International High School [IHS] at LaGuardia Community College, n.d.-b). The program that results from these commitments includes innovative instruction in English as a second language, a dramatically restructured school program and schedule, and more collegial and professional approaches to teaching work. First of all, English as a second language is not taught as a separate course at International. Instead, students learn language skills by engaging meaningful content in their subject matter classes, and by working with one another in small, multilanguage groups that require them to use both their native language and their emerging English language skills. Their tasks are constructed so that they must communicate ideas and directions to one another as they collaboratively produce and evaluate their work.

An Integrated Learning Center supplements other subject matter courses with small-group, interdisciplinary instruction. Classes are organized around themes that help students grapple with essential concepts (such as causality, commonality, interdependence, and relationship) and to develop essential skills, like managing and using information, testing hypotheses, and generalizing. The Center offers courses in communication, language skills, research, and cross-cultural studies, along with an orientation to the school and society. Extended day opportunities allow students to participate in small-group tutorials designed to promote language competence, to extend work in other subjects, to explore career education alternatives, and to participate in extracurricular activities.

Career education is an integral part of the curriculum. Students work in internship settings for half of each school day during one trimester each year. These experiences, generally in social service organizations, allow them to practice their English skills, to develop workplace and life skill competencies, to gain confidence about their ability to cope with the social and cultural environment in their new country, to develop a sense of responsibility, and to explore career ideas. Accompanying coursework activities encourage students "to gain personal awareness through introspection," investigating their interests, abilities, and aptitudes, discussing the world of work, and preparing for interactions in the workplace—practicing job interviews, writing resumes, relating experiences, and suggesting solutions to problems they encounter (IHS at LaGuardia Community College, The Curriculum Committee, 1987, pp. 28–30).

Located on the campus of LaGuardia Community College, International High School offers students access to college courses as well as to its own core offerings. Over time, its internal schedule has evolved both to fit more congenially with the college schedule and to allow for more in-depth experiential and group work. Classes meet for 70 minutes. As teacher David Hirschy[1] notes:

> (T)he longer period encourages small group work, a variety of activities, and an in-depth treatment of topics that makes students more active participants in their learning. (1990a, p. 7)

Students take four classes during each 13-week cycle, while teachers teach three courses each cycle, enabling them to focus their attention on a smaller number of students while extending and deepening the curriculum for their courses. A number of teachers have formed teams to work intensively on an interdisciplinary curriculum with a single group of students over the course of a complete 13-week cycle. In addition, each faculty member serves as an advisor to a "House," which meets for 70 minutes each week.

The schedule supports another critical feature of International's program: collaboration and participatory decision making among teachers. The time allotted for collective staff planning—a half day per week while students are engaged in college and high school extracurricular activities, plus a daily planning period—supports the committee meetings, staff development, peer review activities, and curriculum planning that enable the faculty governance system to operate, and that encourage continual innovation. The faculty's involvement in personnel decisions, curriculum development, and peer review and evaluation has proved to be a central force in the development of experiential learning and authentic assessment opportunities for the staff and, subsequently, for students.

The staff-developed evaluation system at International involves teachers in working with a small, self-selected support team where they set their own goals, observe one another teach while providing feedback, present their work to the panel of other teachers, exchange ideas and practices, and evaluate themselves and each other. Teachers keep their own portfolios, which include observation reports from the principal and from peers; a self-evaluation (which addresses the teachers' contributions in the classroom, to the discipline, to the school as a whole, and to the profession); course evaluation questionnaires from students; course materials representing their teaching work; and examples of student work. Through this process, teacher evaluation teams determine teachers' continuance at the school and their tenure in the school system. Teacher evaluation, traditionally a private process between a supervisor and a teacher, becomes a public process, enlarging the sphere of accountability to the entire professional faculty.

The faculty's peer support, review, and evaluation system became a powerful force in shaping a common set of strongly held values and principles for guiding both the design and practice of student assessment. Over time, student assessment practices have evolved from traditional, periodic tests and quizzes to a continuous process of self-reflection, peer assessment, and teacher assessment, organized around collaborative performance tasks and individual portfolio development. Both the substance and process of the assessments are authentic rather than contrived or removed from the act of learning. The work is hands-on, content-rich, aimed at the development of essential performance abilities and applications of knowledge, and connected to students' lives, experiences, and other coursework. A richly interwoven array of formal and informal occasions for evaluation creates the expectation that learning is a process of continual reflection and improvement, in which every member of the school community is constantly involved.

THE EVOLUTION OF TEACHING, LEARNING, AND ASSESSMENT

Three factors have contributed to the evolution of authentic assessment at International High School:

1. The development and nurturance of a learner-centered instructional model
2. The resulting teacher dissatisfaction with traditional assessments
3. The staff-developed faculty evaluation system.

The Emergence of a Learner-Centered Instructional Model

As Eric Nadelstern, founding director and principal of International High School, emphasizes, International's practices did not begin with assessment. They began with an instructional commitment to student diversity as a generative force for learning. This focus inevitably led to authentic assessment.

David Hirschy, physics teacher, explains: "We wanted to create a total educational experience. We wanted to broaden the context for students' learning and deal with the whole person." In an article published in *Insights*, the school's journal, Hirschy describes how he came to the realization that traditional lock-step approaches to instruction could not meet this goal. Hired to teach physics at International after many years of teaching in a more traditional setting, Hirschy confronted the implications of student diversity in a more vivid way than ever before:

> It became apparent that many of the techniques that I used in teaching, when applied to limited English proficient students, simply didn't work. There were students who just didn't understand when I spoke to the class. There were students who had extensive science preparation in their native countries, and there were students who had very little formal education.
> The attempt to have all students arrive at the same place at the same time was impossible. Now the truth is that it is impossible with native English speakers also. It just isn't as obvious. . . .
> Heterogeneity is not a problem to be solved. In fact when embraced, it is a positive force in the classroom. Students come to us at different stages of development and levels of preparation, and education increases those differences. In the long run, if a student is good at something, we try to encourage the student to pursue the interest, to excel, which results in inequality, differences, heterogeneity. It happens naturally. It is unreasonable to expect that, as a result of our efforts, students should become less heterogeneous. (1990a, pp. 16–17)

Collaboration between and among students and faculty is at the core of the learning environment International has created to celebrate and to use this diversity to enhance learning. The expectation and the reality is that people learn from each other's different experiences and knowledge and from the synergy that occurs in the active process of collaboration and communication, which expands each person's understandings beyond the sum of the parts. As Hirschy explains:

> Collaboration, a combination of individual and small group work, and an environment in which variety is expected, allows us to capitalize on differences. The benefit to the slower student is having a model in the classroom and assistance from peers. The advanced students learn to meet high expectations in an atmosphere where variety is expected and to expand their responsibility to include others. . . . Groups are especially appropriate for limited English proficient students because students need to use language to learn language. They need to talk with each other. They need to read instructions. They have the opportunity to repeat, to review, and to listen. It allows students to experiment with the content and with the language.
>
> The focus is on students learning rather than on me teaching. To paraphrase Piaget, every time we teach a child something we keep him from inventing it for himself. The goal is for students to assume responsibility for their own learning, and to discover how they learn best. (1990b, pp. 18–19)

Hirschy had been long eager to increase articulation between math and science and was interested in Uri Triesman's development of cooperative learning models, especially successful with minority students. In 1990, with the encouragement of Nadelstern, he organized the *Motion Program,* an interdisciplinary, self-contained cluster that includes literature, an integrated math/physics course, and *Project Adventure,* a course modeled on Outward Bound but designed for the indoors.

The kinds of work students engage during the *Motion* course stretch their critical and creative capacities in many directions, while fostering collaboration and the ability to work with and learn from one another. Activities in literature, math/physics, and Project Adventure connect to the theme of motion, and to each other. Many of the activities involve students working in groups on experiments that reveal and test the laws of motion, then developing charts, graphs, formulas, and prose to describe applications of such concepts as acceleration, velocity, and distance. In literature, students create a science fiction story that demonstrates and uses their understanding of key concepts from the physics and mathematics portions of the program, as well as drawing on what they have learned from their study of literary forms and writing. One option is to create a story that involves people on a space journey and takes Einstein's theory of relativity into account. Project Adventure allows physical expressions of "the laws of motion and emotion" (also part of the study of movement and change tackled in the program), while building trust and teamwork among students. Meanwhile, students' views of their physical and social-emotional growth—and the relation of this growth to the themes of the course—become the subject of portfolio essays.

The 75 students enrolled in this trimester-long program spend all of their time each day with the four *Motion* teachers and one assistant principal. The *Motion* Program has become the prototype of the International instructional model. The model is a self-contained, interdisciplinary, theme-based cluster, or a sort of temporary mini-school with its own teachers and students who meet each day, all day, and provide for the students' total education for the duration of a cycle (one third of a school year). Over the course of the cycle, teachers and students get to know one another well. Because of the model's success—all of the 150 students who enrolled have passed—Nadelstern's vision of International has become one of an entire school of such clusters. The model has seven key characteristics:

- Heterogeneous and interage grouping.
- The creation of a learning community.
- Collaboration: Teachers plan together and students work extensively in small groups with teachers alternately coaching, assessing, questioning, and prodding them; within their groups, students work on individual as well as group tasks.
- Emphasis on critical thinking skills and in-depth study.
- Active learning: Students work extensively on problem solving and projects.
- Whole language learning in context (language skills are taught within the context of subject areas).
- Authentic assessment using multiple perspectives.

Other faculty have begun to explore and experiment with the model. Teachers Anthony DeFazio and Charlie Glassman recently formed the *Beginnings Program,* an interdisciplinary program for entering International students. They consolidated two theme-based courses, *Orientation to School and Society* and *Immigration,* with the first course of the three-year *Personal and Career Development Program.* They then added biology to the interdisciplinary mix. DeFazio and Glassman are currently planning to expand *Beginnings* into an all-day, cycle-long, self-contained cluster, similar to *Motion.* These cluster courses, and the assessment strategies they use, are described later in more detail. The cluster concept has now become the organizing framework for coursework throughout the school.

Dissatisfaction with Traditional Assessments

As faculty at International began to find traditional assessments inadequate and inappropriate to their goals, they began to experiment with performance-based assessments. With these early explorations into new approaches, faculty began to invent the learning-as-assessment and assessment-as-learning dynamic that has come to characterize International's practice.

Hirschy, who, in order to cope with the different achievement levels of students in his physics classes, had been giving three different levels of tests, was disappointed with the results. Rather than measuring students' growth, the tests seemed to him to put a ceiling on student accomplishment. Nor did his tests measure skills that would increase learning, such as use of resources or collaboration. Hirschy's dissatisfaction led him to investigate portfolios as a means for evaluating a wide range of student work at a variety of levels over time, and to do so in a manner that could provide incentives for ongoing feedback and revision.

When traditional testing practices failed to accommodate the wide range of students' abilities in spoken and written English, Kathleen Rugger, *Motion* literature teacher, introduced projects that involved both individual and group work. One recent project, for example, involved students pairing up to write each other a series of letters about books they were reading over winter vacation (Figure 4.1). Describing what they were reading and feeling, and asking questions about their partner's book, involved students in a genuine dialogue that motivated their efforts to communicate while allowing them to learn from one another. In another project, students wrote their own myths to explain a physical phenomenon, and then traded them with another student to create different endings. In still another project, students work in teams to analyze a poem and then to write their explanations and interpretations. Rugger, along with her English department colleagues Dina Heisler and Marsha Slater, explains how this kind of work allows them to attain the communication goals that are most necessary and pressing for their students:

> Although the content of an English class is important, we believe that if we only concentrate on teaching facts or specific applications of skills . . . we will do our students a great disservice, for we know that students will need to be able to produce a variety of written and spoken products. If they internalize strategies for reading any text, for accomplishing any writing task, for working together effectively in any group and communicating with each other, then we have fulfilled their basic English language needs. (IHS at La Guardia Community College, The Curriculum Committee, 1987–88, p. 6)

John Stevenson, LaGuardia Community College professor of mathematics, who also teaches the students in the *Motion* Program, asserts that traditional testing practices and pedagogy do not provide students with the independence and collaborative work skills that translate into successful, college-level work. Even worse, traditional assessment practices produced students who, according to Stevenson, "had given over all intellectual and even emotional responsibility for learning to a process that was teacher-dominated," as evidenced by such frequent comments as, "He [i.e., the professor] gave me a C."

Figure 4.1. Student letters

From: Natasha*
To: Alina*

I want to tell you about the book what I'm reading know [sic]. This book is written by Paul Zindel. I never read his books befor, [sic] & it was interesting to open a new writer for yourself. I don't knows exactly, but I think, that this book is about Polish students in America, the only thing, because I think so, that there are many Polish names, may be the author is Polish too. As I said, this book is about students, seniors, which are going to graduate nearly a month. About their relationship. I read a most part of the book, but in this letter I'll tell you only about few chapters.

There are friends Liz & Maggie. Liz is effective, beautiful girl. with strong character. All boys like her & she has a good boy friend, who's [sic] name—Sean. They love each other, & till last time everything is going well. Sean has a car, & they often go to the beach—there -theire [sic] favorite place. They both want to have sex with each other, but they understand that this is impossible. Liz has problems with her parents. Her father died, & she has stepfather, who is dominate on her mother, so the atmosphere in the house is heavy.

Maggie is a nice, good girl, but Liz—a leader in their friendship. Liz's boyfriend acquainted Maggie with his friend, Dennis.

I think, that's it. Now I want to ask you, how do you like your book, what do you think about main characters? I'll wait for your letter.

Bye-bye.
Natasha.

Stevenson believes that if students are given the responsibility for the process of their own learning, they will also take responsibility for the outcomes. In the natural progression of such responsibility, it will not be long before students take responsibility for assessing their own learning. The self and peer assessments used in the *Motion Program* encourage the goal-setting and reflection needed for students to become responsible for directing their own learning.

The Faculty Evaluation System

Nadelstern strongly believes that there is an unavoidable relationship between the ways in which adults relate to one another in a school and the ways in which they relate to students. "If you have an authoritarian, hierarchical school structure," he explains, "the teacher becomes the information dispenser in the classroom. If kids are going to collaborate in classrooms, then teachers have to collaborate in decision-making." At International, teachers are involved in hiring their peers, in designing and developing curriculum, and in developing

Figure 4.1 (cont'd.)

For: Natasha
    Alina

Dear Natasha!
In the beginning of my letter to you I would to wish you happy New Year.
I want to tell you about my book, which I read in the last Chrystman [sic] vacation. I chose very interesting novel. The title of this book is "Lisa, bright and dark." This book is written by John Neufeld. This novel is tolking [sic] about a hard life of the young girl named—Lisa Shiling. The narrator of this book is Lisa's girlfriend Betsy Goodman.
I read just firsts [sic] four chapetrs, but this is very tempting beginning. In the beginning, Betsy is talking more about her friends, which have connections with Lisa. So these are Lisa's boyfriend—Brian and her two girlfriends—Mary and Elizabeth. They was from the same school, from eleventh grade.
Lisa, the first hero of this story had a big problem with herself. She went to crazy. The parsonts [sic] don't heard their daughter.
Lisa was beautiful girl. She had great style, full figure and fantastic legs. She had also a mean sense of humor and big imagination.
Her friends notice her problem on the party in Mary's house. This was day when Lisa and Brian celebrated their first anniversary. Her behavior was different. The party was great and she had good humor. But in one moment she was very nervous and she made a scene for Brian. Then she was like before. Betsy interested her friend. I thing [sic] she want to help her. I'm very interesting what will be next. I like stories like "Lisa bright and dark." If you like stories like this, you must read this story. Please, write what you thing [sic] about my book and about my letter.

Keep smiling!
Alina

and managing the peer support and evaluation system. As the introduction to the school's teacher-developed personnel handbook publication states:

> (S)hared leadership in a high school can foster the professional growth and development of teachers, leading to the empowerment of students as successful learners. . . . If we view ourselves as true educators, we must also view ourselves as learners. We are role models for our students. If we model authority, our students will learn to be authoritarian. If we model self-improvement in an atmosphere of sharing, that is what our students will learn. (*Personnel Procedures for Peer Selection, Support and Evaluation,* IHS at LaGuardia Community College, n.d.-c, pp. 4–5)

Before teachers at International found traditional *student* assessments inappropriate, they first found traditional *teacher* assessments inappropriate:

The traditional evaluation procedure [teachers] had experienced in their many years of teaching was humiliating, intimidating, and punitive . . . viewed as destructive by some, mechanical by others, and not something to be taken seriously by others. Its authoritarian procedure [gave] little or no consideration to the needs and abilities of the teacher. (IHS at LaGuardia Community College, n.d.-c, p. 4)

With encouragement and steadfast support from Nadelstern, who views the idea of supervision with skepticism (He is fond of asking, "Who has the higher vision?"), the personnel committee developed an evaluation system that centers on, supports, and takes responsibility for the professional growth and development of teachers.

As teachers developed their own system for peer review, collegial support, and evaluation, they began to appreciate the power and potential of collaborative problem solving, self- and peer-assessment, and exhibitions of their work for enriching their professional learning and development. The faculty review and observation process has a number of goals, which are remarkably similar to the goals International holds for students' learning as well:

- Exposing faculty to a wide range of methods and techniques
- Enabling them to develop a philosophy of what constitutes effective teaching and counseling
- Encouraging them to view their own behaviors differently, in light of the professional practices of others
- Promoting experimentation with new approaches and strategies observed
- Facilitating the sharing of ideas and insights with their colleagues
- Institutionalizing the process of continuous self-evaluation (IHS at LaGuardia Community College, n.d.-c, p. 6)

The principles undergirding the faculty evaluation system have increasingly found their way into classroom practices as teachers have worked to create the kinds of learning environments for students they find helpful for themselves. Among these are an understanding of and commitment to ongoing assessment, self-directed learning and assessment, evaluation of both process and product, and evaluation from multiple perspectives by multiple colleagues. Their own faculty assessment system has provided a helpful reference point for teachers as they have struggled to make their classrooms learner-centered rather than teacher-centered. DeFazio asserts: "The school is organized to bring out the best, not the worst, in teachers and kids." Nancy Dunetz, teacher and director of career education, offers this powerful analysis:

An American education . . . fosters competition [which] leads to hostility, isolation, secretiveness, and shame. Collaboration, on the other hand . . . promotes a feeling of self confidence . . . a supportive environment [for] presenting what I know is good [and for] examining my weaknesses on my own and with others. . . . Collaboration furnishes recognition for everybody, because each party naturally acknowledges the contributions of the others. It provides a feeling of community, which I haven't experienced in other work environments. . . . Experiencing that environment myself makes it possible for me to provide it to my students. (Dunetz, 1990, p. 5)

Both the spirit and the components of the student assessment process reflect the faculty's assessment system and their experience with their system. Kathy Fine, *Personal and Career Development (PCD)* teacher, says:

I have learned quite a bit from the way we work ourselves as a faculty. Everything sort of trickled up and down. There's been tremendous interplay between what we do as a faculty and how we work with our students. We've all had to deal with issues of discomfort around evaluation that our students would have to deal with and that our students do deal with. It made the school a learning laboratory where evaluation is not just for evaluation's sake, but a service to the person being evaluated.

This stance is clearly evident in the assessment practices teachers have developed for their students as well.

ASSESSMENT THREE WAYS

The basic features of International's faculty evaluation system, a collaborative approach involving self-assessment, peer assessment, and supervisory assessment, are, not surprisingly, central features of classroom assessment throughout the school. Several of the interdisciplinary cluster programs have evolved particularly innovative authentic assessment practices. Three of these—*Beginnings,* the *Personal and Career Development/Internship Program,* and *Motion*—are discussed here to illustrate the range of practices being developed in the school. Although each program's practices are somewhat different, self-assessment and self-improvement are emphasized, as they are in the faculty's assessment system. These similar emphases occur for the same reason: the belief that "individuals have a greater commitment when they identify their own needs, and their standards are higher when they set their own goals" (IHS at LaGuardia Community College, n.d.-c, p. 5).

Of these three programs, *Motion* has the most completely developed system. However, each contains these common components:

- Ongoing performance-based assessments conducted while work is in progress and providing feedback toward improvement
- Summative assessments that evaluate student work according to multiple dimensions
- Assessment of both the processes and products of individual and group work
- Evaluation from multiple perspectives

Table 4.2 summarizes each program's assessment practices.

Below we describe assessment in each of these programs, starting with *Beginnings,* one of the first programs students encounter at International, followed by the *Personal and Career Development (PCD)* strand they follow for three years, and ending with the *Motion* Program—perhaps the most sophisticated set of interlocking curriculum and assessment practices. Each of these provides a different lens on assessment as it can be used to support the different purposes of education.

In the *Beginnings* program, the goals of teaching are to help students learn about themselves and how to live in a new place, to come to grips with the major change that has occurred in their lives, to take stock of who they are and what they want to become, to learn about the United States, and to create new relationships while beginning to learn English. In this program, assessment practices require that students work with one another,

Table 4.2. Summary of Program Assessment Practices

Assessment Components	Program Assessment Tools		
Program	Motion	Beginnings	PCD/Internship
Ongoing assessment (while work is in progress)	Debriefing, exhibitions	Coaching, group work, exhibitions	Group work, seminar, internship site visits
Final assessment	Written evaluations, conference	Conference	Written evaluations
Process and product	Classwork, group work, portfolio	Group work, autobiography	Internship, album
Multiple perspective evaluations	Self, peers, teachers	Self, peers, teachers,	Self, peers, teachers, site supervisors

reflect on their lives and experiences, and communicate extensively both orally and in writing.

The *PCD* sequence focuses on career development, learning about work and oneself, and developing work skills and responsibility. Assessment practices are structured to provide students with feedback from work supervisors as well as from peers and teachers, to focus on the development of a range of practical as well as academic skills, and to provide structured opportunities for reflection on students' excursions into another new terrain: the world of work.

Motion's goals are more traditionally academic, though they are pursued in a nontraditional fashion. In this program, knowledge of physics, mathematics, and literature are as important as the development of communications skills and general problem-solving abilities. Assessment practices focus on mastery of essential concepts and applications of knowledge in these disciplines, as well as on the development of students' abilities to frame and structure problems, conduct experiments, and evaluate what they have learned, generalizing it to new circumstances.

Assessment in the Beginnings Program

The principles of multiple perspective evaluation, of process and product assessment, and of formative and summative evaluation frame assessment in both the *Beginnings* and the *Personal and Career Development* Programs. These programs integrate personal, career, and academic learnings and develop values and habits of work that correspond to those of the workplace.

Beginnings features an interdisciplinary consolidation of three courses— biology, social studies, and English as a Second Language—aimed at those newly enrolled at International. Here, students construct an autobiography including chapters on their childhood, on life in their countries of origin, on their milestones, their immigration, their responses to the United States, and self-assessments of their interests, abilities, and skills in the context of career exploration. They first learn the technology of self-assessment by doing self-assessment. Specific activities guide them through the processes of reflection and decision making so that they are able to identify their interests, aptitudes, and values. They are then armed with information to investigate possible work and career paths.

For example, a student who identifies fashion as an interest and interpersonal relations as a skill, and who enjoys engaging people, might consider exploring careers in fashion sales or public relations. Such a student might then apply for an internship in the fashion field. In fact, students do use the information they derive from these activities to decide later on which internships they wish to pursue, and they select their choice from over 200 possibilities—ranging from human services to profit and non-profit businesses, to technology, arts, and cultural institutions.

Since the autobiographies are developed and revised over the course of an entire cycle, they become major products demonstrating students' achievement at the cycle's conclusion. Throughout the cycle, students, seated around tables in groups of five or six, work independently and collaboratively on their autobiographies. They regularly share their chapters on an informal basis with their peers, who give them feedback for revision. They use one another as resources to help with language difficulties and stylistic considerations. Co-teachers DeFazio and Glassman intersperse these activities with short lessons targeted to specific needs, and coach students as they work individually and in groups.

DeFazio and Glassman want students to develop "an internal standard" that will drive them to work to their potential. The development of a self-motivated work ethic is more important than any other goal to both teachers. Through ongoing reciprocal peer assessment, students learn to expand their expectations and to redefine their standards. Peer assessment creates opportunities for students to enlarge their field of possibilities, extend their imagination, and increase their learning strategies and skills.

The use of collaborative work groups also allows students to see and experience alternatives to their own approaches: alternative habits of work and strategies for learning, which they can adopt and adapt. Reciprocal peer teaching accompanies reciprocal peer assessment. As colleagues give feedback, they also give advice and assistance to members of their group. Glassman underscores the significance of assessment as a learning tool: "Assessment is a mechanism for learning, understanding, and acquiring knowledge, not giving a mark to something. In *Beginnings* [the students] are doing it all of the time."

Assessment is formalized twice during the cycle. Students gather in small groups and make presentations of their autobiographies, evaluating them and receiving feedback from their peers, who also evaluate each work. Evaluation focuses on completeness. Completeness encompasses more than just the completion of all tasks or the inclusion of all parts required by the *Activity Guide*. Completeness is also determined by the impact the autobiography has on the sensibility of the peer readers and their responses to it. Does the autobiography communicate a sense of the whole story to the reader? For example, did the readers want to know more about the various events and places in the autobiography? Did they understand what the author was trying to convey? Did the autobiography sustain the reader's interest? These are not "school" criteria; they are authentic criteria used by readers in real life. From the responses of their peers, students learn whether or not they "did enough" or "got tired and quit." Students rate themselves on the basis of such criteria, designed to focus their attention on the correspondence between product quality and such habits of work as perseverance.

At the conclusion of the cycle, a formal, summative evaluation takes place. Each student meets with the three *Beginnings* teachers and two peers whom he or she has selected. At these conferences, students are expected to exhibit critical thinking skills and a capacity for applying standards in evaluating their work. They discuss their best work. They identify and analyze the elements that make it their best work. They explain the connections they made across content lines. Together with their teachers and peers, they determine a final grade, which ranges from *A* to *NC.* (no credit) The assessment of English language acquisition and proficiency is embedded in *Beginnings'* other assessments because English is the language of public discourse in the class: The conferences are held in English and all student products are expected to be presented in English. Evaluation of English proficiency occurs through teacher, peer, and self-assessments.

Assessment for improvement extends to the *Beginnings* faculty. Students evaluate the *Beginnings* course. DeFazio and Glassman use students' feedback to revise the course, which is still in its formative stage, for closer alignment among goals, activities, instructional strategies, and outcomes. Glassman notes: "We ask them what they don't like." DeFazio adds: "Also, what connections they saw between the various parts of the course. If the answers are not terribly well thought out, then that's a place that we have to work a little harder." Both teachers caution that students tend to say "nice things even if they hate the course." Glassman comments: "You have to want to look at your work with a critical eye," so as to distinguish affirmation from information. Glassman and DeFazio use assessment as a tool for their own learning, for the development of curriculum, and for the construction and refinement of their instructional model. As they use assessment and learning dynamically, they increase their capacity to derive deeper understanding of their students' responses; this then serves to structure increased learning opportunities.

Assessment in the Personal and Career Development Program

The career education program at International consists of a three-year course sequence in personal and career development known as *PCD* 1, 2, and 3 (the first of which the *Beginnings* team has integrated into their cluster) and three internships accompanied by weekly seminars. The program emphasizes informal but ongoing self-assessment as a tool for achieving self-knowledge. Self-examination, which is the thrust of the first *PCD* course, expands in the second course to the examination of workplace issues. *PCD* teacher Kathy Fine explains that concepts "spiral up" throughout the course structure over the three years. Academic and career learnings are integrated as students craft and write resumes and business letters, develop job interview skills, and examine the workplace from a sociological perspective, studying issues such as hierarchy and authority, gender, and organizational structures while they are engaged in their internships.

During the three cycles of internships, students report to their worksite four days a week and to school one day a week. They are expected to learn not only the job they are doing at their workplace but also to develop inter-personal skills as they interact with supervisors and employees, examine the culture and organization of their workplaces, and think about career impli-cations. The seminars help them reflect on and use their work experience to learn problem identification, problem analysis, and problem-solving skills that they can apply at their workplaces. As they develop practical and social workplace competencies, they are better able to make and keep commitments. In many instances, the work skills students need are so basic, they might easily go unnoticed and untaught in a school where self-assess-ment and inquiry were not highly valued. For example, students who have been unsuccessful in scheduling appointments for interviews with work-place supervisors frequently need to learn the discrete steps involved in making appointments, or the strategies for circumventing small but persis-tent obstacles. Others need assistance and assurance in managing the com-peting tensions of responsibility to a supervisor and fear of disappointing adults, so that they will call their worksite supervisor when they are going to be absent.

Fine reports that students transfer the socialization and communication skills they learn in the internship seminar to their internship sites:

> The kids learn to negotiate, mediate, to defend their positions. . . .
> Most of them practice these skills at their internship sites. They
> learn—and we teach them—the importance of being assertive with-
> out being aggressive if they feel they are being used unfairly.

When students invariably complain about problems at their internship sites, the teachers do not intervene. Rather, they present the problem to the class for analysis. After assessing the situation, the class generates possible courses of action to resolve the problem. Students apply the same problem-solving and analytic thinking skills they use to solve workplace problems to academic problems.

In the internship seminars, instructional activity and authentic assess-ment work conjointly. Students construct internship albums that integrate their academic and career learnings. Like the autobiographies in *Beginnings*, the internship albums are cycle-long projects that become both products that demonstrate students' achievement and records documenting their progress. An activity guide outlines the tasks for the album's four chapters. Each chap-ter engages students in a process of analytic self-assessment, along with knowledge and skill building. Students identify their personal and career objectives and articulate their rationales for their internship choices. They describe their job interviews, typical days, job duties, and the organization-al structure, relationships, and roles at their workplace. They interview co-workers and supervisors about their own career development, education, and job satisfaction as well as about the salary range, benefits, and employment opportunities and outlook in their career fields. The interview topics themselves create a framework for thinking about work that will increase students' knowledge about workplace issues. They reflect on and analyze their work attitudes, along with the skills and competencies they are acquiring and need to acquire. They analyze what they have learned about work and about themselves. They compare their current internships with any previous ones. The album used to record these understandings allows students to simultaneously learn about the process of bookmaking and to develop their writing skills.

In the last course of the sequence, *Decision-Making,* students expand their self-exploration to include the external forces that influence them, their behavior, and their decisions: peer pressure, home pressure, and adolescent developmental pressure. Since students take this course in the eleventh grade, when they will start to think about post-graduation career and education plans, they reflect on processes for decision making, analyze their personal decision-making strategies, and prepare for their third and final internship. Once again, the use of self-assessment as a tool for self-knowledge is emphasized.

Learning and assessment are interactive. Working both collaboratively and independently, students regularly share, review, and critique one another's chapters, with the result that they are continuously revising their work. The completed albums become part of a library of internship albums to be read by other students who are researching internship placements. In this way, students' products become curriculum resources for their peers, attaching added value and worth to their work.

The formal summative evaluation includes the multiple perspectives of self, peers, and faculty, and in this case, worksite supervisors. Kathy Fine and Ronni Green, another *PCD/Internship* teacher, formulated the evaluation criteria for both the internship album and the students' performance as interns. In their assessment of the albums, peer evaluators record their reasons for choosing to read the album, their personal reactions to it, and their recommendations for future improvement. On a scale of *A* through *C,* with each letter corresponding to specific indicators, they rate the album on completeness, content (i.e., level of interest, clarity, degree of detail, supportive evidence, and creativity), language usage, and presentation (i.e., aesthetic considerations).

Workplace supervisors rate students on a five-point scale, ranging from poor to excellent, according to nine indicators: attendance, promptness, quality of performance, dependability, cooperation with both co-workers and supervisors, ability to learn, initiative, and growth. The numerical sum is converted into a grade ranging from *A* to *NC.* The students themselves complete a questionnaire in which they assess their albums and their internship performances, taking into account the assessments of their evaluators. If their assessments differ from their evaluators' assessments, they explain their reasons. As in *Motion*, students engage in a process whereby they can square their assessments with those of their judges. Finally, the teacher assesses the students on the basis of both the album and the internship performance. All evaluations are factored into the final grade.

Assessment in the Motion Program

The *Motion* assessment system is multifaceted and cumulative; it contains a variety of occasions for assessment throughout the course that build on one another. The assessment process has three major components:

- Debriefings
- Two portfolio reviews (mid- and end-cycle)
- The final conference

Opportunities for self, peer, and teacher assessments of students' learning processes and products occur in each of the components. In all cases, collaborative work serves both to foster the development and internalization of high standards in the assessment process and to enhance learning so that those standards can be met. Because collaborative work in *Motion* is so central to program design, we first discuss how students experience the process of group work before discussing how each distinct assessment component operates.

Collaboration for Learning and Assessment

The use of assessment to drive collaborative learning turns out to produce one of the most powerful experiences *Motion* students have. Students work in groups to design experiments and solve problems in mathematics and physics, to interpret literature and write to and with one another about books and ideas, and to conquer physical challenges in Project Adventure. Throughout these activities, they must surmount language barriers to communicate with each other—thus being forced to learn and use English for complex, content-rich tasks—and they must surmount the challenges of different styles, approaches to work, and prior levels of knowledge.

These challenges are particularly salient in the culture of American schools and American assessment, where traditional norms view accomplishment as individual and competitive, collaboration as cheating, and the ranking of students against one another as important school purposes. There is a deep-grained fear in American culture that cooperation will make people "soft," will undermine the competitive edge that many believe produces achievement, and will blur the distinctions between the fit and the less fit that Darwinian sorting policies rely upon. At the same time, schools are now being told that the demands of the modern workplace require that students be able to work effectively in teams on solving problems. Strategies for accomplishing this new goal are as yet a mystery to many. The ways in which *Motion* and other courses at International are structured—to enable students to use collaboration to spark greater growth from all students, to acknowledge individual effort along with group achievement, and to increase the levels of achievement for both individuals and the class as a whole—are thus worth taking some time to understand.

Since collaborative group work is used in all four of the courses that make up *Motion*, students develop a complex view of their peers' capacities and of the nature of cooperation and collaboration. Students reveal different strengths in different areas, so that group dynamics are fluid. Natasha Ulanova,* who immigrated from Russia two years ago, articulates the interplay between successful group interaction and learning that is echoed by her peers:

> I always found out that some people know something that I don't know, and I can tell them what they can't do. We learn from each other. There is nobody who knows everything best than somebody else. Once people feel important, that they could be helpers, then they open up and talk. First they are very scared.

Olga Szpilowski,* originally from Poland, explains the fine-line distinctions that lead to group improvement: "The group work depends on how well everybody do. Therefore, it's in the interests of everybody, not to criticize everything possible, but just to improve things."

These positive responses to collaboration are hard won. As Rafael Suarez's* portfolio commentary on group work indicates, the collaborative process includes widely shared frustrations, tensions, and discomfort:

> The best and the worst moments were working in groups. When the group started working on the project, the group wanted to finished it very fast because they will get credit and sometimes they did the project very fast. But when they had to present and give back the papers to the teacher and see if it was right, the project had many mistakes. The students had to do over almost all the project and it made feel angry and sad the students.
>
> When the group was working right and each member was doing and working on the project, it means that each member was giving ideas and adding new things to it. They may sured that each member of the group understood the project . . . that they took the appropriate time to organize the presentation to the teacher responsible of the activity. When the group made a very good presentation the teacher congratulate them because the members of the group demonstrated the organization.

Students must learn to tolerate the competing tensions between individual and collective interests and seize control of opportunities to make the two forces work in tandem. Students progress from feeling conflicted by this double agenda to feeling confident that they can competently cope with their circumstances. Olga reports:

At first I couldn't stand working in groups. I'm used to work on my own. I felt that if I have to do something with other people, I may not get result I want to get. Maybe because they would come late or will not participate. But later on when I got to know them, I feel strong enough to push them to do the work. Then I built up that leader skill in myself. The work in groups really began to work for me. Most of the time people don't cooperate when they don't understand something. So if I knew that they do not understand, I try to explain it to them. Then I get some feedback, maybe they started to understand, and they get some new ideas, and they were feeling comfortable enough to share with me.

WenFu Wong,* a Chinese student who has lived in the United States for three years, articulates the risk of rejection and alienation students surmount when they begin to take responsibility in their groups, especially when they must transcend ethnic barriers by speaking English rather than their native languages and by engaging students from ethnic groups other than their own:

It's so hard. At first, students just didn't want to speak English, including me, myself. It is uncomfortable, because when students have questions, the first language that come up in their head is their native language. They might translate later on, but at first it get on your nerves. You feel left out. You have to talk to the people who do this to resolve the problem.

To help students transcend the barriers to collaboration and communication, *Motion* classes are structured so that students must always sign up to work on activities with students they have not previously worked with or do not know well. As Miguel Melendez,* recently arrived from Ecuador, reports, the most frustrating experience in group work is "when the people doesn't want to work with you." But, he adds, teachers are available to mediate when groups cannot get themselves on course. In the long run, they virtually always do.

Natasha explains the anxiety and doubt students struggle with when the group has not yet begun to collaborate. She understands that different students take diverse paths to collaboration and that collaboration is more than a quid pro quo. She explains the motivational pressure of collective evaluation. When her group was not on task, Natasha felt resentful that lost time would result in lower grades for herself than if she had worked alone. But she found that, over time, as group members formed a bond of trust, the group started to work:

> Time passes. Some people get very scared because they realize they are not going to get credit—you get one credit for all four classes. If you're getting a C, you're getting all four Cs. Some people got interested in the experiments and people built up the trust. But the work in groups started to work. And if you work for the group, if you push them sometimes, and you give them your ideas, then the group will give the feedback to you. They will work for you.

As we describe below, the assessment process skillfully supports this difficult transition from uncertainty and fear to collective capacity for achievement in a variety of interlocking ways.

Debriefings

In each of the four *Motion* classes, assessment occurs throughout the cycle. Whenever a group completes an activity, they participate in a process known as debriefing. At debriefings, the group members make a presentation to their teacher and sometimes to their class to demonstrate their mastery of the content and the collaborative learning process. The debriefing, which allows students to reflect on what they have learned and to explain it orally to someone else, is the means by which the group can achieve credit for the activity. Preparation for and performance of the debriefing also enrich the students' understanding of what they have learned.

The teacher sits with each group and has a conversation in which she or he asks a series of questions that spiral in complexity so that group members can demonstrate their individual levels of mastery. In this example from the publication *The Motion Program,* during the study of inertia, the questions students will be asked in the debriefing would range from "What is inertia?" to "If you took two tennis balls [which the students have been experimenting with in the activity] into a spaceship in a weightless environment, how could you tell the difference between them?" (IHS, Middle College High School, & LaGuardia Community College, 1991, p. 213). The levels of mastery and capacities for explanation will differ because the groups are heterogeneous and students' English-speaking capacity varies. Although each individual in the group must demonstrate an understanding of the concepts in the activity—e.g., inertia—*the group,* not individuals, receives credit. The group credit strategy provides students with the incentive to collaborate, to use and learn English while they are learning subject area content, to learn and practice collaboration and social responsibility, and to persevere during frustrating and discouraging moments. Without incentives to persevere, it becomes all too easy to retreat to isolated and isolating learning strategies.

Debriefings provide teachers with critical feedback on the effectiveness of the curriculum and of specific activities. This information forms the basis of curricular revisions. Debriefings enable teachers to see what students know, to understand how they got to know what they know, and to get to know the students as individuals and learners. Hirschy explains:

> By the time the portfolio comes along, we've sat with all of these groups maybe ten or twelve times in conversations with them about the work that they've done. And in those conversations, it starts to emerge who really masters this. It comes out in those conversations. We don't necessarily mark it at those times, but everybody gets to know each other. You get a pretty good idea of how people approach and solve problems and have an assessment of their ability to solve problems.

Because the debriefing process is designed to strike a balance between a common rigorous standard and differences in ability and achievement both between and within groups, it supports and sustains heterogeneity as both a pedagogical strategy and a democratic value. Students may differ in ability and achievement levels; however, they need not feel either embarrassed or underchallenged, because the diverse questions give all students multiple opportunities to demonstrate their intellectual capabilities. At the same time, the different levels of students' responses set a standard of possibilities: Students experience a range of responses toward which they can aspire. Because each member of the group must demonstrate an understanding of each activity's concepts in order for the entire group to receive credit, the debriefing process reinforces interdependence and responsibility among group members for the group as a whole. When a group does not receive credit for an activity, it reconvenes itself and reviews the activity until all members can perform adequately.

A debriefing conducted by Hirschy illustrates a number of the points mentioned above. A *Motion* group, having completed a series of activities requiring them to examine the relationship between the Fahrenheit and Celsius temperature scales, presents their results to Hirschy. Using both scales, the students have individually measured the temperature of seven different places in the school, recorded their data on charts, and plotted them on graphs using different axes for each scale. After having interpreted one another's data, they converted them into linear equations.

At the debriefing, Hirschy notices that the data the students have collected do not match the data displayed in the computer graph they have produced. After he challenges the data on their computer graphs as "invented," the students understand that they must return to the computer to replot their data. Emilio Cruz* questions Hirschy to clarify his assessment. Amalia Fresne* rephrases Hirschy's responses using her own constructions. The two remaining members of the group listen. Emilio takes the lead at the computer, replotting his data as three girls watch, occasionally offering suggestions. After a few tries, Emilio gets it right. When he begins to key in the data for another member of the group, Hirschy wants to know if the girls are letting him do the work because they are uncomfortable with the computer. They assure him they are not and become more active in directing Emilio's actions, although they do not make any effort to work at the computer themselves. After the graphs are printed, Hirschy and members of the group listen to one another as they recapitulate the processes they used to convert the data on their charts to the graphs.

They must now reconstruct their equations. Again, Emilio takes the lead, articulating the process to convert their data into equations. However, as he plots out the process, he becomes aware that he is not quite confident of it, and the three girls reveal that they are also unsure. Hirschy directs them back to a previous activity on mass in which the steps for writing equations were explicit. (In contrast, their current task requires the consolidation and application of prior knowledge and skills.) Hirschy wants the students to reinforce for themselves the concrete process of constructing equations so that it becomes intuitive. Hirschy's redirection helps the group recall the process they used to construct equations in the mass activity. As they recapitulate the process, their discussion grows livelier, with all group members contributing actively. Having observed the working of the team, Hirschy later suggests that they create an activity for another class, perhaps an activity on conservation of momentum. He will give the students equipment as well as material to read. Hirschy suggests that they experiment until they come up with a clear and accurate procedure for their activity, which they can record for another group.

Hirschy has punctuated this debriefing with challenges that allow for differentiated responses from students. His questions and directions have emerged, not from a preconceived agenda or lesson plan so much as from his analysis of the immediate and specific context of the particular encounter, his knowledge of the group, its members, and its dynamic, his knowledge of physics and mathematics, and his pedagogical craft, all of which enable him to orchestrate the learning situation. Effective debriefing requires teachers to use their combined knowledge of content, pedagogy, and individual students to create an occasion for assessing and stimulating learning that sets standards without requiring standardization, that values a variety of student outcomes, and that is respectful of developmental variation.

The Portfolio

If the debriefings provide a moving picture of students at work, then the portfolios are series of snapshots reflecting student progress and achievement at two points in time: mid-cycle and end-of-cycle. The *Motion* portfolio has four components:

1. A data summary and samples of students' work
2. Personal statement: a self-assessment essay
3. Mastery statement
4. Self, peer, and faculty evaluation: assignment of grades

Following is a description and discussion of each component and a reproduction of the Mastery Statement (Figure 4.2).

Data Summary and Samples of Students' Work.   For both the mid-cycle and end-of-cycle portfolios, students provide data on the number of times they have been absent or late, the number of activities they have completed, and the titles of the work samples they have included in the portfolio. These data are recorded separately for literature, math/physics, and Project Adventure. Except for two required entries for the end-of-cycle portfolio—a reading log identified as successful by the student and a math/physics problem entitled, *The Hunter and the Monkey*—all of the student work samples in the portfolio are selected by the students themselves as representative of their best work during the cycle. Although students have an opportunity to rework the activities they plan to submit in the portfolios, the faculty encourages them instead to record and substantiate their growth in the Mastery Statement, a documentation of accomplishments, combined with demonstrations of mastery of core concepts and reflections on learning (described further below).

Almost any combination of the sixty-plus activities in the *Motion* curriculum can be found in a sampling of students' portfolios. Students' literature entries are illustrative: Students may include a myth they wrote to explain a natural phenomenon or a science fiction story they created to demonstrate their understanding of key concepts in physics and math, such as Einstein's theory of relativity. These also demonstrate students' understanding of literary forms and their developing writing skills. They may choose from other imaginative literature activities, such as Graphing Lives, and Laws of Motion in Life and Mind Movement. They may include a piece of autobiography they wrote illustrating an important decision, or submit reading logs they wrote while working their way through a piece of literature. The autobiography included in one student's portfolio (Figure 4.3) illustrates a task that enables students to connect their reading and writing to their own lives.

From the physics portion of the program, students can include charts, graphs, and formulas they have developed in the course of problem solving for activities such as "Statis-Ticks," an exercise in which students use statistical methods to calculate the level of danger of the deer tick population in a particular location, or "Temperatures," which leads students through experiments and calculations that establish the relationships between Celsius and Fahrenheit and help them learn to develop and graph equations.

Figure 4.2. Mastery Statement

What did you see in the movie "The Gold Rush" that relates to what you have learned in physics, math, literature, and Project Adventure? Explain.

Through the cycle, you've followed the concepts of motion as expressed in a variety of literary forms. For each activity, consider the following categories:

Fiction	*Poetry*	*Science Fiction*
Non-fiction	*Novel*	*Biography*
Drama-play	*Legend*	*Autobiography*
Dialogue	*Essay*	

List the readings and writings you have completed. State which category or categories it fits into. Explain.

Which is your favorite form to read or write? Explain.

Consider Newton's three laws. State them in simple language. Give examples. What would a world which did not obey Newton's laws be like?

We have been using graphs to help us understand relationships. Examples are: the graphs of distance, velocity, and acceleration for objects in free fall. Each of these has a different shape. Think about these graphs. Draw each of them. Explain what each means. How are they connected to each other? What does a straight line or a curved line mean on a graph? What does the slope tell us? What would the graphs of distance, velocity, and acceleration be like for objects moving at constant velocity?

In several of the math activities we have drawn graphs and expressed the relationships in an algebraic equation (The Mystery Container, Temperatures). Draw a graph with a linear relationship between two variables. Write the equation for it. What do the Y-intercept and the slope represent (for your variables)?

Select the two most challenging elements on the ropes course.
Describe or draw the element.
Describe your experience on this element.
How did it help you learn trust, problem solving, and self-confidence?

How can the skills learned in Project Adventure help you solve problems in you life? Refer to specific experiences in or out of school.

Use as many pages as you wish to answer these questions.

The International High School/Middle College
The Motion Program

Figure 4.3. Autobiography in a student's portfolio

MY AUTOBIOGRAPHY (decision)

My name is _____ and I'm 14 years old. I come from Atlantico-Columbia. Atlantico is a state, but I lived in the city of Barranquilla. I lived in the city of Barranquilla. I lived in Barranquilla all my life and I lived in a city with my mother, sisters, cousins, uncles, aunts and grandparents.

One of my big decisions is when I had to move from Colombia to the United States. It was a big, big decision that I had to make because I didn't want to leave my family and my friends. My family is to big and I love and I love them all and my friends. I had a lot of friends in the school, neighborhood, in the town where my grandmother was born and in other cities. I miss those people that I left in my country because where I lived everybody is so friendly, and it is so beautiful.

But I had to move to this country because my Dad was here (New York) and he wanted to be with us. He wanted me and my sister studying here and he needed to be with us because he could see us only in December and he didn't want to form a family like that. Someday I want to move again to my country because I miss all my friends and family. This decision was hard for me because I had to change my life because now I can't have my family with me, and I lost my friends. Also, there is a big difference in the languages. English and Spanish are so difference and it's difficult to learn another language. In this country everybody needs to speak in English. Other differences are the food, customs, education and the people.

My parents like my country too, but we have everything here and now it's difficult move again. "It's another life, another world." I feel strange in this country.

!This decision changed all my life!.

Work samples may also include discussions on the applications of such concepts as acceleration, velocity, and distance.

Project Adventure entries may include narratives on the physical expression of the "laws of motion and emotion" as well as responses to activities like *Trust Activities, Decision Making* and *Problem Solving,* and *The Ropes Course.* In the Project Adventure entries, students' views of their physical and social-emotional growth—and its relation to the themes of the course—become the subject of portfolio essays. These also emerge in the personal statement and mastery statement described below.

The two activities required for the end-of-cycle portfolio assess students' consolidation of their learnings. The Hunter and the Monkey is an activity that consolidates many of the concepts in the math/physics course: "free fall, projectile motion, reaction time, formulas for constant speed and accelerated motion, and the independence of horizontal and vertical motion." It requires students to demonstrate skills they have developed during the course: the capacity to assess initial conditions and assumptions in predicting outcomes (IHS, Middle College High School, & LaGuardia Community College, 1991, p. 232).

Olga's response to The Hunter and the Monkey illustrates a clear understanding of the concepts of gravity, acceleration, velocity, and reaction time, and a capacity to apply mathematical and practical reasoning skills. The start of this answer, in response to a scenario posing a hunting situation, is a good example of how students have learned to reason through problems in the *Motion* class:

> The hunter may or may not hit the monkey because we don't know the D from what hunter is shooting. This is very important, and without D we can't give the exactly answer. Let's try to count the minimal D from what hunter will hit. This means, if he'll shoot from the more D than the minimal he'll miss, if he'll be closer he'll hit. In order to count the D, we need the t ($D_m = V_{bullet}$ x t). t = 2s/g (s = $gt^2/2$). If the hunter aimed in the middle of the monkey, s = 1/2 x 0.30 = 0.15. t = 2 x 0.15/ g, 8 = 0.175 sec. $D_m = V_b$ x t, D_m = 700 x 0.175 = 122.5m. As you see, if hunter will shoot from the 122.5m or less than this D, he will hit, if more than 122.5m he'll miss because monkey will have time to pass the danger area.

The student goes on in similar manner to evaluate the reaction time of the monkey, the trajectory of the bullet, the effect of gravity on the monkey's motions, and the relative safety of the monkey if he responds to the light of the rifle shot versus the sound of the shot.

In an excerpt from his written assessment of this portfolio, teacher John Stevenson reveals his goals for student work and criteria for evaluation:

> Your work on the "hunter-monkey" was inspired. The analysis was sophisticated, subtle, lengthy, and original—it represents exactly how mathematicians and scientists really operate. What's more you seemed to enjoy working on the problem for its own sake—not for fame or praise. . . . Your commitment to clarity and precise articulation has not only enhanced your own linguistic skills but also established you as a "go-to-person" for the class. Others will go to you for clarification, discussion, etc.

This kind of exercise allows students to integrate what they have learned and demonstrate their capacity to apply concepts to new problems. At the same time, it allows teachers to see how they have succeeded in developing students' deeper understanding of core ideas and thinking processes. Embedding such tasks within a broader array of work samples selected for the portfolio by the student gives both students and teachers an opportunity to reflect on areas of proficiency and areas of progress in terms of both mastery of content and development of communications and personal skills.

Personal Statement.   In the personal statement essay, students reflect on and express the progress they have made as individuals and as members of work groups. In the mid-cycle portfolio, they assess their strengths, areas of difficulty, and goals in six areas: language and communication skills, individual work and responsibility, group work and participation, work with adults, academic growth, and overall progress. In the end-cycle portfolio, students assess the personal goals they have achieved. They articulate new goals, accomplishments they are proud of, and their learnings from collaboration with others. Rafael, who is originally from Honduras and has been in the United States for less than one year, writes:

> I was very unsure in the first days of school . . . [but] the teachers
> and the students included me to all the activities. . . . I developed
> my English, *not because it was willingness. It was because the system*
> *which this class has practicing* [Italics added]. . . . I learned many
> vocabulary from those activities: "Jabberwocky," "The Road Not
> taken," "The Pit and the Pendulum," "The Eye and How You See," the
> light project in physics . . . physics equations, the name of the
> equipment of the physics room . . . the symbols of the slope of the
> graphs . . . and the ropes and the knots in Project Adventure. For all
> of this activities, I am now feeling surer when I speak English.

From Rafael's perspective, the *Motion* learning environment fosters personal and interpersonal learning, develops competence in language skills and content, and creates a foundation for growing self-confidence. Despite his still-developing competence in English, the portfolio process allows him to demonstrate his ability to clearly articulate his insights about the group process. His limited English proficiency is not an obstacle to his learning. He effectively communicates his views, priorities, and areas of learning. The honesty of his assessment and his willingness to expose his vulnerability is a tribute to the trust he has in his audience and their respect for him. The personal statement gives Rafael's teachers access to his agenda and to his learning processes, needs, and values, while informing them about the impact of their curricular and instructional decisions.

The personal statement reveals that what is most important to Rafael is improving his English. While he is glad to have been well accepted at International, where all of the students are immigrants, he remains convinced that acceptance by his new society is contingent upon his acquisition of English. His increasing self-confidence is directly related to his perception of his increasing language competency. As he refers to the new vocabulary he has learned, we are reminded of the power of naming, of the liberation and self-assurance that follow from confident identification, and of the sense of personal empowerment effective language use confers on human beings.

Amina* records the goals she has achieved: "concentrating on the activities we are doing, and having more friends." Students commonly set making friends as a goal and view it as a gateway to their academic achievement. The newer the students are to International, the more prominently the goal of friendship figures.

The personal statement essays of other students indicate that, throughout the *Motion* Program, academic learning occurs within both personal and social contexts and acquires meaning through an increased sense of personal competency and interpersonal connectedness. As in the faculty evaluation system, conscious and reflective personal assessment in the context of a supportive but demanding community is the cornerstone of growth. While assessment is aimed at mutual learning rather than at "catching" students' failings, the press for achievement and for constantly raising one's sights and standards is also very obvious.

Natasha assesses her progress as she recalls how limited her initial response to the concept of motion was. At first, she thought motion meant "go." After some time in the program, her concept of motion expanded considerably:

> I learned a lot of new things and have many new ideas and insights about motion and movement. There are 21 people in our class, and everybody has personal ideas about this. Sonia* asked very philosophical question: "Is there life without motion?" I think no. Life is impossible without motion, it connected with motion. But, mechanical motion is possible without the life. Bullet from the rifle is in motion, but not alive. The end of movement means the end of life, but the end of life doesn't mean the end of motion.

Students articulate their achievement of personal goals, significant accomplishments, and what they have learned about working with others. They assess their progress in the areas of language growth, communication skills, individual and group work, task completion, reliability, and use of resources. Olga writes, "I am especially proud of my reading. I read the book which has 300 pages. It's my first book which I read in English." The personal statement essay of Sherif Baha el Din,* from Egypt, communicates the significance of his learning English:

> Before I came to U.S.A., I didn't learn English so when I came here I had many troubles because I didn't know it. Now my English got better. On every subject I have to speak English because is some one who doesn't understand Arabic, so I speak and by doing this I'm improving my English skills.

Mastery Statement. The mastery statement is a set of essays written by students to demonstrate the degree of mastery they have achieved over the concepts and skills presented in the course. A set of tasks laid out in the directions for the mastery statement guides students in demonstrating their capacity to synthesize their knowledge and critical thinking skills within and across all four content areas. They are asked to recontextualize, apply, and extend the knowledge they have acquired. A sampling of mastery statement tasks over various cycles of *Motion* indicates how they loop students back to their work and learning during the cycle, encouraging them to use prior knowledge to make new connections:

- A scientist who studies fish goes to a small lake with a net. Describe a good procedure she might use to learn about the fish in the lake.
- Select the two most challenging elements on the ropes course [in Project Adventure]. Describe or draw the element. Describe your experience on this element. How did it help you learn trust, problem solving, and self-confidence?
- Consider Newton's three laws. State them in simple language. Give examples. What would a world which did not obey Newton's laws be like?
- How are the four classes of motion connected? How are they different?
- What did you see in the movie "The Gold Rush" that relates to what you have learned in physics, math, literature, and Project Adventure? Explain.
- In *To Build a Fire, Autobiography, Southbound on the Freeway, Being Moved, The Paw,* and *Graphing Lives,* you saw the concept of motion used in a variety of ways. Select two of these activities and describe in detail how a person or character can be in motion in ways that are physical and not physical.
- In several of the math activities we have drawn graphs and expressed the relationships in an algebraic equation (*The Mystery Container, Temperatures*). Draw a graph with a linear relationship between two variables. Write the equation for it. What do the y-intercept and the slope represent [for your variables]? (IHS, Middle College High School, LaGuardia Community College, 1991)

Natasha's mastery statement, reproduced in Figure 4.4, answers six questions concerning what she has learned about writing, about connections between the work in math and physics and work in literature, about Newton's three laws, about distance, velocity, and acceleration, about linear equations, and about herself, through her work in Project Adventure. Her statement raises common themes and understandings that pervade the portfolios of other students as well. Although she is still learning English, she can now explain what she understands about how to write, how to think through problems, and how to tackle new ideas by drawing on earlier learnings. Her written explanations of Newton's laws and of the concepts of velocity and acceleration in free fall, further explicated with hand-drawn

Figure 4.4. Mastery Statement

---

1. What have I learned about how to write well from your writing experiences in literature?

I have learned about it a lot of things. First when we begin to write we have to know about what problem to write. Then make plane [sic]. Most of us I know that almost every work like Reading Log has three parts: introduction which says about what are you going to write, next is the main part which talk about problem more extensionly [sic], this part reveal introduction and the last part it is usual some conclusion from everything what did you say before, or your own opinion or thoughts about work problem. If you use it, I mean these three parts when you write something it makes your work better. Plan can help you to make order in your thoughts and of course in your work. Also what I have learned about how to write well, I can say that you have to write as easier as you can. It make your work more understanding for you and for your readers.

2. How does the work you have done in Literature connect to the work in math and physics? Give examples from at least two of the activities you have done since mid-sycle [sic].

The four activities I have done which was real connected literature with other subject. The Paw, What is science, Alice in Wonderland, and South-bound on the Freeway. How it connected? When we do some activity we answer a lot of questions, some of them is about physics and math. For example "The Paw" is activity about measurement which we used in math in activity "My Ruler". "Alice in Wonderland" we after reading we talked about falling and we had to give our knowledge of physics about fall, to support this answer we used information in physics and in math also. In activity "Southbound on the Freeway we talked about mistake like we can make similar in math in "Statis-sticks". The connecting literature and physics and math is very easy. We use our knowledge which we get in physics and math to explain something in literature. But this connecting is very important, and the idea of "motion" make us more connecting everything, connecting different topics and combine difference knowledge.

3. Consider Newton's laws. Play with them in your mind. State them in simple language. Give examples. What would a world which did not obey Newton's laws be like?

Newton's 1st law in own words: When somebody rests or moves with constant velocity and some force acts on it, this object will start to move or accelerate or this force will compel the object to move slower to states of rest. In another words, is after acting some force object changes its position.
Examples: You run and somebody push you opposite why to your own direction you can't stop suddenly, but in a few seconds you'll stop runing [sic]. It means that some force in situation is pushing force acted on you and you changed your state of motion. Another thing if you set somewhere and somebody pull you or push you, you start to move or if you moved already you accelarat [sic].

(cont'd.)

Newton's 2nd law in own words. When some object has acceleration it produced by a net force which is resulting force, and accelaration [sic] directly proportional to magnitud [sic] of this force which act with the same diraction [sic] as a net force and inversely proportional to the mass of the body

$$a \sim F \qquad a \sim \frac{1}{M} \qquad a = \frac{F}{M}$$

Examples:

Me and my friend we try to push the big box together but she push with one force for example $F_{her} = 10$ N and $F_{my} = 13$N $m_{00x} = 3000gz = 3$ gz $\rightarrow$ $\leftarrow$ the net force it'll be equal $13 - 10 = 3$N, the accelaration [sic] which will be produced by this net force equal

$$a = \frac{3N}{3kg} = 1 \frac{N}{kg} = 1 \frac{mkg}{kgs^2} = 1 \frac{m}{s^2}$$

And if we together try to pull it with one diraction [sic] it produced more accelaration [sic]

$$a = \frac{13 + 10}{3} = 7.7 \text{ m/s}^2$$

From this examples we can see that if the net force increase and mass is the same, accelaration increase too.

Newton's 3rd law in own words. For every force exist another force which exerts opposit diraction [sic] and equal to the first force. Action force equal reaction.

Examples:

The book lay on the table it doesn't move, but book act on the table. If the book has states of rest it means some equal force act on the book.

I think that without these laws everything will spill, go to pieces.

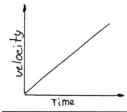

4. We have been using graphs to help us understand relationships. One example is the graphs of distance, velocity and acceleration for objects in free fall. . . .

This graph is velocity vs. time. The slope of this line, wich [sic] looks like line, represent accelaration [sic]. Accelaration [sic] doesn't changing. Accelaration [sic] is equal changing velocity in 1 time interval devided [sic] by changing in time.

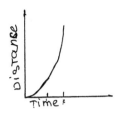

This graph is distance vs. time. The slope of this line represent velocity because the object, which movement is showing here, in time interval discovered one distance and in the same interval but a little later is discovered much more distance. This graph looks like parabola and we can say that parabola means changing, I mean what slope represent is not constant. Speed every time changed.

This graph is acceleration [sic] vs. time. This graph sais [sic] that acceleration is constant. In free fall acceleration constant. In anytime interval the changing in velocity was equal.

They are connected to each other two different way. First is shown in figure number 1. Let's take the graph distance vs time. Take one point in the parabola's line and find the slope (m) in this point. How we already know that this slope represent velocity it means that in that time (x-intercept) it was m-velocity. Now find x-intercept (which equal time in that moment) in the grap [sic] velocity vs. time. $T_D = T_V$. Look at point which represent this time in the line and then find y-intercept. This number it will be closer to slope in point (distance vs. time). The same situation with connection velocity graph and acceleration graph.

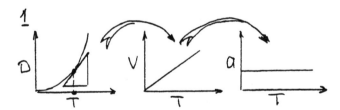

They connected also a back direction if you now [sic] accelaration [sic] and time interval you can find velocity, and if you now velocity in time you can find distance and of course using these graphs.

In general I'll try to give the determining about what does the slope tell us? The slope is ratio of our axis which number is changing of axis to corresponding to it in another axis.

(cont'd.)

Fig. 4.4 (cont'd.)

If the objects move at constant velocity the graphs look like I show.

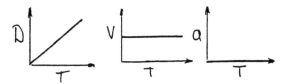

5. In several of the math activities we have drawn graphs and expressed the relationship in algebraic equation (The Mystery Container, Temperatures.) Draw a graph with a linear relationship between two variables. Write the equation for it. What does y-intercept and the slope represent (for your variables)?

From these two activities I did Mystery Container. It's real interesting work. Here I draw graph with linear relationship between totel [sic] mass of container and number of container. This is not exactly what we had, this point was took very simple to make how it must be. We can suppos [sic] that there are kind of coin in container which increase in mass from container to container represent. This slop [sic] represent changing mass of container. Now I said already that some coin increase we can say that the slop [sic] represent mass of coin. The slope is the line and we can say that increase in container is constant x- it is y-intercept in the graph, what represent mass of empty container. The equation for it,

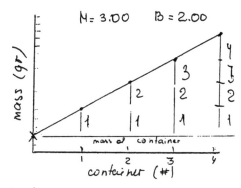

$$M_{totel} = M_{coin} \times N_{coin} + M_{cont.}$$

$$M_T = 3 \times N_{coin} + 2$$

Another way.

We have totel [sic] mass of each container.

M_{totel}	#1 = a	$a - M_{coat} = m_a$
M_T	#2 = b	$b - M_c = m_b$
M_T	#3 = c	$c - M_c = m_c$
M_T	#4 = d	$d - M_c = m_d$
...	= ...	... = ...
M_T	#N = N	$N - m_c = m_n$

$m_a, m_b, ... m_n$ without mass of empty container

We don't know what kind of coin is inside, maybe two different together. We measure different coins like panny [sic], dime etc. Than we have to try all combination which is possible, what can be inside each container, and what number'll be closest we can defin [sic] what is inside. In our situation we recieved panny [sic].

6. Do you think your work in project adventure changed the way you worked in class? Did you find out anything surprising about yourself?

I like project adventure and I think that this subject make our "motion" life more interesting. When you set in literature, in math and in physics you have to be concentration, almost everytime you have to think, write, read. And when you go to gym it make your life more fun, more interesting and it make us more doing something in other subjects. But don't think please that in literature, math and physics I feel terrible and only project adventure make me feel fun, happy. Everything what I said means that my opinion in this question is positive. I really think that my work in project adventure changed the way I worked in class. What I can say about surprising in myself, that I started to observe something interesting in myself. When we did some activity for example climbing and when we were in net, before I felt what I had to do to be more accurately and later it was like I felt. I think it is very important becaus [sic] sometimes the people don't have this feelings. I think that is intuition It's important because it means almost like can to see, hear etc.

---

graphs and illustrations, demonstrate the kind of thinking and expression of mathematical reasoning urged by emerging professional standards in mathematics and science, as well as by other disciplines.

Though Natasha's work is more clearly written than some, it is not atypical of students' conceptual understanding. While Natasha illustrates Newton's second law with an example of herself and a friend pushing a box, first from opposing directions and then from the same direction, calculating net force and acceleration for each instance, Olga's calculations use the example of a small boat pushing a larger boat. Yolanda Bermudez* illustrates her explanations of Newton's Law of Inertia: To underscore the principle that objects at rest tend to stay at rest, Yolanda draws a cartoon of a young boy swiping a table cloth off the table leaving the objects on it perfectly in place. The wide variety of examples described in students' portfolios reveal that they have made the connection, in various ways, between these abstract concepts and real world events.

Students also use their knowledge of physics to inform their imagination when they conjure up a world without Newton's laws. Typical is the response of David Han,* a Korean student:

> According to what I understand about Newton's 3 law, if there is a world which not obey the Newton's law, when you lean against the wall, you might fly away from the wall because the wall lean against you back more force than you lean on against the wall.

Similarly, students have obviously thought hard about what they have learned in other areas. Natasha describes how the three parts of a written composition—the introduction, the main part, and the conclusion—help organize one's thoughts and convey one's ideas more effectively. Amina distills her newly learned writing skills into these personal principles of composition: "thinking about what to write before starting; concentrating on one theme; writing clearly—easy to understand; dividing the composition into paragraphs; using the punctuation symbols correctly."

Throughout mastery statement essays, students also connect their experiences in Project Adventure to the development of trust and the interpersonal skills they use to work effectively in their academic groups.

Self, Peer, and Faculty Evaluation.   Portfolios and classwork are rated with grades ranging from *A* to *NC* by the students themselves, two peers, and two faculty members who have been selected by the student. Additionally, each evaluator writes comments about the student's portfolio, classwork, and interpersonal interactions, focusing on areas of strength and recommendations for improvement. The student in turn writes a summary of the commentary of his/her peers and teachers. Each of these commentaries, as well as the ratings, are part of the portfolio.

Although the evaluation procedure is systematic, it is personalized so that individual differences and needs are taken into account. In the evaluation of Rafael's portfolio, each reviewer commented that he or she had found working with Rafael pleasurable. They commended him on his progress in English and on the clarity, organization, and industry his portfolio demonstrated. One peer and one teacher directly but sensitively critiqued aspects of the portfolio for insufficient detail. They would have liked to know more about his feelings and thinking. Rafael's response summarizing their commentary indicated that he was unclear about what details he omitted. This ambiguity would be discussed at the conference.

The individual ratings for classwork and the portfolio that are assigned by the five evaluators will be factored into one final letter grade at the conference. The final grade will also range from *A* to *NC* since International has a "no fail" policy. Students who receive NC can fulfill the unmet requirements with other courses or reenroll in the same course. The *Motion* Evaluation Guidelines, which are distributed to students at the beginning of the program, clearly articulate teachers' expectations and the criteria that will be used to judge students' achievement.

Judgments in the two categories of classwork and portfolio entries are made on the basis of six indicators each. Indicators used to judge classwork are:

1. Number of absences and number of times student was late
2. Amount of work completed

3. Understanding of classwork
4. Working with others
5. Concentration
6. Communication growth

Indicators used to judge the portfolio are:

1. Explains clearly and completely
2. Gives specific examples
3. Shows what the person has learned
4. Is well organized
5. Is neat and easy to read
6. Explains the connection between classes

The indicators were designed collaboratively by both the faculty and the students. Interestingly, each group came up with the same criteria independently, except for "communication," which only the teachers thought of. Upon discussion, however, the students agreed that communication was an important criterion to include. Students also participated in developing the guidelines corresponding to the letter grades for classwork. To reinforce the value of collaboration as an important and necessary skill, the evaluation guidelines used in scoring the overall portfolio for the cycle place equal weight on "working with others" and "understanding of classwork." The student and his/her committee of peers and faculty comment on the extent to which the student supports and helps others and concentrates on his/her work, along with the extent to which the student has completed work adequately and can explain it to others.

Motion students come to understand and independently apply the standards in several contexts. First, standards are written in the portfolio. But effective communication of standards requires more than providing students with a list of terms and grade correspondences. Students must have opportunities to experience standards of performance. *Motion* students do this while they are working in different groups. Rugger explains: "They begin to notice what other people are doing and make their own distinctions." Ruthellen Weiner, assistant principal, elaborates: "They make distinctions when they are doing the first portfolio. They look at their work and the work of their peers. Going through the process [of assembling the portfolio and writing the personal evaluation, statement, and mastery essay] gives them a clearer idea of the standards."

But even the success of group interactions is insufficient for students to fully understand the standards for portfolios. Because students needed models demonstrating standards of excellence to fully comprehend what excellence looked like before they could achieve it, teachers assembled model portfolios with particularly insightful mastery and personal statements demonstrating standards of excellence. As students' access to the models and to one another's work increased, they developed, says Stevenson, an "I can do it attitude."

Internalizing standards enables students both to achieve at higher levels and to be thoughtful evaluators. In addition to a sense of standards, *Motion* students explain that self-assessment and peer assessment require fairness, which requires them to learn to resolve conflicts of trust and loyalty. Students have had to become conscious of these conflicts and to learn strategies for negotiating them. Olga has learned that fairness is more than an attitude. She explains the effort required for students to develop the skills of being fair:

> How fair can we be about giving ourselves a grade? Through the whole Motion class, we try to develop the skill of being fair not just to ourselves but to others. We do it in the Project Adventure class— develop the trust and being fair to yourself and to everybody else.

Luz elaborates on negotiating the fairness/loyalty conflict:

> Being honest about the grade is very important. When you do all the experiments with all groups, you learn how to be fair to everybody, especially if you have a friend in your group. Even if he did a C or a B portfolio, you have to give him a fair grade. *The most important thing is what you learn and what you experience.*

Natasha explains how structure, values, and norms, and the socialization mechanisms in the class culture, enforce fairness despite the tensions and internal conflicts prompted by the impulse toward self-advancement:

> It's very hard to grade yourself. You know how hard you were working and everyone else knows how hard you were working, if you did it last night or if you were working on it through the whole time we had. Everybody tries to be very fair for the grades for themselves. They know if they put a lower grade, then the teachers will think— because the teachers put a lot of trust in us—then the teachers will think, "Well, I think that he did better, but if he thinks that he deserved a C or a B, let's put him a B." Then it makes you think, "Maybe I should get a higher grade." But then when you put an A for yourself, inside yourself, you know you deserve a C+ or B. Then your friends will come to you and say, "You know, I think you should try harder next time. But this time, I think that you don't deserve the A." *It's a very friendly atmosphere that makes you fair.* [Italics added.]

The temptation to abuse adult trust is mediated by the knowledge of the community's values—as articulated by Luz: "The most important thing is what you learn and experience"—and the power of the peer culture: the trusting atmosphere that students are unwilling to risk.

After the evaluations have been completed, the evaluation statements and grades provide the basis of the conversation for the conference.

The Conference

After the portfolios have been evaluated, each student and his or her peer and faculty evaluators convene for a conference of 5–8 minutes, the ostensible purpose of which is to determine a final grade. This is important for three reasons. First, the conference formally validates the student's achievement. Second, since students often do not know how their grades are determined, the conference is an opportunity to review the correspondence between performance, growth, achievement, and the grade. Third, if the student and his/her evaluators disagree on their assessments, especially where students rate themselves higher than their peers or teachers, the conference becomes an opportunity to clarify the rating criteria and process, the rating itself, and the rationale of each rater. The conference respects the perspective of the learner while adding other perspectives and a sense of external criteria as well.

The conferences also have a forward-looking purpose, which is to set the course for future improvement, growth, progress, and commitment. Their tone is hushed: sensitive and supportive, but serious. The student and his/her four judges sit around a table with the thick portfolio and its ratings in the center, attesting to the student's progress and achievement and available for public view and review. The center placement dignifies both the work and the worker.

Peer evaluators tend to comment primarily on the student's acquisition of English and behavior in group settings. Although, according to custom, they begin with complimentary statements of the student's strengths and contributions, they do not demur from criticism for students who "fooled around too much." Students being evaluated tend not to be defensive or resistant to the critiques. They seem readily to admit their errors, usually with reasonable explanations, though not excuses. They show a clear-headed capacity to critique their own performance, as these conference comments reveal:

- I really didn't do a good job on this.
- I didn't maintain my momentum.
- I didn't work hard at the beginning, but then I did and I think my work shows the difference.

Teachers take this opportunity to affirm the student's achievements and potential and to explore in depth with the student strategies that can improve performance. They ask questions intended to help students formulate new goals and the next steps to achieve them. Thus, plans for improvement are self-generated, emerging from students' own assessments of their needs and capabilities as stimulated by those of their teachers and colleagues. Once again, assessment is a tool for learning. Once again, the school's fundamental premise that assessment is linked to empowerment of students is reaffirmed. As an instrument of empowerment, the conference emerges as *Motion's* ritual for the renewal of commitment: an individual's commitment to themselves and their community and the community's commitment to the education of its members.

Because the system of assessment in the *Motion* Program is simultaneously a system of instruction that intricately and inextricably interweaves learning and assessment, they become as inseparable as the flip sides of a coin. Assessment and learning serve each other so dynamically in *Motion* that students have an unusual capacity to reflect on, articulate, and utilize the "hidden" curriculum as well as the overt curriculum. As correction and self-correction become natural in the course of learning—teacher as well as student learning—self-improvement becomes inevitable.

INTERACTIONS OF TEACHING, LEARNING, AND ASSESSMENT

The principles and practices of assessment identified in the three programs discussed above have had far reaching effects because they function as instruments of both learning and evaluation. They are integral to the daily life of classrooms in which assessment has become a habit of work rather than a special, feared, or surprising event. Because the teaching and learning process is laced with assessment, a feedback loop of teaching, learning, assessment, and validation has evolved, providing students and teachers with ongoing information about their performance, their work, and their outcomes. This approach provides all members of the school community with the systemic and personal capacity to obtain that information on a regular basis in either a private or a public forum.

By creating a system in which assessment is habitual and supportive, International increases the probability that students will be able to improve their personal competence throughout life because they have internalized a capacity for self-reflection, constructive interaction with others, and responsive problem solving. Stevenson explains: "We are always in interaction with the students so that the kinds of questions, the kinds of dialogue you may have with the students indicates to them how to think about the issues." Dialogue is both assessment and instruction in how to think about work, work problems, and work quality. Hirschy adds that these conversations with students inform teachers' practice. As teachers learn what and how students are thinking, says Hirschy, "they understand what is really being communicated." Changes in teachers' practices and changes in the portfolios have consequently promoted further changes in students' learning and performance. He says: "As the questions [in the portfolio] got better, the portfolios got better. Reading the portfolios is often a validation of what we're doing, and it gives us insights as to what they're really doing."

Evaluating student work from multiple perspectives is another form of validation for the members of this learning community. When evaluations by teachers and peers confirm students' assessments of themselves, the results can be very powerful, whether the grade is an A or a C. Students are frequently silenced by the unabashed admiration of their peers and teachers, who take great pleasure in describing their strengths and the details of their growth. Such attention makes students feel valued. Criticisms are delivered sensitively and within the context of both the students' potential and peers' and teachers' belief in that potential. Great pains are taken not to compromise the self-esteem of students whose self-evaluation is inconsistent with the evaluations by their peers and teachers. Time is taken to help students concretely and discreetly sort out the disparities and accept what is usually a lower grade than they have given themselves. The unspoken but nevertheless palpable refrain of these interactions is one of reaffirming shared commitment.

Effects on Teaching, Learning, and Student Performance

Information creates the possibility and the capacity for self-correction without which learning outcomes cannot improve. Stevenson explains that, in *Motion*, "Students have the opportunity to figure out why they're not getting it. They can find the thing that causes them not to get it." The regular opportunities for formal and informal feedback among peers and faculty create an intimate and respectful learning community that can support students' admissions of "not getting it," their investigations of "why they're not getting it," and their uncovering of "the thing that causes them not to get it." Luz Mercado,* a Puerto Rican student, explains: "You're not afraid to make mistakes in front of people you know. You express your ideas and then you sort them out. You're not afraid to tell someone else you think they are wrong. You feel free with one another."

WenFu emphasizes the significant role of intimacy in the clusters that keep students together all day with the same group of peers and teachers: "Because you are with the same kids every day, you get to know them well. You feel close." Through this process of socialization in a protected environment, a culture of inquiry and self-correction develops, making it safe for students to take responsibility for their outcomes. In fact, taking responsibility is the norm, as portfolio conference confessions reveal. This process paves the way for discovering *the thing that causes students to get it.*

Rugger explains that *Motion* students learn to assess themselves for the purposes of self-knowledge, self-correction, and self-direction. She underscores the connection between understanding one's thoughts and actions, being able to change them, and thus being able to grow; her remarks place in relief the difference between students' experiences with this form of assessment and the traditional form in which they "receive" a grade, but frequently do not understand it and are unable to use it to guide their future work and decisions. She says: "Students are always in the position of [looking at] where they've gone, what they're doing right then, and where they want to go."

Natasha confirms Rugger's observation:

First they are very scared and they go, "I'll never be able to write two pages in English of Personal Evaluation. I'm not good [at writing English] at all." Then once they started to write, they perform beautiful. And when we read it, the teacher goes, "Oh. you wrote here that you didn't make such a progress, but look here. You wrote two pages in English." People feel proud and that helps a lot.

Because the assessment processes encourage students to connect their past and present to their future—to reflect regularly on their growth—it increases their faith in their capacity to grow and their willingness to risk, especially when unfamiliar demands are made on them. As they take risks and grow, they gain confidence and a greater sense of control over their learning and progress. The connection between work and outcomes is demystified. Glassman observes that in *Beginnings*, because students confront their work on a daily basis, there are no surprises about grades.

Nancy Dunetz, career education coordinator, notices that students who have completed the *Motion* Program have the ability to think more deeply about problems than do other students. The students themselves point with pride to the recent student government elections in which *Motion* students occupied 90% of the positions on the slates. Teachers notice changes in students' performance: reductions in cutting, longer retention of information, and a repertoire of problem-solving and social skills.

The programs' assessment practices have changed teachers' roles, but not without anxiety. Teachers have had to learn to trust the group process in their classrooms and to resist the impulse to overcontrol. Rugger writes about her own "odyssey" from a traditional teaching approach to a group-oriented, learner-centered style:

For years I had been encouraged and required to be in total control of the classroom, and now I was in a school where the philosophy of education is to work in groups. I understood and applauded the reasoning behind this, but to put it into practice day after day was daunting. For one thing, there is often a lot of noise. People are talking to each other trying to explain. Sometimes this is going on in several languages at once. They may be arguing about points that are being made. At times, someone needs to get up to get supplies, or go across the room to get answers to questions. It appears to be confusion. People are not sitting in rows and whispering. I had visions of the principal or other teachers opening the door and asking "What's going on here?"

But working in a class where the students speak five different languages, none of which I speak, and range from total nonspeakers of English to people who have been in this country for three years and have picked up a lot of English, made me realize that group work was the only system that would work. We depend on each other to share knowledge and experience, so we both learn. I had to give up my role of total expert, and realize we were learning things together. (Rugger, 1990, pp. 36–38)

Nadelstern sees his role as one of continually rearranging and reshaping the organizational pieces so that teachers can explore the instructional initiatives that interest them. Contrary to the underlying assumptions of most schools, asserts Nadelstern, International is organized on the assumption that students and teachers are trustworthy.

A trusting environment is not, however, a laissez-faire environment. Teachers exert a strong classroom presence, by becoming facilitators and coaches, casting off the role of disseminators of information. They have learned to demonstrate to students that they value more than the mere completion of activities. As a result, *Motion* teachers, for example, developed questions requiring students to apply their learning to new contexts. They learned to take the role of what Hirschy calls the "wizened guide." Rather than answer students' questions, teachers restate or recontextualize them and direct the group to resume their struggle in search of solutions. This response not only gives students a new handle on the problem, but it models a strategy they can use whenever they get stuck.

Beginnings teachers also see themselves as modeling the kinds of learning behavior they want for their students. DeFazio and Glassman, who team teach, talk about modeling collaboration. DeFazio says: "It's a good model for the kids to see how we take different roles."

How Assessment Informs Curriculum

Assessment has prompted instructional and curricular changes in all three programs. Student feedback in *Beginnings* has led DeFazio and Glassman to reorganize the curriculum. They have refined some activities and added new ones. Revision based on students' feedback, asserts Glassman, customizes curriculum to the developmental needs of students. As a result, the revisions increase students' capacity to produce increasingly sophisticated products and more in-depth analysis. This is corroborated by the *Motion* team. The more feedback the teachers receive on what students are and are not learning, the more they can target exactly what they want students to learn.

In all three programs, assessment has supported a shift in curriculum priorities from coverage of content to mastery of skills. That does not mean that rigorous, substantive, or traditional content has disappeared. Students in *Motion* still do experiments in physics, generate algebraic equations, and read classical literature. Students in *Beginnings* study the American historical perspective on immigration. Students read and report on famous biographies in the *Personal and Career Development Program.*

In all of these cases, however, engagement with content functions in the service of developing essential skills and performance abilities. Content becomes a vehicle for students to develop intellectually, to demonstrate critical thinking skills, to generalize, to recontextualize, to synthesize, and to apply their learning to new situations. Moreover, content offers opportunities for students to develop, practice, and perfect the life, study, and work skills that will make a difference in their success in post-secondary schools or the workplace. They develop the skills of perseverance, task engagement, time management, prioritization, interpersonal relations, collaboration, communication, responsibility, reflection, and assessment.

Glassman says that students in *Beginnings* must learn strategies for presenting and giving feedback. He teaches his students presentation skills for their exhibitions. He teaches them to have a sense of pride during their exhibitions, to make sure that everyone is watching their presentations, and to take responsibility for engaging members of the audience who are not paying attention. He says:

> Everyone has a job. The presenter has a job of keeping everybody's attention, the listeners have the job of listening. If a kid's attention wanders during a presentation, the presenter must learn skills such as saying, "How do you like this, Nancy?" Such skills are not learned in two shots or three or four. It's a long process. You do a little at a time.

The assessment used in all three programs has supported the development of interdisciplinary, thematically based curriculum that focuses students on the development and use of thinking skills rather than on the mere memorization of content. *Motion* teachers report that as students progress, they spend less time on recapitulation—redoing, neatening, or completing activities that they plan to include in the portfolio. They spend correspondingly more time on the portfolio tasks that demand a reconceptualization and synthesis of their experiences across the curriculum and an analysis of their learning and growth.

Internship seminars demand that students engage in analysis of the workplace from multiple perspectives: they assess their own performance at their sites, they assess their supervisors' assessments, and they assess the sites organizationally from the perspectives of benefits, worker satisfaction, and structure. This enables them to understand and appreciate many points of view and to reflect on the different criteria various parties bring to their assessments, tasks, or situations. In *Beginnings*, students' participation in peer assessment helps them learn to read critically and responsively and to develop internal criteria for judging what they read.

The practice of self- and peer assessment has demanded a new curriculum for communication and social interaction. Most traditional schools and classrooms are organized to avoid peer communication and social interaction, or at best to tightly control them. Almost all of the teaching, learning, and assessment in the programs we have described at International, however, take place through social interaction and collaboration. This is a particularly important prerequisite for the development of those generic, work-related skills of teamwork, cooperation, and interpersonal problem solving that are so frequently cited by commissions and reformers striving to persuade schools to prepare students for their later life experiences.

Natasha explains that Project Adventure activities promote social interaction skills. Because activities such as belaying[2] make students responsible for one another's safety and for their lives, they teach students to trust each other, despite temporary disputes and disagreements. She comments on the difficulty of remaining angry at someone when you quite literally have their life in your hands: "The responsibility puts things in a perspective." The belayed partner, as well, learns that trust can be a responsible choice that transcends disagreements and anger. WenFu concurs, explaining how Project Adventure activities develop communication skills that build trust:

> The teacher would give us a situation and a problem and time to think of a solution. Through this I think that a lot of us have learned about giving each other time to listen to their ideas. Learn to trust each other and we learn to listen to each other rather than to shout out. Through listening to other people, you might come up with better ideas instead of just your own ideas.

Fine describes how assessment becomes curriculum that teaches students to assume responsibility. In one of her *PCD* classes, she asked students to create a report card for which they had to develop evaluation criteria. They spent a week debating which criteria would be best, as Fine worried if she would ever get to the content. Once students settled on the evaluation criteria, however, the criteria began to drive their behavior, as assessment often drives curriculum and teaching. Suddenly, students who cut class found themselves accountable, not to the teacher's rules, but to the rules of their peers—and, worse yet, of themselves! Students were less likely to cut and more likely to exert effort in the ways suggested by the criteria they developed. Fine believes that the change in power relations liberated the students to take responsibility for their behavior.

CHALLENGES AND CHANGES

Because International was still a new school when it began its work on assessment, it has been spared the problems typically encountered by schools trying to reform long-standing traditions and behaviors. The only internal challenges have been initial student resistance and the need to invent the technology to implement the assessment. External stumbling blocks, including local and state policies that influence staffing and curriculum, are more problematic because they require changes outside the school's control.

New Roles and Responsibilities

The internal challenges have been met in the collaborative spirit that supports most activities in the school. When Fine's students resisted direct self-evaluation, she heeded Glassman's advice by introducing the album. Students took to assessment when it was embedded in concrete learning activities. She recalls:

> The biggest problem students had was viewing assessment experiences as learning opportunities, evaluating on a regular basis, asking, "Where was I and how far have I come?" [With the album] every single assignment is an evaluation of what's going on in their internship, what they're learning, and how they're doing.

Unless teachers help students negotiate their fear of the unknown, they are unlikely to accept new approaches. As DeFazio explains, the hardest thing is

> getting the kids to buy into the assessment, to see that there's a lot of value for themselves in it, that it will make them feel good to do it. Since they've never experienced it, they're scared of it, like all of us. But once you encourage them enough and create an atmosphere so they experience it, they feel great showing off their work.

Students also sometimes resist adopting new roles, especially active and interactive roles that release them from their powerless station in the school hierarchy where, traditionally, they have had no involvement in or recourse to their evaluations. "Getting kids to learn the skill of the process, how to look at something [i.e., the work of their peers] critically, how to offer helpful feedback, is a major problem," DeFazio notes. Learning the skills of the process, struggling for language, making the effort to communicate are all symbolic of accepting a new role, a role that demands increased involvement, commitment, and responsibility from students. It is the foundation for reconfiguring the classroom community so that everyone is accountable to everyone else.

Standards Without Standardization

By far one of the most exciting challenges International has confronted is the dilemma of standards. The issue of standards in the context of authentic assessment is controversial and complex. Here, the faculty's navigation through this barely charted territory has been thoughtful and provocative.

The *Motion* team confronted three issues: (1) the establishment of standards; (2) the communication of standards; and (3) the teaching of standards. Teachers brought a wealth of knowledge and experience about traditional standards from their former practice in other schools, where they had taught tracked courses. But the instructional model the *Motion* team developed called for standards combining a collaborative learning process with a multifaceted product—the portfolio. This is complicated. Hirschy explains:

> We have a multiple set of standards. Although it's very difficult to be exact about what constitutes an A, it's very clear to faculty and students when students fall in an A area or in a B area. . . . It's a composite of a group of individuals looking at a variety of areas and then putting together one picture.

The ambiguity is not indicative of confusion or sloppiness but rather of the team's desire to develop standards that capture the broadest range of achievement: achievement that is both conventionally and unconventionally demonstrated and that is social and personal as well as academic. The process is one of weighing and balancing various aspects of performance that are ultimately equally valuable for student development and success in later life. Rugger explains:

> An A student can generalize to something else, take knowledge and use it someplace—in written form, in artwork, in the physics lab. There are students who can do this less well, but their leadership skills help others to reach that A level and everyone acknowledges that. . . . They may be in the B+ range as far as the ability to generalize. But they are a powerful force in the class. And they can get an A. They may be able to verbalize their generalizations better than writing them.

International teacher Simon Cohen has articulated some of the various factors that he has found important to consider in his quest to "assist younger people to go as far toward realizing their potential as I could in the time they were with me, an older professional" (Cohen, 1990, p. 30). These reflect the questions teachers at International wrestle with consciously and intentionally on an ongoing basis:

1. How do we balance various factors, for example, homework, classwork, attendance, punctuality, group work, individual work, etc.?

2. How much do we credit students' growth in a subject, and how much
   their mastery of the material?
3. How much credit can we give for language development, and how much
   should we give for content acquisition?
4. How much do we take a student's individuality and uniqueness into
   account, and how much do we hold the student to a set of standard
   expectations?
5. How much do we credit affective and behavioral aspects and how much
   do we credit cognitive growth? (Cohen, 1990, p. 31)

Cohen posits that the appropriate weight for each of these factors may
shift over time for individual students. Behavioral concerns may weigh
more heavily at the beginning of a student's experience, and cognitive concerns may weigh more heavily at the end; it may be critical to emphasize
and reward language acquisition initially, with content acquisition gaining
in importance later on.

In this spirit, the *Motion* team acknowledges the importance of both
academic and social standards, as well as the salience of both personal and
group standards. It has acknowledged the value of collaboration, interpersonal relations, and communication as being as powerful as academic
achievement itself. While this equation is unorthodox in secondary schools,
it is common in the workplace, where interpersonal skills that increase and
improve productivity are highly valued and rewarded. In redefining standards, the *Motion* team has raised the question of what knowledge is of
most worth in schools.

Hirschy explains that the multiple perspective evaluation system produces multiple sets of standards against which individuals assess their
progress and achievement. This helps maintain multidimensional standards.
In the *Motion* assessment system, internal standards are applied in the self-
evaluation, group standards are applied in the peer evaluation, and broader societal standards are applied in the faculty evaluation. Actually, these
multiple sets of standards exist in all classrooms, but, except for the teacher's
standards, they generally remain hidden, unacknowledged, and without
voice. This contributes to many students' reasons for opting out of the formal system, feeling it does not value what they deem important.

Through the *Motion* assessment process, these multiple sets of standards
become visible and public. They influence one another. They get discussed,
negotiated, and revised as students have access to them and to one another's achievements and strategies for achieving. The standards are also
inevitably raised and enriched as students interact and engage their peers
and teachers, as teachers see a wider range of possibilities, and as they
develop the teaching technology to obtain improved student outcomes.

For example, when students in Hirschy's physics class independently
extended their learning to invent activities, he included some in the physics
curriculum. This action acknowledged the role of students as legitimate cur-

riculum developers. Hirschy's discovery that students demonstrated their mastery of content by generating their own activities led him and his colleagues to expand the indicators of student expertise, thereby both increasing the level of challenge in the program and increasing students' opportunities to demonstrate their expertise. They revised the *Motion* curriculum to include a student-invented activity—the special project—that teaches concepts of the course. In *Motion*, student outcomes are not the culmination of the learning experience; instead they become a starting point for new learning opportunities, as their products feed back into curriculum and instruction.

If standards are not immutable, how are continuity and constancy maintained? Teachers continually check their consensus on standards by analyzing the degree to which their evaluations of students' classwork and portfolios are compatible. This process guides the continuous construction of standards by students and teachers, which, asserts Rugger, "is the only way to take the cap off achievement." Ultimately, the validity of such a system rests in the knowledge and expertise of the teachers overseeing it. Having seen the process in action as well as the products of students' work, it is easy to believe the observation of Dunetz: "Over the years, teachers' standards have become higher and higher and kids' products better and better."

Supportive Policies

At the heart of International's integrated teaching, learning, and assessment system is its creative and energetic faculty. Here, too, International has had the good fortune to be able to seek and hire like-minded teachers on the basis of their qualifications and commitment to the school's educational mission and innovative practices. At the time of this study International was one of only two schools out of over 900 in New York City that had been granted a much valued waiver from citywide personnel policies that authorize the central office to randomly assign teachers to schools and permit senior teachers to automatically transfer throughout the city wherever there is a vacancy in their license area. But the waiver must be requested anew each year, and, since there are no guarantees that it will be granted, International's control over its destiny is uncertain.

An additional challenge is a continuing constraint on the shape of the curriculum. As the school seeks to go further in the direction of an interdisciplinary curriculum organized around active, collaborative learning, the New York State Regents Competency Tests (RCTs), particularly those in content areas (e.g., social studies and science), increasingly "get in the way," according to Nadelstern. Still grounded in an outmoded theory of learning emphasizing the memorization of discrete facts, and an outmoded form of testing using primarily multiple-choice exercises, the RCTs grate against integrated project and activity-based curricula that are seeking to get students to think in greater depth and to perform in more complex ways.

Though students at International succeed on the Regents tests, the tests deflect time and attention from what the school sees as more important kinds of learning activities. International faculty look forward to a day when the state's approach to assessment supports the kind of successful teaching and learning they have developed. Recent initiatives by the state's Council on Curriculum and Assessment promise to place assessment systems like those at International and CPESS at the forefront of state-wide changes that are transforming testing and the goals of teaching (New York State Council on Curriculum and Assessment, 1993). In the new system, local schools and districts will develop portfolios of student work supported by state performance assessments, and an assessment bank providing access to models and exemplars.

CONCLUSION

The assessment practices at International make school a workplace where the processes and the products of individual and collaborative student work are at the center of the entire enterprise. Students learn a work ethic founded on effort, pride in one's achievements, acknowledgment of mastery and expertise, and a capacity to accurately and adequately assess what they have done and how it can be continually improved. The expectation is that all students will ask themselves if they are working up to their potential. The teachers want students to develop and internalize the drive to achieve their potential.

There is no division at International between academic and vocational skills. Critical thinking, goal setting, accurate self-assessment, effective communication and relationships with peers and supervisors, collegial collaboration, self-motivation and initiative, and application of learning to new contexts—all features of the assessments—are valuable in both the school and the workplace. Teachers report that students demonstrate higher levels of cognitive skills, greater capacity to retain and generalize what they know, increased self-reliance, and a repertoire of problem-solving strategies and social skills. They possess self-knowledge about their capacity, potential, and effort.

In contrast with traditional assessments, where the test is about the work but at an abstracted level, at International the test *is* the work, whether the work is an activity, a product, or a portfolio. Despite the fact that the artifacts of authentic assessment require more intense and demanding work, whether they are portfolios or products such as the internship album or the *Beginnings'* autobiography, students prefer them to traditional tests. Glassman is fond of pointing out that no student has ever lost his/her autobiography. According to Natasha, the process of assembling and organizing portfolios encourages students to construct knowledge and respects them as learners because it reflects their achievements in their own terms.

Portfolio is important because you build, you put everything together, all your experiences during the cycle in the class. . . . You look at the work and you are able to see what you did and how you did it. When you do the tests [a reference to traditional tests], you study, you learn by heart, next day you pass the test, that's it—out of your head. You will forget about it. I guarantee.

Olga concurs that portfolios are better than tests, illustrating how they double as learning opportunities.

Portfolios are better than tests. . . . You are learning it while you are writing it. Once you present it [at debriefings or before the class], you know it for sure. It's forever.

But is the assessment at International forever? Without policies that support it, does it have a chance to become the norm rather than the exception to the rule? Will there be a time when International cannot obtain the waivers necessary to carry on its work? Now that International has a $600,000 federal Academic Excellence Award grant for the purpose of replication, will other schools have to traverse an obstacle course of regulations in order to replicate International's success? Will other schools, inclined to adapt International's practices, but with leaders and faculty who are less resourceful, less resolved, or less lucky than Nadelstern and his teachers be willing and able to change without policy supports in place?

These are the $64-million questions that school reformers must ask—and answer—in order for International's accomplishments to become a foundation for their own and other schools' further growth and success.

NOTES

1. Teachers' names are unchanged. Students' names have been changed and are marked with an asterisk.
2. "Belaying is a technique used in rope climbing, involving concentration and focus on the person who is climbing. . . . The belayer maintains physical control of the rope. It is the belayer's responsibility to manipulate the rope to assist the climber, and to insure safety." From Alan Krull, "Project Adventure: An Adventure in Growth and Maturation," *Insights,* p. 27.

5

THE PRIMARY LANGUAGE RECORD AT P.S. 261

Linda*[1] was initially characterized by her first grade teacher as an "extremely slow" learner with "reading problems." The teacher's view of Linda began to change, however, after she worked with her in a literature-based reading program, supported by careful observation, using the *Primary Language Record*. Based on her assessment of Linda's needs and interests, the teacher read regularly with Linda, using books featuring lots of repetition and poetry. As a result of an ongoing process of individualized work, guided by careful observation and documentation of her learning, Linda's reading problems began to disappear, and her path to literacy opened up.

One of Linda's favorite books was Cowley's *The Monster's Party* (1983). She read it over and over again, approximating the text by using the pictures, by using her own sense of the story's meaning, and by using her memory of previous readings. Linda's teacher gave her support by praising her as a reader, encouraging lots of contextual guesses, and giving her clues when she was stumped.

After many reading sessions in which they worked on developing multiple strategies for getting at the meaning of print, Linda's teacher asked her if she wanted to make her own book based on *The Monster Party* format. Linda was delighted. Her story, entitled "A Little Girl's Party," modeled the language pattern of the original book. Linda chose and dictated to her teacher what the girl could do, drew pictures to give herself the needed clues, and finally *read* it aloud to a smiling and appreciative class audience.

She can dance
That's what she can do.

She can jump.
That's what she can do.

She can skip.
That's what she can do.

SHE CAN READ!
That's what she can do.

The *Primary Language Record (PLR)*, an authentic measure of young children's literacy development, has influenced teaching and learning in over 50 New York City public elementary schools that have been engaged since 1990 in a process of developing alternatives to standardized testing in the early grades. These schools, along with community school districts and the New York City Office for Research, Evaluation, and Assessment (OREA), have all been developing and testing alternatives, seeking to invent and support schoolwide and classroom options. These include performance-based assessments in a variety of subject areas, portfolio assessments, and strategies to support teachers' observation of students. The *Primary Language Record*, developed in England and increasingly used in the United States, is one example of a support for teachers' observations of student learning. It involves teachers in collecting guided reading and writing samples of students' work, in interviewing parents and students, and in documenting students' literacy behaviors in a wide range of settings and tasks. In England and in California the *PLR* has been expanded to cover a full range of disciplinary areas—mathematics, science, social studies, and the arts. The *California Learning Record,* for example, provides a means for documenting student growth and learning across subject areas at both the elementary and secondary levels.

In New York City, teachers' initial efforts to use the *PLR* have focused thus far only on the original literacy assessments. These are currently used to supplement other traditional and nontraditional means for assessing and reporting student growth, including traditional standardized tests and report cards in many schools, and new portfolio and performance assessments in others. *PLR* study groups, assistance from facilitators, and other supports have been provided by OREA, the Fund for New York City Public Education, the Center for Educational Options, and local networks of schools and teachers, including the Center for Collaborative Education and the Elementary Teachers Network. The hope of these groups is that strategies like the *PLR* will eventually be woven into a fully developed set of authentic assessment practices in schools across New York City.

The *Primary Language Record* was introduced at P.S. 261, a racially and economically mixed neighborhood elementary school near downtown Brooklyn, in the summer of 1991. P.S. 261 is similar to many other elementary schools in New York City—a fairly large, traditionally structured school of about 700 students, with about 35 teachers and other support staff. The school's principal, Arthur Foresta, first learned about the *PLR* from District Superintendent William Casey. Arthur was intrigued by what he heard, especially since he had already begun encouraging a "whole-language" approach to literacy development and had stopped buying basal readers for the school. He supported two teachers' attendance at an intensive, month-long *PLR* summer course sponsored by the Lehman College Institute for Literacy Studies. These teachers were asked to share their knowledge about the *PLR* with the school community at several workshop presentations early in the fall of the following school year. As a result of the meetings, all eleven of the Pre-K through Grade 1 teachers in the school agreed to try the *PLR* with several children in their classes. These teachers were supported by regular classroom visits from Jill Benado, an OREA facilitator, and by voluntary weekly lunchjtime meetings at the school. Four teachers also attended a biweekly, after-school study group led by Jill that focused on issues raised by the use of the *Primary Language Record.*

In the spring of 1992, an additional six middle grade teachers became involved in the project. They began using the *Primary Language Record* with two children each and met for guidance in this work with Jill in after-school sessions. A second summer session in July of 1992 involved more teachers at both beginning and advanced stages of The *PLR*'s understanding and use. In this way, over a period of time, a new approach to literacy development and assessment was introduced throughout the school by teachers studying a strategy, sharing their knowledge with other teachers, trying it out, working through questions, adapting their approaches, and working through more questions. This was not a quick fix or an externally mandated reform, but rather a flexible lens through which to look at growth and learning; the *PLR* became part of—and a major support for—other learner-centered efforts P.S. 261 was initiating.

THE PRIMARY LANGUAGE RECORD

The *Primary Language Record* (Barrs, Ellis, Hester, & Thomas, 1988) was conceived in 1985 by educators in England who were searching for a better means of recording children's literacy progress. Teachers, school heads, staff developers, and central office representatives developed it together as a way of reflecting and supporting existing good teaching practices. It is designed to meet the following criteria for good assessment:

- Assessment practices need to support and inform day-to-day teaching in the classroom.
- Assessment practices need to provide a continuum of knowledge about children as they pass from teacher to teacher.
- Assessment practices need to be able to inform administrators and those responsible in the community at large for children's work.
- Assessment practices need to provide families with concrete information about children's progress.

The *Primary Language Record* is a vehicle for systematically observing students in various aspects of their literacy development—reading, writing, speaking, and listening—using particular classroom events and samples of work as the basis for recording students' progress and interests; for recommending strategies for addressing needs and building on talents; and for discussing ideas and perceptions with the students, their parents, and other faculty. By virtue of what teachers are asked to observe, the *PLR* offers a coherent view of what constitutes progress and development in language and literacy learning. It is grounded in the philosophy that literacy acquisition develops in a manner similar to language acquisition—through immersion in meaningful and purposeful activities. It recognizes that developments in language and literacy do not take place in isolation but in diverse contexts that span the curriculum. It encourages teachers to identify children's strengths and note their growth points, to regard errors as information, and to analyze patterns of errors in a constructive way.

In these ways, the *PLR* reflects an overall shift in thinking about the learning process—a shift that recognizes that good teaching is based on intimate knowledge of the child as well as on knowledge of the curriculum and teaching strategies. It also represents a shift in thinking about the purposes and uses of assessment—a shift that acknowledges the importance of documenting growth over time in rich, informative ways; a shift that provides for congruence between values, goals, instruction, and assessment practices.

Essential Principles

The *Primary Language Record* is designed around the following essential principles.

Parent Involvement. The *PLR* encourages parent involvement in schools in two important ways. First, it provides for an ongoing exchange of information between teachers and parents about a child's language and literacy growth. It offers a fuller and rounder picture of a child's progress than is given by any standardized test score. Second, it values the knowledge of parents as the child's first teacher by eliciting and utilizing the information parents have about their child in the learning process. In these important ways, an ongoing parent/school relationship develops throughout the year.

Respect for Family. The *PLR* values each family's knowledge about their children and respects each family's cultural and linguistic background. It takes special note of home language and offers positive support for the gathering of information about language and literacy development in languages other than English. By asking parents to reflect and report on their children's literacy behaviors, it enables them to recognize growth, and it further encourages activities that are related to literacy development in the home.

Respect for Children. The *PLR* values children in two important ways. First, it recognizes that children come to school with prior knowledge and experience as language users. It looks at them individually, noting growth over time rather than comparing them to other children or classes. It provides authentic information about children—a picture that focuses on and values each child's strengths, what each child *can* do, rather than a picture obtained through the lens of a deficit model. Second, it values children's knowledge about themselves. It provides them with the opportunity to be actively involved in the evaluation of their progress and the planning of their own work.

Respect for Teacher Knowledge and Professionalism. The *PLR* builds upon teachers' understandings and enhances teacher professionalism in several ways. First, it draws out and enriches teachers' knowledge and uses it as the basis for educational and instructional decisions. In doing so, it acknowledges teachers—those closest to the learning situation—as the best assessors of children's growth and the most knowledgeable decision makers regarding instruction. Second, the flexibility of the framework allows for and respects differences among teachers in much the same way as it does for children. Each teacher is able to decide how to manage the frequency, format, and style of observations. Third, it supports both individual and collaborative teacher reflection and learning—about children and about teaching practice. The *PLR* is designed to allow all teachers who teach the child to be involved in compiling a full picture of the child's progress and to ensure that their special insights are incorporated into the child's picture and plan.

Format of the PLR

The structure of the *Primary Language Record* provides a framework in which teachers can observe, document, and learn about the learning of their students in order to provide more adaptive instruction. It is a way of organizing information and synthesizing that information in order to look at an individual student's growth over time. While it offers a format for recording continuous observations about particular aspects of development and learning, it does not mandate a particular time, schedule, or manner of observing or reporting (see Appendix to this chapter). Each teacher is free to decide how, when, and where to record information. The structure provided by the *PLR* is in its conception of the teaching and learning process, rather than in an insistence on uniform reporting procedures.

The *Primary Language Record* is organized to include the elements presented below.

Parent Interview. A discussion is held between the teacher and the child's family member(s) and recorded at the beginning of the school year. The purpose of this discussion is to encourage communication and to establish a partnership between home and school. In this interview, parents' knowledge of the child, both at home and at school, is shared. Parents have the opportunity to comment on what the child reads, writes, and talks about at home, as well as on what changes or developments they have noticed. The interview also elicits parents' observations, concerns, hopes, and expectations about their child and his or her experiences of school. (See Figure 5.1.)

The information gained through this discussion supports children's learning at school by providing the teacher with a full picture of the child's development to which the teacher can refer throughout the school year. Teachers learn about such important influences on children's development as the family's primary language, interactions with brothers and sisters, television viewing, likes and dislikes, and changes that have occurred in the child's language and literacy development. This information helps teachers understand how much children know and how much they are involved in a range of language and literacy-related activities in their home and in their community. At the end of the conference, the teacher and parent(s) agree on the points to be recorded in the *Primary Language Record*. This summary becomes part of the child's permanent record. For example:

A1—Record of discussion between child's parent(s) and class teacher
Juan* likes videos, Mickey Mouse, Charlie Brown, Casper, cartoons, Sesame Street. Sometimes says letters and numbers. Mom teaching him alphabet. Just recently started talking in a way that Mom could

Figure 5.1. Suggested parent interview questions (developed by Jill Benado and colleagues)

1. What kind of reading does your child enjoy at home?
2. What are some of his/her favorite stories?
3. How do you think your child feels about reading in school? At home?
4. What observations have you made about your child reading at home? Does your child pick up books and read on his/her own? Does your child prefer to be read to at home?
5. What are some of your child's favorite stories or books?
6. What are some of your child's favorite stories?
7. What are some of your child's special interests at home (i.e., toys, comics, TV programs, games)?
8. What are some of your child's favorite poems, songs, riddles?
9. What kind of writing and/or drawing does your child do at home?
10. Have you noticed any change in your child's language or reading since school began?
11. How is homework handled at home? Discuss the routine for homework. Who helps your child?
12. How do you think your child feels about homework (includes 20 minutes of being read to)?

understand. (Last year at age 3). Before that spoke baby talk. Has never had hearing checked (has appointment next week). Mom sits and watches TV with Juan. He gets excited as he watches; screams, expressing feelings physically—banging, squealing. He has ABC book, number book, Charlie Brown book. He looks at the pictures. He imitates what cartoon characters do—especially videos he knows well. Understands Mom most of the time. Always does what Mom says. He's very energetic.

Language/Literacy Conference Between the Child and Teacher.   This conference is designed to give children an opportunity to discuss their experiences, achievements, and interests with the teacher. It, too, takes place at the beginning of the school year. It is meant to enhance already existing dialogue between students and their teacher and to provide a formal opportunity for the students and teacher to develop a joint working plan. For the teacher, the conference reveals the students' interests, preferences for different learning styles and contexts, and reasons for making particular choices. It also provides insights into the ways in which the students' language(s) are developing and supporting their learning. For each child, the conference provides an opportunity to reflect on his or her reading and writing activities and interests, to assess his or her own progress, and to play an increasingly active part in his or her own learning. (See Figure 5.2.)

A record of Juan's conference is provided below.

Figure 5.2. Suggested student interview questions (developed by Jill Benado and colleagues)

Ask the student to bring his/her own selection of books and writing.

1. Do you enjoy reading? What does reading mean to you?
2. How do you feel about reading? What kind of a reader are you?
3. Do you remember how you learned to read? Spanish? English?
4. What kinds of books are you reading now (i.e., mysteries, stories, easy books, chapter books)?
5. What kind of books do you enjoy reading in school? At home?
6. Tell me about the books you have at home.
7. What are some of the TV programs you watch? Which do you like best?
8. Does someone read to you at home? At bedtime?
9. What is your favorite story or book? Why?
10. How often do you go to the library? Do you have a library card?
11. How do you feel about writing?
12. What does writing mean to you?
13. Tell me about the stories you write in school. At home?
14. How do you feel about the reading and writing you do here in school?

A2—Record of language/literacy conference with child
Juan brought a book over to show me—*Hello School* (book title). As
he looked at pictures, he said: "Baby doing." "Putting coat." "Is baby."
"Juan." (said his first and last name) "Butterfingers and bubble gum."
(Said this in his own pronunciation. I understood because I've heard
him say it to Mom and asked what he meant. Said "butterfingers and
bubble gum" as he pointed to picture of little boy going home from
school. His Mom buys him this on their way home every day.) Said a
few other things that I didn't understand. "Finished."

Observations Focused on the Child as a Language User. This section of the
report is completed toward the end of the spring term of the school year.
It is compiled from concrete evidence—the day-to-day observations and
records kept by teachers throughout the course of the year. In this section,
the child's strategies, approaches, and behaviors in the areas of talking, listening, reading, and writing are all noted. The record asks for notations
about particular aspects of development in each area: for example, the
child's ability to reflect critically on what he or she reads; the range, quantity, and variety of writing in all areas of the curriculum; the child's involvement in writing narrative and non-narrative pieces, both alone and collaboratively; the influence of reading on the child's writing; and so on.
Although the various aspects of language development are separated in this
section of the record, they are all interrelated in that the progress noted in
each area mirrors and supports the progress noted in the other areas.

Two kinds of entries are made for each aspect of language development: (1) observations on the child's progress in that aspect of language
learning; and (2) a description of any experiences or teaching that have supported the child's development in that aspect of language learning.

Also included in this section are special notes regarding the child's use
of both primary and secondary languages, any concerns about the child's
progress, any ways in which the child's progress is exceptional, or any special educational needs the child may have.

Social and curricular contexts of the classroom are important dimensions
of the learning environment that are also explained and included in this section of the *Primary Language Record*. Assessments of the child's progress
in all aspects of language development are matched against descriptions of
opportunities provided in the classroom for each of these aspects to develop. Below are samples of the talking, listening, and reading portions of this
section of the record.

B1—Talking and listening
*Please comment on the child's development and use of spoken language
in different social and curriculum contexts, in English and/or other
community languages: evidence of talk for learning and thinking;
range and variety of talk for particular purposes; experience and confidence in talking and listening with different people in different settings.*

Juan's speech is becoming clearer. I understand at least one or two words every time he speaks. Some words are so clear that I now recognize when he is using a Spanish word. He loves talking about his work, i.e., block buildings, Legos, Duplos, pattern blocks. Often he screams out my name excitedly (many times) to show me. He is beginning to use "talk" to initiate contact with other children. He understands and follows through on most directions given by me. Sometimes he needs to be shown what it is I'm asking him to do. He listens intently at story time, often with lots of facial expressions. He participates in large group discussions. I now understand some of his words. When he doesn't like what is being said to him, he turns his head (often pouting and blinking intensely) and disregards you. When asked a question of a problem-solving nature—he responds by repeating the question.

What experiences and teaching have helped/would help development in this area? Record outcomes of any discussion with head teacher, other staff, or parent(s).
HELPFUL EXPERIENCES—Interactions with small groups, with teacher present to interpret what he is saying for the other kids. Modeling use of full and complete sentences. Singing songs. Talking with him as he works, verbalizing his actions. Giving him *very verbal and sensitive partners*. Providing clear, slow model of pronunciation of some words.

HOW TO SUPPORT FURTHER DEVELOPMENT—Continue above; provide him with options for solving everyday problems; model/scaffold problem solving. Verbalize as we go through the motions.

End of Year Comments from the Child and His/Her Family.   Spring conferences are held with the child individually, as well as with the child's family, to comment on their feelings and judgments about the child's work and progress over the year.

Information for the Child's Teacher for the Following Year.   This section is a final assessment of a child's progress in all aspects of language and literacy learning. It is meant to provide the next year's teacher with up-to-date information about the child's development. It allows current teachers to pass on their experience and understandings of the child and to make suggestions about the kind of support they think the child needs.

Reading Scales.   Reading scales are an additional feature of the *Primary Language Record*. They provide yet another means of noting growth and development. They are directly informed by the evidence teachers gather through observation and documentation of children's growth during the school year. The scales, which are longitudinal measures that can be used to describe a reader's progress over a period of years, outline the processes involved in becoming a competent and experienced reader. They serve to help teachers think about children's progress across a wide age range—to offer some helpful ways of describing what a child is able to do, with increasing ease, on the road to developing as a reader. They can also be used to identify children whose reading development is causing some concern.

One reading scale for younger children (Figure 5.3) charts children's progress as readers on a continuum from *dependence* to *independence*. Another reading scale for older children (Figure 5.4) plots the developing *experience* of readers and looks at the ways in which readers broaden and deepen their experience of reading many kinds of texts.

In addition to their usefulness in identifying individual children's progress in a shorthand format, these scales can also be used annually to monitor the reading levels of groups of children. Scale scores can be aggre-

Figure 5.3. Becoming a reader: reading scale 1

	DEPENDENCE
Beginner Reader 1	Does not have enough successful strategies for tackling print. Relies on having another person read the text aloud. May still be unaware that text carries meaning.
Nonfluent Reader 2	Tackling known and predictable texts with growing confidence but still needs support with new, unfamiliar one. Increasing ability to predict meanings and is developing strategies to check predictions against other cues such as the illustrations and the print itself.
Moderately Fluent Reader 3	Well-launched on reading but still needs to return to a familiar range of texts. Simultaneously beginning to explore new kinds of texts independently. Beginning to read silently.
Fluent Reader 4	A capable reader who now approaches familiar texts with confidence but still needs support with unfamiliar materials. Beginning to draw inferences from books and stories that are read independently. Chooses to read silently.
Exceptionally Fluent Reader 5	An avid and independent reader who is making choices from a wide range of materials. Able to appreciate nuances and subtleties in text.
	INDEPENDENCE

From Barrs et al., 1988. *The Primary Language Record Handbook for Teachers.* © CLPE, 1988.

Figure 5.4. Experience as a reader across the curriculum: reading scale 2

INEXPERIENCED

Inexperienced Reader 1	Experience as a reader has been limited. Generally chooses to read very easy and familiar texts where illustrations play an important part. Has difficulty with unfamiliar material yet may be able to read own dictated texts confidently. Needs a great deal of support with the reading demands of the classroom. Overdependent on one strategy when reading aloud, often reads word-by-word. Rarely chooses to read for pleasure.
Less Experienced Reader 2	Developing fluency as a reader and is reading certain kinds of material with confidence. Usually chooses short books with simple narrative shapes and with illustrations and may read these silently; often re-reads favorite books. Reading for pleasure often includes comics and magazines. Needs help with the reading demands of the classroom and especially with reference and information books.
Moderately Experienced Reader 3	A confident reader who feels at home with books. Generally reads silently and is developing stamina as a reader. Is able to read for longer periods and cope with more demanding texts, including children's novels. Willing to reflect on reading and often uses reading in own learning. Selects books independently and can use information books and materials for straightforward reference purposes, but still needs help with unfamiliar material, particularly non-narrative prose.
Experienced Reader 4	A self-motivated, confident, experienced reader who may be pursuing particular interests through reading. Capable of tackling some demanding texts and can cope well with the reading of the curriculum. Reads thoughtfully and appreciates shades of meaning. Capable of locating and drawing on a variety of sources in order to research a topic independently.
Exceptionally Experienced Reader 5	An enthusiastic and reflective reader who has strong, established tastes in fiction and/or non-fiction. Enjoys pursuing own reading interests independently. Can handle a wide range of texts, including some adult material. Recognizes that different kinds of texts require different styles of reading. Able to evaluate evidence drawn from a variety of information sources. Is developing critical awareness as a reader.

EXPERIENCED

From Barrs et al. (1988), *The Primary Language Record Handbook for Teachers*. © CLPE, 1988.

gated to indicate the number and proportion of students reading at different levels. Using the scales in this way can enable schools to obtain an overall picture of the reading performance of their students, and to consider instructional strategies accordingly.

Research with over 4,000 students in London schools has found that the scales are useful to teachers and schools in several ways. They help teachers to be better observers of children. They provide a conceptual framework for understanding development, and they enable teachers to identify students' difficulties and strengths. This supports teaching practice by giving teachers information as to the range and variety of materials, books, and experiences they should plan to use.

The scales also provide continuity in understanding and reporting a child's development. They provide a shared view and language for student progress among teachers and across grades. They help teachers to speak with and report to parents by providing a meaningful vocabulary and framework based on real development (Centre for Language in Primary Education [CLPE], 1990).

Two surveys carried out in England by the Research and Statistics Branch of the Inner London Education Authority (ILEA) have provided additional information about the reading scales. In addition to validating the scale scores' potential for assessing reading achievement at least as well as other assessments (CLPE, 1990),[2] the surveys indicated that the reading scales provide more wide-ranging information on a pupil's progress than do standardized tests. Finally, the surveys revealed that the reading scales can be effective as a diagnostic tool, indicating not only which students require extra help with reading but also pointing to what kinds of supports these students need.

This evidence supports the broad potential of the reading scales for monitoring reading performance in schools along with assessing individual student progress. This kind of regular, longitudinal assessment can enable teachers and schools to respond to the needs of all children, and especially to the particular needs of students who are found to be developing in different ways or at different rates. The kind of assessment offered by the *PLR* provides detailed and useful information that simultaneously performs two functions—it informs instruction in classrooms and it can serve to inform the community at large about schoolwide student performance.

A LOOK AT A CLASSROOM—THE PLR IN ACTION

Before coming to P.S. 261 to teach first grade last year, Mark Buswinka taught for five years at an alternative program in another district. Mark's classroom shares common characteristics with the classroom practices of other teachers involved in using the *Primary Language Record*. Opportunities for students to be actively engaged with a wide array of literacy activities permeate the way his classroom is arranged, the kinds of learning activities offered, and the ways in which he interacts with students.

The classroom space is organized into areas well-stocked with a rich array of materials. Besides an extensive library of children's literature, there is a block area, a dramatic play area, an animal/nature area, an art area, and an area where manipulative math materials are organized. Desks are clustered in groups. Children's work is attractively displayed both inside and outside the classroom walls. These displays surround the children with meaningful, interesting, and relevant print that has developed out of their classroom experiences. A mural entitled "Animals Are Different" reflects an extensive study done by the class about different animal species. Drawings of books by favorite authors make up another display. Under each book title are comments by the children. Some of the comments about Ezra Jack Keats' *Regards to the Man in the Moon* (1987, MacMillan Child Group) are:

"I like it when they went to the space ship."
"I didn't like the monsters."
"I like the way the sky looked in space."
"I like when the boy uses his imagination."
"He went up to the moon."

The daily schedule of this class is structured so that long stretches of time are available for children to actively engage in different experiences in the various areas of the room. While some periods of time may be devoted solely to literacy activities, within this time children have many different choices. For example, both reading and writing take place simultaneously during the morning. Some children sit alone or with a partner, reading books. They choose books according to their interests and tastes. Some choose the famous "Clifford" books; some choose folk tales like *Why Mosquitoes Buzz in People's Ears* (V. Aardema, 1978, Puffin Books); some choose books based on the popular "Ninja Turtle" movies; some use small, easy reader books imported from England. In one section of the room, a small group of boys take turns reading out loud to each other. They appear almost to have memorized these texts. They show each other how to use the pictures to help figure out unknown words.

Some children are in the Listening Center—an area in the classroom set up for playing cassette tapes. Here children read their books along with a taped version of the story. Other children gather together on the rug around a "Big Book." It is the size of giant easel paper, has large pictures, oversized print, and phrases that have a catchy rhythm and pattern to them. The children read it together by pointing to each easily distinguishable word as they go along.

Brown bear, brown bear, what do you see?
I see a red bird looking at me.

Red bird, red bird, what do you see?
I see a yellow duck looking at me.

Yellow duck, yellow duck, what do you see?
I see a blue horse looking at me.

(Martin & Carle, 1967, pp. 1–6)

Sometimes Mark reads Big Books to the whole class. Sometimes the whole group chants the story together. Lots of discussion about the action takes place afterward.

Writing activities are also underway. Children express themselves in a range of ways: Some children draw, some make marks of unrelated letters, some use "invented spelling" (self-initiated phonetic spelling of words), and a few use words written in conventional spellings. Pencils, crayons, markers, glue, and an old typewriter are all used for these purposes.

This array of activities goes on easily and casually while Mark moves about the room, note cards in hand, assisting children and facilitating different situations. After answering the questions of a group of children who are writing together in one corner of the room, he sits individually with a succession of children. He helps one child read by pointing to the words as they go along. He helps another by reading back to her what she has already written. He helps yet another child by taking dictation of her story in the little book that she made and illustrated, and still another by encouraging her to identify initial sounds of the words she wants to spell. With each child he jots a few notes down on his note cards to remind him of the nature of their interaction.

At the end of the work session, a sharing meeting takes place. The children gather on the rug and take turns presenting their pieces of writing to the group. The child who is presenting sits on a chair in the circle while the other children gather around on the floor. The presenter reads his story while showing the pictures. When finished, he calls on other children for comments and questions. These provide the authors with useful feedback that affirms their efforts and can sometimes help them revise their work.

As the children conduct the meeting, Mark sits toward the back of the circle taking notes. Occasionally he asks a question that provides clues for other children about how the writing process was done. For example, to a girl who read a journal about her recent vacation, he asks: "How did you know what to write about on what day?" She answered: "At the end of each day, I wrote about what happened so that I would remember it."

The sharing session is not exclusively for written compositions; it accommodates many forms in which writing is used. For example, one boy shares a game he made called "Fake Money." It was inspired by a story Mark read to the class about a boy who won things in a game. It has a colorfully decorated, home-made envelope with hand-made picture game cards inside. The game's enthusiastic reception by the group reflects Mark's acceptance and valuing of many forms and expressions of language learning.

Mark feels that his teaching practice connects to the documenting and observing process of the *Primary Language Record.*

> I use what I learn about the kids from observing them to help support them in their work. The observing makes me more precise. It also makes teaching harder (but more interesting as well) because it makes me demand more of myself and ask more questions about my teaching. For example, I want to know more about the kids who are struggling with reading. I want to figure out better what they need and refine how I work with them. How do you do sound/letter correspondence with kids who don't hear sounds? Do you help develop other strategies? Or do you work on it more? This work has made me extremely aware of how wide the gap gets between children for whom reading and academics come easily and those for whom it doesn't. What do you do? How much do you focus on it? How much are they stalling and in need of support? How much do you say, "You need to practice"? And if you say that, what message are you giving them about reading?

As he reflects on children's learning, Mark asks questions that allow him to examine his own practice and to evaluate the consequences of his decisions for children's motivation and learning strategies. These questions enable him to undertake a deeper inquiry into the range of possibilities for teaching.

A Look at a Child through the Lens of the PLR

Mark has learned a lot about Carla,* a child he has followed with the *PLR* all year. He interviewed both Carla and her mother in October to complete the initial section of the *PLR*. By systematically collecting samples of her work and by regularly writing down his observations of her throughout the school year, Mark has compiled a portrait of Carla's growth over time. His note cards document things that Carla *can* do. For example, he notes that on 10/24, she copied words from desks, read "given," stenciled shapes, read "Kim, Mikey, Nakia, Brian," and told him she knew these names "because they all begin with different words." Drew an "n" and told him "this is an N for No, No." He also notes that she stenciled ABC's backward, and read it right to left. She had missed some letters, and while singing, she corrected for some. All of these notes help Mark develop a detailed understanding of which aspects of reading Carla is beginning to grasp, and which aspects are next to be worked on.

Mark's observations are correlated to specific pieces of work that Carla has completed. For example, from one piece collected in October, showing figures with print-like lines above and below, Mark learned that Carla knew the difference between pictures and print. From her backward stencil, he learned that she did not yet understand the concept of directionality. From a page of words that she had copied from signs and materials around the classroom—"cat" "frog" "teddy bear" "inkpad" "stamps" "markers and crayons"—he learned that she was aware of uses of print in her environment.

From a running record made during Carla's reading of Ezra Jack Keats' book *Whistle for Willie* (1964, Viking Children's Books) in February, Mark noted that she relied heavily on the pictures for making meaning of the text. (See Figure 5.5.) In a running record, the teacher documents a child's oral reading of a text by noting on the text exactly what the child reads, how she reads, and what strategies she uses for decoding. At that time, Mark also noted that Carla showed an awareness of letters, an interest in print, and that she knew what she did not know.

Mark summarized his observations in the reading section of the *Primary Language Record,* noting Carla's progress from Level #1 on the *PLR* Independence Scale (beginning reader) to Level #2 (nonfluent reader).

B2—Reading

Please comment on the child's progress and development as a reader in English and/or other community languages: the stage at which the child is operating [refer to the reading scales at the end of Chapter 2]; the range, quantity, and variety of reading in all areas of the curriculum; the child's pleasure and involvement in story and reading, alone or with others; the range of strategies used when reading and the child's ability to reflect critically on what is read.

Carla is in love with books. She enjoys reading them and uses some book language if it is a known text. Carla uses the pictures to keep up a story line. Her attention to meaning causes her to disregard one-to-one to keep going. Carla reads back her own writing—focusing on initial consonants. She has gone from a beginning reader to a non-fluent reader (#2).

What experiences and teaching have helped/would have helped development in this area? Record outcomes of any discussion with head teacher, other staff, or parent(s).

Carla likes to reread big books that have been shared. She practices with friends and likes books that have song lyrics as text. We could effectively use these known texts to focus on one-to-one. Knowledge of initial consonants should be encouraged and expanded. "Story Box" books could be used to build confidence and reinforce use of pictures one-to-one and confirming guesses with initial consonants.

When Mark shared these and other observations gained from his ongoing documentation of Carla's work with his colleagues at a lunch-time teacher meeting, they made note of the many things Carla *could* do:

Figure 5.5. A running record of Carla's reading

WHISTLE FOR WILLIE

Willie ✓ ✓ _can_ ✓
Oh, how Peter wished he could whistle!

His friend is ✓ ⌣ ⌣ _and he turned himself around and around_
He saw a boy playing with his dog. Whenever the boy whistled, the dog ran straight to him.
in circles

And ✓ ✓ _turned_
Peter tried and tried to whistle, but he couldn't. So instead he began to turn himself around—

around and around he whirled...faster and faster....

forwards?
(Then he went ✓ ✓ ✓ ✓ ✓ _back and forth) and_
When he stopped everything turned down...and up...and up...and down... and around and

around.

This, he had, There was a boy on the street
Peter saw his dog, Willie, coming. Quick as a wink, he hid in an empty carton lying on the

sidewalk. "Wouldn't it be funny if I whistled?" Peter thought. "Willie would stop and look

And he ✓ ✓ ✓ ✓
all around to see who it was." Peter tried to whistle - but still he couldn't. So Willie just

walked on. _And the dog kept on walking_
_he_ ⌣⌣ ? ⌣⌣⌣ _haltingly_

Peter got out of the carton and started home. On the way he took some colored chalks out of
So he made ✓ ✓ ✓ _(excitedly)_
his pocket and drew a long, long line.

right up to his door. He stood there and tried to whistle again. He blew till his cheeks were ‖⎯

tired. But nothing happened. ∨

✓ ✓   _fast and_
He went into his house and put on his father's old hat to make himself feel
more grown-up. He looked into the mirror to practice whistling. Still no whistle! _sketchy_

She is aware of the purposes for reading and writing.
She understands book protocol such as "by Carla."
She knows what a title is.
She shows knowledge of and attention to initial consonants.
She correlates pictures and words.
She uses pictures to find meaning in the text.
She has developed her own strategies to identify letters and words.

She knows the difference between letters that make words and those
   that don't.
She is writing more words on her own as time goes by.
She is on the road to connecting it all.

In discussing work together in this way, the teachers are doing more
than learning about an individual child. They are actually examining their
teaching practice and sharing their knowledge about the process of learning to read. They are also sharing strategies about how best to support children's literacy growth. As they answer each others' questions, they also raise
many new ones. For example, Mark's description of Carla reminded everyone of a common occurrence:

What should a teacher do when a child writes something one way
but reads it back as something else? Should you write what the child
is saying on the text or should you leave it alone?

In reflecting on this question, the teachers agreed that respect for the
child should be expressed by not altering her work. However, many alternative suggestions were made:

Write post-its on the back so you can remember what the child said.
Don't write in front of the child but *do* jot down what is said.
Only select some pieces to save and record. The child will read back
   what is really meaningful and you can note that.
Keep an ongoing record of growth.
This seems to be happening because Carla appears to be attending
   more to print in writing than in reading. Take dictation from her
   and have her read it back.
Point when reading with her to help her develop one-to-one corre-
   spondence of words with sound.

Through discussions such as these, teachers participate in a process that
is both *teacher research* and *professional development*. As part of this
process, they are investigating the learning paths of individual children, they
are examining many different approaches to learning, and they are learning about themselves as teachers.

THE INFLUENCE OF THE PLR ON
TEACHING, LEARNING, AND ASSESSMENT

Teachers' work with the *PLR* influences many aspects of school and classroom life, including the climate and culture of the school and the nature of
teaching and learning.

Influences on Teaching

The use of the *Primary Language Record* has affected different teachers in different ways. It has provided tremendous validation to those teachers whose long-established practices are congruent with the *PLR's* philosophy. To those teachers for whom this philosophy is new however, The *Primary Language Record* has been an opportunity to test out new ideas and to try out new practices with guidance and support.

The Experienced Teacher

Alina Alvarez has been teaching for fourteen years and is presently an early childhood teacher at P.S. 261. She finds the *PLR* to be a tremendous support to her longstanding efforts to seek out and build on children's strengths.

> As a pre-kindergarten teacher I've always tried to build on children's strengths, rather than classify them by their weaknesses. It has always made me angry when children with special needs, or children who speak languages other than English, or children who come from poor or working class homes are described by our school system as "deficient."
> The Primary Language Record has supported my view of children and of learning by encouraging observation of student's reading, writing, speaking, and listening in the context of classroom activities. It offers me a framework in which I can pull together and organize these observations. This provides me with concrete information about each students' learning process which then guides my teaching in a way that standardized test scores and preconceived developmental checklists simply cannot do.

The most important learning that Alina attributes to her involvement with The *Primary Language Record* is a result of its approach to the participation of parents.

> As part of my PLR work, I interviewed the parents of all the children in my class. In the past, I always thought that I had respect for parents, but I was amazed at how much I could learn from them about literacy. I was struck by how much parents know about their kids in general and about their literacy development in particular. For example, they would tell me that their kids could read a "walk" sign or a supermarket flyer.
> I was also amazed at how much I didn't know about the parents themselves. I gained a heightened awareness of and respect for their backgrounds and cultures. I learned to be more sensitive to questions that implied value judgments, such as, "Do you read to your child?" Instead, I learned to phrase questions in a non-judgmental way geared towards getting useful information, such as, "Tell me about

when your child watches TV, reads, looks at magazines, etc." I learned to listen to parents differently and to help them develop a positive, sometimes different, perspective on their child by reflecting back to them what they already know. This has enabled me to develop a partnership, rather than a one-sided relationship, in which I am the expert telling them what I know.

Working with the *PLR* has also increased Alina's respect for and knowledge of children. The child interview section of the record has "given me an indication of how much kids know about their own learning process." The cumulative effect of using the *PLR* has been that Alina has enriched her knowledge of her own teaching. She attributes this in large part to the reflecting, talking, and sharing she has done with other colleagues.

If a teacher just did this on her own and didn't talk to anyone else about it, I don't think it would foster reflection. But when teachers talk with each other in a group about kids' strengths and weaknesses, there's a mixture of different kinds of thinking, and that helps us look at kids and figure out how to help them grow.

The Newer Teacher

For many teachers, the form of record-keeping and assessment that the *Primary Language Record* presents is new. Its use often encourages them to change certain things about the classroom as well as to develop new teaching strategies. One teacher describes it this way:

The PLR presupposes that learning takes place within a social context, and that the responsibility for growth doesn't lie only with the teacher but is shared with children and parents. And it presupposes that classrooms are set up in flexible ways. For instance, how can you record kids' talk if they are not able or allowed to talk to each other in the classroom? Teachers have to change things in order to do the PLR and changing those things changes how they teach. (Alvarez, 1991, p. 11)

Mark Buswinka credits the *PLR* with helping him learn how to teach reading in a developmentally grounded way:

The Primary Language Record has helped me learn how to teach. It is the first real reading course I've ever taken. No one ever said, "Look at kids" to me. Courses I took just said, "Do this to them, or do that to them." But with the PLR I can really watch kids and see how they develop. It helps me know what to look for. By watching them I can learn. I'm working *with* them, not doing things *to* them. The PLR lays it right out. It is a framework for the kind of teacher I want to be.

Mark also believes that the behavior of the children changed as a result of his use of observing and recording children's work. For example, he keeps track of his students' reading behaviors by noting them on file cards that he keeps hanging on a hook. When his students asked him what he was writing about, he told them he was noticing what, when, and how they read. Since then, he notes, not only do they read more, but they also point out to him when and how they are doing it.

Supports for "Teaching to the Child"

Teachers who use the *Primary Language Record* find that it enriches the way they look at children, the way they look at families, and the ways in which they teach. The *Primary Language Record* supports teachers in better understanding how children learn by providing a framework with which they can examine their students' learning strategies. It helps teachers to see their students even more closely as individuals. The *PLR*'s essential process of observing and documenting the growth of individual children makes each child's actual growth more visible to teachers and consequently enables them to be more appreciative and supportive of each child's strengths. Rather than "teaching to the test," teachers are supported in their desire to "teach to the child."

Third through 6th grade teachers who attended an after-school study group spoke about the new things they learned from using the *PLR*:

> From doing child interviews we all found out more than we knew, all that's not revealed so clearly in the classroom.
> We may have known what the social worker's or psychologist's report said about a child's home life, but talking to children one-on-one for the PLR interview is different. We developed an intimacy. We were struck by how eager the kids were to connect.

For teachers, the process of writing observations goes beyond recording information. It informs their pedagogical thinking and often expands their instructional practices as well. By carefully observing and reflecting on their observations, teachers gain a heightened awareness of the different strategies children are using in learning to read. They are then able to provide more knowledgeable interventions by analyzing strategies, supporting those that are being used, and introducing those that are not.

Careful observation of one child may reveal that the child has a grasp of syntactic and graphophonic cuing systems but needs more support in phonetic skills. A close look at another child may reveal something entirely different: The child has phonetic skills but has not been able to connect those skills with the general meaning that the text is generating. A teacher who is observant and knowledgeable about these differences can use this information to support children's reading growth.

These pedagogical understandings and skills lead to and support a communication-rich environment in the classroom in which the reading and language arts program is carried out. Generally, a teacher using the *PLR* is providing times for reading in the classroom where there is significant time spent listening to individual students, a great deal of peer and group work, and substantial autonomy for students. The reading time is generally structured so that the teacher can move about while children work independently or in small groups. This gives the teacher opportunities to observe, record, and assist children individually. The teacher functions more as a reading facilitator than as a reading instructor.

The conceptualization of reading instruction that develops as a result of the *Primary Language Record's* use often spills over to influence the entire classroom environment. In fact, the usefulness of the *Primary Language Record* in England led to the creation of a *Primary Learning Record,* which uses similar strategies for observing and assessing student's progress in science, mathematics, social studies, and other subjects. The *Primary Language Record* supports teachers in developing not just keener understandings of literacy development, but also enriched understandings of the teaching/learning process in general. This is evident in the more open, flexible classroom arrangements of *PLR* teachers, as well as in their general use of more diverse learning materials and experiences. It is also evident in the more flexible scheduling of their day, which provides for greater integration of all subject matters and which connects literacy development to study in all the disciplines.

PLR teachers see the need for learning experiences to be placed in meaningful and purposeful contexts. They understand that learning is a social process, and they provide more opportunities in their classrooms for discussion, dialogue, and exchange of viewpoints. The *PLR* supports their recognition of the importance of concrete materials for learning new things, and they are encouraged to stock their rooms with materials and experiences that lend themselves to active inquiry: manipulatives for mathematics; a range of materials for expression in print and other art forms; animals, plants, and cooking materials for the study of science; trips to develop social studies concepts; and so on. These teachers also value a diverse range of learning styles and diverse forms of expression for that learning. Children's approaches, dispositions, and strategies for learning are appreciated as much as their products.

The presence of a district-funded assistor, Jill Benado, has been critical to the process of integrating these practices into classrooms. She has spent several years in the school, working with teachers from diverse backgrounds and viewpoints who represent a spectrum of grade levels and subject areas. Together they have been formulating common, child-centered goals and practices. Jill's twice weekly presence in the school has supported teachers in a variety of ways. She visits classrooms regularly and works side by side with the teachers involved in the *PLR* project. She provides resources and materials for teachers to use in their work with the children, as well as articles for their own professional growth. Her presence in the classroom gives teachers the opportunity to discuss their practice in depth with another colleague. She is a mirror to them as well as a sounding board for their ideas.

The teacher meetings she facilitates give teachers the opportunity to collaborate with their peers. At the lunch and after-school meetings, teachers share concerns with one another and jointly reflect on what have they have learned and what else they can do to support the literacy development of their students.

Jill has established a sense of trust and acceptance with the teachers at P.S. 261 by clearly exhibiting how much she respects and values their work. Her understandings of the realities of classroom life, of the teaching/learning process, of literacy development, and of the needs of teachers have enabled her to both facilitate discussions and to provide direction to collaborative work. In an unobtrusive manner, she has undertaken those tasks, however small, that make it possible for the staff to forge plans, to follow through on projects, and to make sure that the projects actually happen; she even takes care of such details as regularly ordering food for lunchtime meetings.

An important characteristic of Jill's work is her skill at asking probing questions that aid reflection, such as: "What new things did you learn?" "What surprised you?" and "How do you think you'll use what you've learned?"

These questions are intended to help teachers construct and synthesize their own understandings. The "right" way is never dictated or imposed. By working in this manner, Jill is able to tap into teachers' implicit knowledge and to make it visible to all. Her approach also encourages teacher collaboration by promoting a sharing of information, strategies, and resources.

As a consequence of these opportunities for collegial inquiry and reflection, both long-time and newer teachers experience a sense of personal growth and development. They see the in-depth examinations of children and their learning as an impetus for knowledge building. They see asking questions as a means of developing new possibilities in their teaching. They find themselves increasingly able to replace judgments about children with compassion and understanding. They also become more confident about what it is that they know, and they are more comfortable talking about it.

Influences on Learning

The professional growth of teachers that is encouraged by the *Primary Language Record* translates directly into student growth and improvements in their attitudes toward reading. Reading, writing, and the school experience in general are more pleasurable and productive when teachers are able to connect with children and their work on an intimate level. Alejandra,* a kindergarten child who is bilingual, describes her learning life in this way:

> I *love* writing! I wrote this [referring to a paper with her marks on it]
> with all the different colors. It's for my mother and my father. I like to
> go to Block Area. I made a big, special building. I like to go to
> Housekeeping Area. I like it *all*. *All* the time! I like to play at Drawing
> and Writing and Easel too!

Catherine, a 7-year-old first grader, also finds enjoyment in books:

> Reading is fun. I like books to play with. I read the title of books I
> know. I look at the pages inside of it, and then I start reading. I play
> with the books at home . . . play school. I read to Grandma and
> Mom and Dad and my aunt and myself and my doll.

Children's literacy development, as well as their educational growth in
general, is supported by having teachers who are more observant of what
they actually can do and who use this knowledge to inform their teaching
practice. Relying on the concrete evidence of children's work leads teachers to look at children through their strengths rather than through their
deficits. This is helpful to all students. It appears to be especially so for children with special needs—those with special learning challenges and those
whose first language is not English. Lucy Lopez, a kindergarten-through-sec-
ond-grade bilingual teacher, recounts how keeping a diary of her observations has clarified her understandings about particular children and subsequently has affected her ability to help them learn.

> Jeremy* had me confused. He doesn't speak in complete sentences;
> sometimes he'll only talk in Spanish. I thought he didn't understand.
> But from watching him in different settings and from interviewing
> him for the *PLR,* I learned that he *can* talk appropriately and he *does*
> understand.
>   There is another child, Jorge,* whom I used to think was not
> learning—that he was hyperactive. I used to focus more on his
> behavior. Now it doesn't bother me as much. I focus on what he *can*
> do. I found that if things are presented to him in context, if he has
> visual aids around him, he *can* get it.
>   Using the *PLR* has helped me to focus on the kids more—to see
> what they say and about what. It has helped me to understand them
> more, to understand their language in different situations, to focus
> more on how they communicate, to see their needs and their strengths.

Students' learning is thus supported by the increased knowledge and
understanding that teachers get from their exposure to the *PLR*. The benefits of their teachers' professional development are evident in the help students receive in refining their skills. They are strengthened by their teachers' recognition of the complexities of the learning process. Their growth is

enhanced by the fact that their teachers are less likely to categorize them in static ways and more likely to descriptively observe nuances in their strengths and learning styles. Children are given greater room for the expression of their individual styles, paces, and interests because the classroom environment is more open to diversity. They thrive in a dynamic that supports the strengths, and that values the complexities, of learners.

One other benefit of the *PLR* for students is that they have input into their learning process through the use of student interviews and conferences. These serve to inform teachers about children's prior knowledge and interests, about what children presently understand, and about what children also know about their own learning style and process. The result of this is to enhance teacher responsiveness to student needs.

In a conference with her teacher, Catherine* revealed how much she knows about the purposes of print:

> You make nice people, nice writing, pictures of cats. Then you put the words. Then you write what it is about, then you show it to the people that like it. If it is for them, you give it to them.

In this same conference, Catherine also revealed several of her own learning strategies:

> If I don't know [something], I ask what it says. Then I watch them [Mom, Dad] read it to you and then you know the title and what it is about. Then you can read it by yourself. If no one is there, you figure it out yourself by listening and thinking. When you get it, you show your mom what you can do.

Influences on Home and School Relationships

Partnerships between home and school are strengthened through the use of the *Primary Language Record*. It fosters sensitivity and support for family cultures and languages. It values and uses parent knowledge. It promotes enhanced communication between home and school by offering greater opportunity for family input into the learning process.

The *PLR* serves as a support to family education in that it provides parents with concrete examples of their child's literacy acquisition, grounded in developmental understanding and research. In family conferences, teachers are able to clearly demonstrate to parents the growth of the children based on the evidence they have compiled throughout the school year. Teachers can share with parents such developmental markers as the books that children read, the strategies that children use most readily, the strategies in need of support, and the interests and approaches that children bring to their learning. Through concrete examples found in children's work, teachers are also able to interpret and explain to parents innovative teaching practices, such as "invented spelling." The result of such communication is the conscious building of a community that is knowledgeable and supportive of children's learning. One parent reflects on what she has learned about her child: "I've learned how to look [at my child] from areas of strength. I've gained confidence in what is happening with him."

Another parent says:

A lot of stuff that [the teacher] exposed me to made sense to me as a parent. I'm learning to relax, learning to help my children with less anxiety. It's been very very helpful. It's helped me to understand my own learning in a more objective way. It's important to understand how you learn because it helps you understand how others learn. It's made learning a lot more fun. Parents want to be a part, feel relaxed and at home, so that they can do more for their kids.

Influences on the School

The school's principal, Arthur Foresta, has done a great deal to facilitate the rapid introduction and implementation of The *Primary Language Record* throughout P.S. 261. He views the *PLR* as supportive of his overall educational vision and goals.

My goal for this school is to have teachers know the individuality of each child—each child's strengths, knowledge, experiences, needs, and family circumstances—in order to enact the most effective plan of instruction. I will bring anything into this school that will encourage the adults to look closely at individual children and to help them become more understanding and compassionate.

Arthur encourages all kinds of programs and staff development initiatives at P.S. 261 to foster this belief. In addition to the *Primary Language Record,* staff are also engaged in using The Descriptive Review of a Child (Prospect Center, 1986), a collaborative faculty process of carefully describing and discussing a child to address a specific question or concern. In the areas of literacy and language development, the *PLR* builds on a number of other compatible approaches to teaching, learning, and assessment: a "process" approach to writing (Calkins, 1986; Graves, 1983), which encourages writing in a natural manner and setting; the use of "running records" or "miscue analysis" in reading (Goodman, 1979, 1982; Goodman & Burke, 1972; Goodman, Watson, & Burke, 1987), an assessment technique that identifies individual children's reading strategies and strengths and that charts change in these strategies and strengths over time; and the use of reading logs—lists kept by children of what books they have read, the dates they have read them, and their comments on the readings.

Teachers keep writing and mathematics portfolios—collections of children's work compiled by teachers with the input of students, and dated and chronicled over the course of the school year (or years). Teachers also prepare alternative report cards that provide narrative descriptions of children's growth and development supported by detailed teacher observations of children and their work. A Reading Recovery Program (Clay, 1985) provides a holistic, individualized support program for children in Chapter 1 (a federal compensatory education program) who require additional literacy supports.

Arthur's intention in bringing all of these approaches into the school is to support the growth of both teachers and children:

> I want to help teachers get away from looking at what children *can't* do and to focus instead on what they *can* do. I want the kids to be terrific readers who love to read. They will do well on the tests if we teach reading well. The tests will not drive the curriculum in this school. Hopefully, our good teaching will show up in test scores. But we won't start drilling kids from September.

Arthur believes that the *PLR*, used in the broader context of other learner-centered practices, strengthens all parts of the school:

> The *PLR's* support of teachers' development promotes an atmosphere of continual learning in the school. It increases teachers' understandings, enhances their commitments, and promotes professionalism and a sense of community. This impacts on the children by supporting their growth as readers and learners.
>
> The *PLR's* inclusion of family input provides a vehicle for respectful partnerships between home and school. As an alternative to relegating parent involvement to bake sales and other fund-raising chores, it offers a meaningful way to include families in the life of the school.

Arthur also sees the *PLR* as a useful instrument for administrators to use in demonstrating how their school is accountable to children, families, and the larger community. The fullness of the picture the *PLR* provides for each child demonstrates the school's integrity and thoroughness with regard to individual children. The process of keeping the record itself permits teachers to be accountable in a comprehensive way and supports the quality of instruction. In addition, the reading scales can be used to aggregate meaningful, quantifiable data on groups of children, if that is necessary or desired.

Implications for Accountability

Staff at P.S. 261 see their use of the *Primary Language Record* as an important part of their strengthening accountability to students, to themselves, and to their community. The day-to-day observations of children that form the basis of the record guide teaching in more child-centered ways. This makes it harder for students to "fall through the cracks" because teachers keep track of what and how their students are learning. Close examination of their students' work, combined with reflection on and discussions of their teaching practice, build teacher knowledge about literacy and the learning process.

The joint sharing of information in the interviews and conference portions of the record—from family to school, from school to family, from student to teacher, and from teacher to student—also make for a more thorough and rounded accountability picture. The summary in the record that is written for the child's next-year teacher provides a unique opportunity for continuity of knowledge about a student to be constructed and shared throughout the school. This collaborative following of a child's growth from year to year, along with the essential, ongoing dialogue among teachers that is a critical part of the *PLR's* use, promote a professionalism in the school that strengthens its accountability to all parties involved.

Lessons for Using Assessments like the Primary Language Record

The story of the *Primary Language Record's* use at P.S. 261 provides a portrait of how changes in assessment practices can influence teaching in ways that support the growth of both children and adults. This story describes how one approach to assessment can involve parents meaningfully in the education of their child, recognize the diverse strengths and knowledge that children bring with them to the school experience, support the integrity and professionalism of teachers, and value different cultures and languages.

What stands out from this examination of the *PLR's* use at P.S. 261 is that, more important than the new procedures and processes it presents, the *PLR* supports a new way of thinking about teaching and learning in general and about literacy development in particular. It offers a holistic framework for observing and documenting the growth of children that allows for differences in teachers as well as in children. It enables teachers to understand better how children learn and thus to teach in more child-centered ways. By focusing on children's strengths, by looking at them individually, by celebrating their diversity, it supports the overall quality of school instruction. Successful use of strategies such as the *PLR* throughout a school depends on some fundamental requirements. One of these is leadership that endorses, promotes, and facilitates its use. Another is the ongoing support and resources of a staff developer who can help teachers find their own way when they feel overwhelmed by the hard work of change, when they bump up against the reality of the change process, or when they find they want additional information, ideas, feedback, and opportunities for problem solving.

A change in thinking about professional development grows out of, and is essential to, the use of assessment strategies that look deeply at children and their learning as a means for shaping teaching as well as of providing information. Professional development must be understood as a process of teacher dialogue and reflection rather than as a body of information to be learned through workshops with staff developers. Instead of being a packaged set of teacher activities and lesson plans, this kind of professional development is an encouragement to teachers to synthesize for themselves what they observe about children, what they know about child development, and what they also know about literacy acquisition. From this frame of reference, the instrument of the *PLR* is really a vehicle for ongoing teacher growth that improves instruction by focusing on children. Without this perspective, the *PLR* could simply become another in an endless series of technical innovations that have come and gone in the world of schools, leaving little impact on the nature of teaching.

Finally, the success of strategies like the *PLR* rests with several major structural challenges: One challenge is how to provide the time needed for the observing, recording, and conferencing work that the *PLR* requires. Included in this requirement is the time teachers need for the individual and collective reflection and dialogue that is a part of the process of doing the *PLR*. Ultimately, this requires fundamental restructuring of school time so that shared planning time is a regular part of every week, and teachers' time for working on curriculum and assessments is acknowledged as teaching time (Darling-Hammond, 1990a, c).

Another challenge is how to restructure current reporting structures and practices (conference schedules and reporting systems) so that there will be communication between family and school that is consistent with the conceptualization of teaching and learning that the *PLR* promotes. This requires a much more holistic view of change that reshapes all aspects of schooling around a common conception of teaching, learning, and student and family responsibility, rather than one that tries to change one element—whether it is assessment or any other single aspect of schooling—in ways that exacerbate the inconsistencies students and families experience when they deal with schools.

Perhaps the major challenge is how to lessen the grip of traditional, standardized tests on teaching, so that the tension between the values and goals of these different approaches to learning are minimized. The barrage of tests given each year to students in the New York City public schools (and many other school systems) reflects views of literacy development that conflict with those that shape the practices of the *Primary Language Record*. While the *PLR* values a student's growth over time in a wide variety of literacy areas, the tests make judgments of a student's progress based on his performance on a multiple choice instrument in a few hours of one day during the life of an entire school year. While the *PLR* assesses reading, writing, speaking, and listening in real-life, purposeful contexts, the tests assess a limited form of silent reading in isolated, esoteric paragraphs that often are far removed from the students' frame of reference. Tests do not evaluate oral reading, writing, speaking, or listening at all. While the *PLR* comments on a student's individual growth and then rates that student on a descriptive scale that is easily translatable from and to experience, the tests compare students on a numerical percentile ranking that provides little information useful to instruction or to the growth process of the student.

As the value of approaches such as the *PLR* becomes more widely recognized, it will be important for overreliance on traditional, standardized tests to be reduced. An increasing number of states and school districts are doing so: A number have eliminated standardized testing in the primary grades entirely, and many are moving toward more authentic forms of assessment throughout the grades, using standardized tests sparingly for statistical reporting purposes and alternative forms of assessment for useful information about students and instruction.

Each school faced with the challenge of developing teaching and assessment practices that support children's growth must find its own way, indigenous to its own culture and needs. What P.S. 261's experience has shown is that the *Primary Language Record* can provide one useful framework for this journey.

NOTES

1. Children's names have been changed and are noted by an asterisk. Teachers' names are unchanged.

2. The ILEA's 1989 validation survey found high correlations between scale 2 levels and London Reading Test Scores. Another study of 400 students in Lewisham found that the first reading scale also correlates highly with other forms of assessment, including the British national curriculum's Standard Assessment Tasks and teacher assessments ($r = .84$) (Feeney & Hann, 1991).

Primary Language Record

School   School Year

Name   DoB   Summer born child ☐

☐ Boy   ☐ Girl

Languages understood   Languages read

Languages spoken   Languages written

Details of any aspects of hearing, vision or coordination   Names of staff involved with child's language and literacy
affecting the child's language/literacy. Give the source   development.
and date of this information.

Part A To be completed during the Autumn Term

A1 Record of discussion between child's parent(s) and class teacher *(Handbook pages 12-13)*

Signed Parent(s) _____   Teacher _____

Date _____

A2 Record of language/literacy conference with child *(Handbook pages 14-15)*

Date _____

©ILEA/Centre for Language in Primary Education, 1988.   Published in the U.S.A. by Heinemann Educational Books, Inc., 70 Court St., Portsmouth, NH 03801

Part B
To be completed during the Spring Term and to include information from all teachers currently teaching the child.

Child as a language user (one or more languages)   *(Handbook pages 17-18)*

Teachers should bear in mind the Authority's Equal Opportunities Policies (race, gender and class) in completing each section of the record and should refer to *Educational Opportunities for All?*, the ILEA report on special educational needs.

B1 Talking and listening   *(Handbook pages 19-22)*

Please comment on the child's development and use of spoken language in different social and curriculum contexts, in English and/or other community languages: evidence of talk for learning and thinking; range and variety of talk for particular purposes; experience and confidence in talking and listening with different people in different settings.

What experiences and teaching have helped/would help development in this area? Record outcomes of any discussion with head teacher, other staff, or parent(s).

B2 Reading   *(Handbook pages 23-28)*

Please comment on the child's progress and development as a reader in English and/or other community languages: the stage at which the child is operating (refer to the reading scales on pages 26-27); the range, quantity and variety of reading in all areas of the curriculum; the child's pleasure and involvement in story and reading, alone or with others; the range of strategies used when reading and the child's ability to reflect critically on what is read.

B2 (continued)

What experiences and teaching have helped/would help development in this area? Record outcomes of any discussion with head teacher, other staff, or parent(s).

B3 Writing   *(Handbook pages 29-34)*
Please comment on the child's progress and development as a writer in English and/or other community languages: the degree of confidence and independence as a writer; the range, quantity and variety of writing in all areas of the curriculum; the child's pleasure and involvement in writing both narrative and non-narrative, alone and in collaboration with others; the influence of reading on the child's writing; growing understanding of written language, its conventions and spelling.

What experiences and teaching have helped/would help development in this area? Record outcomes of any discussion with head teacher, other staff, or parent(s).

Signature of head teacher and all teachers contributing to this
section of the record:

Part C To be completed during the Summer Term* (Handbook page 35)

C1 Comments on the record by child's parent(s)

C2 Record of language/literacy conference with child

C3 Information for receiving teacher

This section is to ensure that information for the receiving teacher is as up to date as possible. Please comment on changes and development in any aspect of the child's language since Part B was completed.

What experiences and teaching have helped/would help development? Record outcomes of any discussion with head teacher, other staff, or parent(s).

Signed: Parent(s) _____　　Class Teacher _____

Date _____　　Head Teacher _____

*To be completed by the Summer half-term for 4th year juniors.

Observations and Samples (Primary Language Record)

attach extra pages where needed

Name: **Year Group:**

1 Talking & listening: diary of observations

The diary below is for recording examples of the child's developing use of talk for learning and for interacting with others in English and/or other community languages.

Include different kinds of talk (e.g. planning an event, solving a problem, expressing a point of view or feelings, reporting on the results of an investigation, telling a story ...)

Note the child's experience and confidence in handling social dimensions of talk (e.g. initiating a discussion, listening to another contribution, qualifying former ideas, encouraging others ...)

The matrix sets out some possible contexts for observing talk and listening. Observations made in the diary can be plotted on the matrix to record the range of social and curriculum contexts sampled.

(Handbook pages 37-39)

LEARNING CONTEXTS	SOCIAL CONTEXTS				
	pair	small group	child with adult	small/large group with adult	
collaborative reading and writing activities					
play, dramatic play, drama & storying					
environmental studies & historical research					
maths & science investigations					
design, construction, craft & art projects					

Dates	Observations and their contexts

©ILEA/Centre for Language in Primary Education, 1988. Published in the U.S.A. by Heinemann Educational Books, Inc., 70 Court St., Portsmouth, NH 03801

2 Reading and Writing: diary of observations
(reading and writing in English and/or other community languages)

(Handbook pages 40-44)

Date	Reading
	Record observations of the child's development as a reader (including wider experiences of story) across a range of contexts.

	Writing
	Record observations of the child's development as a writer (including stories dictated by the child) across a range of contexts.

4 Writing Samples (writing in English and/or other community languages)
Writing to include children's earliest attempts at writing   *(Handbook pages 50-54)*

Dates			
Context and background information about the writing: • how the writing arose • how the child went about the writing • whether the child was writing alone or with others • whether the writing was discussed with anyone while the child was working on it • kind of writing (e.g. list, letter, story, poem, personal writing, information writing) • complete piece of work/extract			
Child's own response to the writing.			
Teacher's response: • to the content of the writing • to the child's ability to handle this particular kind of writing • overall impression			
Development of spelling and conventions of writing.			
What this writing shows about the child's development as a writer: • how it fits into the range of the child's previous writing • experience/support needed to further development			

Please keep the writing with the sample sheet

6

THE BRONX NEW SCHOOL:
WEAVING ASSESSMENT INTO THE FABRIC OF
TEACHING AND LEARNING

In 1987, parents and teachers from diverse neighborhoods of a local school district in New York City came together to found the Bronx New School (BNS)—a small, public elementary school of choice. Their goal was to create a school that would be "learner centered"—that would build on children's development, involve families, ensure diversity and equity, and achieve high standards of learning for all. These commitments were the basis for decisions about how the school would be organized and governed and how curriculum and teaching would be developed. The school was organized into heterogeneous, multiage classes and structured to encourage and enhance collaboration among faculty, students, and students' families. Classroom environments featured an interdisciplinary approach to learning, active involvement with materials and experiences, peer interaction, and many opportunities for children to develop and display their interests and their strengths.

The school was an autonomous unit, though it was administratively attached to a larger school for purposes of New York City bureaucratic management. This was because it was led by a teacher-director rather than by a principal. Opening in 1988 with a small staff and about 100 students in kindergarten through 3rd grade, its population was selected through a public lottery of applicants to intentionally reflect the diversity of the district—one third African American, one third Latino, and one third other racial/ethnic groupings. Each year it added a new grade and new teachers so that it could carry children through the 6th grade.

Shortly after the Bronx New School was founded, it became a member of the Center for Collaborative Education, a network of elementary and secondary schools comprising the New York City affiliate of the Coalition of Essential Schools. Within and outside this network, BNS was recognized for its application of developmental understandings to curriculum, for its comprehensive authentic assessment practices, for its atmosphere of professional development, and for its inclusion of families as part of a collaborative learning community.

After several years, political upheavals at the district level brought about changes in the school's leadership and personnel, as well as in its organization and structure. A new superintendent took steps to incorporate the school into the larger school under whose auspices the school was administratively lodged, intending to place it under the more direct administrative control of the principal of that school and thus of the district, despite the philosophical and pedagogical differences that BNS was founded upon. Parents were so distraught at the prospect of losing the kind of education created by the school that they took their case to the local board and to the central New York City School Board and finally to the courts. As a consequence of their efforts, the school eventually regained its autonomous status and was declared a "regular" public school, although some faculty had left by then. The parents won the right to select their own principal rather than accepting a principal selected by the central office.

Even given these changes, the school's founding values survived and remain intact today, along with many of its original practices and policies— a testament to the strength of the school community and to its beliefs, and the extent to which the school's commitments were deeply rooted in the structures, norms, and operating practices of the organization. This story focuses on the school's first 3 years, a time when a comprehensive assessment system was designed and used throughout the entire school.

CONTEXTS FOR TEACHING AND LEARNING AT THE BRONX NEW SCHOOL

The assessment system at the Bronx New School emerged out of a conception of teaching that places students at the center of the learning environment. Classrooms are structured to encourage active inquiry and are stocked with a wide range of concrete materials meant to be used for direct investigation. They offer diverse experiences that provide multiple entry points into learning. Math manipulatives (bundling sticks, powers of ten blocks, hundreds boards, inch cubes, fraction strips, geo boards, and attribute blocks) are available in every classroom, along with science materials for direct exploration—batteries, bulbs, magnets, wires, household chemicals, scales, balances, weights, and other natural materials. Art materials such as clay, plasticine, papier-mache, paints, and pastels are regularly used as tools for learning and expression. Libraries containing a range of children's literature are standard in every classroom as well. These rich, hands-on research materials, considered to be extras in many schools, were purchased with the savings obtained by not buying expensive workbooks and texts—here considered a serious drain on limited funds that provide much less useful grist for learning.

Students in BNS classrooms are also regularly engaged in opportunities to exchange ideas and to collaborate with peers. Extended work periods allow for in-depth study independently and in groups. The school day is organized to accommodate the rhythm and pace of the children. The intent is to

> Provide a setting that engages learners, seeks to involve each person wholly in mind, sense of self, sense of humor, range of interests, interactions with other people in learning; that suggests wonderful ideas to children . . . different ideas to different children . . . and that lets them feel good about themselves for having them. (Duckworth, 1987, pp. 1, 7, 134)

To put this vision of education into practice, teachers need to understand human development and learning theory, content matter and teaching strategies, and, most of all, their students. Much of this information derives from an assessment approach that places observation of students and their work at its center. As teachers observe what their students know and can do, the particular strategies their students use as they learn new things, they then use this information to build bridges between past and future skills and understandings. The experiences of the Bronx New School also demonstrate how engaging in this process also enhances teachers' general understandings of teaching and learning, building their capacities as professionals and providing a culture of continuous inquiry that becomes an integral part of school life.

DOCUMENTING CHILDREN'S LEARNING:
THE FOUNDATION OF ASSESSMENT

The Bronx New School assessment system was designed to inform instruction and support teaching and learning through the collection of descriptive records of student growth. Teachers and school support staff across grade levels developed a common plan that systematically looked at various forms of learning in a variety of meaningful, real-life contexts. Borrowing from the work of others across the country and developing tools and instruments of their own, the staff created a system involving multiple sources of information collected over an extended period of time: Teacher-kept observations, student-kept records, and samples of student work are used in combination to develop a picture of each child's learning. These sources of direct evidence of student growth are enhanced by regular input from students' families. Assessment methods focus not only on students' accomplishments but also on students' special strengths and the strategies they use in their learning. A developmental framework provides a general guide for expectations of progress. The accumulated information is then used for planning appropriate learning experiences and for developing curriculum responsive to students' needs and experiences.

The assessment system also documents the progress of groups of children, provides opportunities for teachers to reflect on their assessments of children and their work, and involves families in the life of the school. All of these occasions for reflection, learning, and communication have influenced curriculum, instruction, and teachers' professional development.

Unlike assessment systems that rely predominantly on tests that evaluate children through prescribed questions against standardized expectations, the primary purpose of this assessment system is to inquire *about* children—to look closely at students' thoughts, strategies, and skills to find the most effective means of supporting their learning (Chittenden & Courtney, 1989). While the staff adopted common methods and guidelines, these are neither as rigid as those required by standardized tests nor as informal as teachers' own private record-keeping. The methods and guidelines allow the flexibility needed for responsive teaching yet provide information necessary for accountability to families, other teachers, colleagues, administrators, and the community at large.

The school defined "accountability" more broadly than just the provision of information about student learning. Teachers wanted the assessment system to address how their commonly agreed-upon goals for learning were being met. They developed standards for work and general indicators of progress. These were then used as a framework in which to view student growth, constructed for levels of development rather than for specific ages or grades. Teachers were careful to ensure that this framework did not emphasize standardized outcomes at too early a stage. Teachers based this framework on the knowledge that growth in the early years takes place unevenly and over an extended period of time (National Association for the Education of Young Children [NAEYC], 1988); they felt strongly that too narrowly defined expectations of progress, such as the accomplishment of specific skills by the completion of specific grades, place students at risk of being prematurely labeled "unsuccessful" when, in reality, students might only need more time and support to master needed skills and to make sense of their learning.

In addition, teachers believed that achieving the "right answers" and getting students to perform in specified ways often gets in the way of developing genuine understanding (Kamii, 1985, 1989; NAEYC, 1991; National Association of State Boards of Education [NASBE], 1988; National Council of Teachers of Mathematics [NCTM], 1989). They wanted assessments to support and reveal a wider range of understandings than those generally demonstrated by conventional methods. As they worked with their students and talked together about these ideas, their teaching environments and accompanying assessments increasingly called attention to diverse student strengths, talents, and abilities.

Assessment of Individual Students

Teachers collected their records of student learning and growth, samples of student work, and students' own records of work across disciplines in portfolios that traveled with each child from grade to grade and from teacher to teacher. The portfolios also informed families and students themselves about what students can do, as well as about the particular strategies, strengths, styles, and interests they bring with them to their learning experiences.

The portfolios were both cumulative and authentic. They were "cumulative" in that they contained evidence of student progress from each year of a student's school career. They were "authentic" in that the records and samples within them were not produced specifically to fulfill a set of predetermined assessment requirements but were collected to demonstrate the range of students' activities in the natural contexts of the school's everyday life.

Information about a student's progress was placed in the portfolio at the beginning, the middle, and the end of the school year to provide a portrait of the student's development over the course of time. In addition to showing what the student had learned, the information was gathered specifically to portray particular growth issues, significant developments or interests, or an occasional sample of what the student considered to be his or her best effort at that particular point in time.

Because the Bronx New School is small—it was only 100 students at the time of this study, although it has currently grown to about 250—and because it has continuity of philosophy, values, and teaching practice throughout the grades, portfolios can build a continuum of information about the child over several grades, enabling the staff to come to know all the children well and to share understandings and strategies with one another about how best to support each child's growth. This produces a community of supporters for children, exemplifying the ancient African proverb, "It takes a whole village to raise a child."

Teacher-Kept Records

Teacher-kept records in the portfolio included documented observations of students, inventories and checklists of student skill development, and notes from conferences held between teacher and students about their interdisciplinary projects. These were dated and entered into the records at least once a week for each child. They were then used to inform narrative reports, completed at the middle and the end of each year, which commented on a child's general approaches to learning (i.e., each child's particular learning styles, themes, interests, and so on), as well as on that child's progress toward the acquisition of specific skills and knowledge in reading, writing, mathematics, and other discipline areas.

In addition to helping teachers think systematically about students' progress, teachers' observations also expanded their conception of "the intellect." The more they observed, the more sensitized they became to the diversity of student talents and abilities. They began to recognize linguistic, logical, numerical, musical, bodily, spatial, social, and other strengths (Gardner, 1983). This, in turn, influenced the way they thought about curriculum and teaching. Over time, they moved away from a standardized, static curriculum—calling for everyone to do and to learn the same set of things in the same way—to one that left lots of room for different ways of exploring common themes, presenting content and skills in contexts responsive to students' interests and prior experiences. They came to understand that no uniform curriculum or teaching strategy could be equally effective for all students.

Over time, teachers also recognized the limitations of uniformity in their own use of the assessment instruments. Just as they found that no one method of teaching was best for each student, they also discovered that no one documentation strategy was best for each teacher. Different teachers favored different formats for record keeping. Some jotted down observations on note cards, others used "stick-ems" that they pasted into a notebook at the end of the day, and still others carried a notebook that had sections demarcated for each child in which they would enter quick notes during the course of the day and longer reflections during preparation periods, lunch, or after-school hours. Some reviewed these records and notes regularly, jotting down a few summary lines about five children once a week. In a little over a month, a review of information about every child in the class was compiled. By the end of the school year, a substantial record of each individual's growth was accumulated.

As they experimented with different approaches and shared their experiences with one another, teachers came to understand that the assessment commonality they were seeking was not in the specifics of the instruments they used, but rather in the ways they looked at children and, subsequently, supported student learning. This was not easy to do, however, and they soon discovered that they did not really know as much as they wanted to about how and what to observe about children. For example, they found themselves using evaluative rather than descriptive language, attaching judgments and labels to children rather than describing exactly how and in what context something occurred. The tendency toward summative evaluation did not enhance the teaching process. Compare, for example, these two evaluations. First there was an early attempt at noting Stephen's*[1] progress, which evaluates his work but tells nothing about how he does it or how it might be built upon.

Stephen has an excellent vocabulary.
Stephen does outstanding work.
Stephen has excellent math skills.

A later version shows why Stephen's teacher originally considered his work to be "excellent" and "outstanding."

Stephen uses a rich variety of descriptive words in his writing.

Stephen works independently and intensely. He thinks critically, takes risks in putting forward new ideas, and is thorough in attention to details of presentation.

Stephen is fluid in his thinking about number concepts. He can generally find several solutions to a problem and is able to explain them to others in a clear way.

Other teachers also struggled with this issue. They learned from children's language and work, placing their observations in the framework of developmental progressions, thinking about how a child puts ideas together. When teachers, children, and their parents received this kind of feedback, it helped them to better understand what students do, to recognize their strengths so they could build on them further, and to identify areas in need of support in order to make plans for how to address them.

As teachers documented the work of their students in these ways, many of them were overwhelmed by what seemed like the enormity of the task. They felt that it took too much time to write notes on each student, and they thought they could just as easily keep much of this information in their memories. However, through their experiences of writing down their observations in a variety of settings in a variety of ways, most learned so much more about their students than they had previously known that they eventually became staunch advocates of keeping written records. They saw that memory of the details, and the nuance that makes each child visible, does indeed escape them in the blur of time; that only by writing down observations can teachers achieve a perspective of each student's unique growth over time.

Jotting down, reflecting, assuming the researcher stance thus became part of their way of life. They set aside time to have conversations together, which continually clarified their values and deepened their understandings about children and teaching and assessment. At the same time, they created a policy allowing each teacher to select his or her own preferences from a variety of philosophically compatible assessment tools.

A number of checklists and inventories on literacy development were among their collection of tools. A universal favorite was one checklist that identifies significant elements of early literacy growth: Observation of Reading Behavior (Davidson, 1985), shown in Figure 6.1. All of the primary grade teachers also used another instrument: Settings for Assessment of Children's Reading in Primary Classrooms (Educational Testing Service [ETS], 1989), shown in Figure 6.2. It lists the various primary classroom settings and occasions in which literacy learning takes place—such as story time, writing time,

Figure 6.1. Observations of reading behavior

Name _____   Year _____
Age _____

	Date	Comment

Recognizes name
Prints own name
Can indicate cover of book
Can indicate front of book
Can indicate back of book
Can indicate title
Can indicate print
Can indicate picture

Knows where to start reading
Knows which way to go
Knows to move left to right and
    return to beginning of next line
Knows first word
Knows last line

One to one matching
  • becoming established
  • well established
  • uses as cue for self-correction

Can indicate a word
Can indicate the space between
    the words

Can indicate a letter
Can indicate a capital letter, e.g., M
Can indicate a small letter, e.g., m
Can match capital and small letters
Knows some letters
Letter identification *test* score

Can indicate a full stop
Can indicate a comma
Can indicate a question mark

Knows some basic vocabulary
Word test score

Is writing letters
Is writing parts of words
Is writing words properly sequenced
Is writing groups of words
Is writing simple sentences

Figure 6.2. Settings for assessment of children's reading in primary classrooms

Setting	Examples of child's activities
Storytime: teacher reads to class (response to story-line; child's comments, questions, elaborations)	
Independent reading: book-time (nature of books child chooses or brings in; process of selecting; quiet or social reading)	
Writing: (journal, stories, alphabet, dictation)	
Reading Group/Individual: (oral reading strategies; discussion of text; responses to instruction)	
Informal settings: (use of language in play, jokes, storytelling, conversation)	
Books and print as resource: (use of books for projects; attention to signs, labels, names; locating information)	
Other:	

independent reading, and informal settings—providing an organized way for teachers to record their anecdotal notes of various activities.

Many portfolios in the early grades also included running records, sometimes referred to as "miscue analyses" (Davidson, 1985). Running

Figure 6.3. Running record of Fly with Me

TA=Teacher Assistance
11=Pause

Child's name _____
Teacher _____ Grade ____
Date _____

Fly With Me   *Teacher read title*   1st Read

w TA
Fly with me.   *isolated "w"*

                        TA — looked back to page 2
Fly with me up and up.   *Re-read sentence on page 2*
                          several. Then Read 'and'

Fly with me down and down.

Fly with me into the clouds   *Looked at picture*

TA   TA   TA
and around and around.   *Looked back to page 2*
                          but this time couldn't
Long   *remember 'and'*
pause Let's go fly over
         Look out for the hill.   *added "over"*

         let's go fly over a river
         Look out for the bridge.   *added "over"*

         Let's not fly   *omit again*
         Look out for the ground!

(40 words)

text	Substitution		text	Substitution
with	"w"		the	a
and	--		bridge	river
around	--		ground	again
look	let's			
out	go			
for	fly			

records (see Figure 6.3) systematically document students' oral reading in a way that helps teachers become aware of the strategies children use in their efforts to make meaning out of print. As a student reads a chosen text, the teacher follows along on a Xeroxed copy, indicating the number of overall errors that the student makes, the number of words the student reads incorrectly but substitutes with meaningful alternatives, the number of words the student omits, the number of times the student is able to self-correct, the fluency of the reading, and the number of times the student needs teacher assistance. This is an especially helpful tool to guide instruction when students are beginning to be independent readers but are still struggling with different aspects of fluency.

At the Bronx New School, running records were kept at monthly intervals, providing a comprehensive picture of the specific skills and strategies students were developing as they progressed through different texts. The information obtained from running records was especially helpful in demonstrating reading progress not revealed by standardized tests. Karen Khan, the school's Reading Support teacher, recalls her work with one student:

> The documentation that I kept of my work with Roberto* showed the ways he grew as a reader that were not evident from his scores on the reading tests. He was a third grader who was not yet fluent in his reading and he got overwhelmed by all those long, boring, complicated paragraphs on the city/state reading test. As a result he received a very low score. The running records I had regularly kept on him, however, demonstrated the changes he had made over the year and showed how much he actually could do. They documented how he was recognizing more words, how his miscues [mistakes, errors] were becoming increasingly related to the meaning of the text, how he was correcting himself more frequently, and how he was reading longer, more complicated passages. This reassured me, as well as Roberto and his family, about his progress and gave me concrete suggestions for how they could support his reading at home.

The *Primary Language Record, (PLR)* (Barrs et al., 1988) was yet another choice of literacy assessments in student portfolios. Its framework for observing and recording children's literacy progress informed teachers about the full spectrum of the developmental stages involved in becoming a reader. The *PLR*'s scales, noting points of growth along the literacy continuum (described in the previous chapter), chart children's progress as they become increasingly independent and experienced with many kinds of texts. These scales helped Bronx New School teachers think about and characterize children's progress, offering helpful ways of describing what a child was able to do on the road to reading. Scale ratings were reported on the mid- and end-of-year narratives. The score given to any particular student was arrived at on the basis of evidence gathered through teacher observation and documentation of that student's growth during the school year.

Student Work Samples

At the heart of the Bronx New School portfolios were collections of student work selected by teachers and students to represent a range of media from all discipline areas. Writing samples demonstrated literacy development while journals of mathematical problems and accompanying narratives showed progression in mathematical thinking. Drawings or photos of art projects, along with reports of science experiments and other projects, provided information about learning as it took place across the disciplines. Photos of three-dimensional work unable to be saved (block buildings, woodworkings, results of cooking, constructions of bridges or buildings) and photos of students engaged in activities with others (reading, tending to animals, sports, music, or dramatic play) gave a sense of each student's interests and learning styles. Items were dated to give a sense of progress over time.

At the end of each year the portfolios were reviewed to ensure they contained adequate information about all discipline areas, as well as about the uniqueness of the child. Teachers selected a representative sample of items from each of the areas of study at the three intervals (beginning, middle, and end of the year) to save for the following year. These were selected to show growth over time; to include literacy, mathematics, and science and social studies projects; and to show the range of the student's work and his or her particular strengths. In total, about 12–20 items might be selected to document these various aspects of children's learning. In the early grades especially, the teacher's observations of literacy development through checklists, profiles, and running records would be included in the pass-along portfolio. The remaining items were then sent home for families to keep.

Student-Kept Records

Children kept their own records of their reading and writing, their interdisciplinary projects, and their responses to teacher/student conferences. All students kept logs of their reading, listing what they read, and sometimes also *when* they read it and what they thought about it. These took a variety of forms, including lists kept in notebooks, on oaktag bookmarks, or on teacher-designed forms.

Reading logs provided continuity and a sense of concrete accomplishment for students, as well as instructionally useful information for the teacher about who was reading what. This enabled teachers to both chart students' reading interests and the levels of difficulty of the books individual children were tackling, and to inform their suggestions of books for students and the activities they designed to help students progress. Since the Bronx New School did not rely on conventional methods of charting reading progress—basal readers, workbooks, or ability-tracked reading groups—this record-keeping was also especially useful in demonstrating to families how students' reading was coming along. It also helped students recognize what they were learning (a real motivation) while it gave them a sense of responsibility, control, and ownership of their work.

This approach to student-kept records was tried in some classes with other subjects as well. For example, some teachers used math journals. They would assign three or four problems at the beginning of the week that required thought, time, and the ability to use an array of skills and understandings. The problems often had more than one right answer. Students would work them out in their journals and share them at the end of the week. Math notebooks would also be used to record student-invented math problems or teacher-designed, individualized problems that students would complete during open-ended math activity times.

Some teachers also had children keep project folders. These would describe what students did during the daily classroom time allocated for project work, the questions that arose, how they proceeded to answer those questions, and what they learned as a result. One student, who spent considerable project time engaged in an investigation of an ant farm, included his detailed drawings and descriptions of it in his project folder. The student drew the farm and its tunnels on subsequent days, recording the changes he had noticed from his observations as well as the inferences and conclusions he was making as a result of his study.

Children also shared these records of their work with their classmates, so that they became exposed to a wider world of information and ideas. Each child received questions and comments from classmates that clarified their thinking and stimulated new directions for work. This developed a shared body of knowledge for the class without everyone having to do the same project.

Akeem's* story, told below, demonstrates how this documentation of student learning actually worked in practice. Akeem was a child who was struggling to find a way to find a positive identity and path to learning in school. For this student, careful observation called attention to previously hidden strengths, which were then used by his teacher as a teaching resource that greatly enhanced Akeem's learning and self-confidence.

AKEEM'S STORY

Akeem came to the Bronx New School when he was a 3rd grader, after three difficult years in a troubled, overcrowded school. Standardized teaching and testing in that environment had already marked him as a failure. His records indicated that he had scored in the lowest percentiles on the norm-referenced reading and math tests administered to all New York City public school children. In addition, his official school cumulative record folder was filled with checks in the unsatisfactory columns. No other information about him was available. Only by accident, at an informal conversation during a district meeting, did his teacher, Susan Gordon, learn of his troubled past—

that he had been suspended from his former school for throwing a desk at a teacher.

What prompted this behavior remained a mystery throughout Akeem's first days at the Bronx New School. But difficulties soon became apparent, motivating his teachers to find out more about him. Akeem had intense swings in mood, almost what appeared to be two distinct postures—one always in constant motion, the other quiet, gentle, and still. He loved to run, jump, climb, and stretch. Sometimes the school setting seemed almost to constrict him; his long legs and large hands often bumping into things, his hands always tapping his thighs or his cheeks or playing with a paper clip, rubber band, or eraser. At other times he seemed quiet, closed, almost sorrowful. His head would hang low, his shoulders hunched. At these times it would not take much to move him to tears.

At classroom meetings Akeem fidgeted endlessly, talking, singing, popping his cheeks, or humming. Sometimes he sneered, grumbled, or muttered to himself; sometimes he teased, smiled, or giggled with others. When frustrated, he would throw things: pieces of cork, plastic, cardboard. His forehead, brows, and mouth would all scowl simultaneously. When reprimanded, he often denied what he had done, stomping angrily out of the room engulfed in a dark, stormy cloud. On several occasions, in fits of frustration, he overturned chairs or threw other large objects, frightening and angering those around him.

Akeem was openly considered a disruptive presence in the class, particularly during group meetings. There was an implicit expectation that he would do something to disturb everyone. This was lost on no one, least of all Akeem.

Susan,[2] desperate to understand and contain his behavior, observed Akeem carefully, noting the contexts in which he lost control. She soon discovered that he could not independently read or write and that he had difficulty with even simple mathematics and that his disruptive outbursts generally began when he was called upon to use these skills. From this evidence she inferred a number of possible rationales for Akeem's behavior: that he was trying to avoid participating in activities at which he was convinced he would fail; that he hoped his disruption of an activity would cause it to cease; or that rather than being known for *not* being good at something (school-related learning), Akeem preferred to be known for being good at *something* (in this case that something was being "the disrupter").

Together with other school staff, Susan searched for ways to help Akeem. Since Akeem's disruptive behavior bouts seemed to correlate with assignments to do things he could *not* do, they hypothesized that the logical way to avoid further disruptions was to involve him instead in what he actually *could* do. What those things were, they didn't know. They suspected that Akeem didn't know either.

Susan began by allowing Akeem to choose his work from the many rich and varied interdisciplinary activities available in his flexibly scheduled, workshop-style classroom. It was organized into centers of interest that had tables, a meeting area for discussions, a library area, shelves filled with math games, blocks, paints, clay, sand, water, wood, fabrics, and tools. It also had materials for cooking, for construction, and for "messing about" (Hawkins, 1965) in science: found objects, wires, batteries, bulbs, magnets, household chemicals, and an array of recycled junk. This variety of materials was regularly available.

Susan structured the classroom around several long work periods every day. These gave opportunities for Akeem and his classmates to involve themselves deeply, and for extended spans of time, in areas of their particular interest. She encouraged the students to be active, to find their own avenues of self-expression, and to revisit the activities of their interests whenever they chose. Her classroom learning environment was structured to help students get to know each other's ideas through conversation and to utilize each other's knowledge through peer teaching.

The plan to help Akeem also included giving him special permission to make his own schedule and excusing him from the group meetings that he had continually disrupted. Susan observed him closely as he explored the classroom, tested things out, and settled into a few types of activities—legos, building blocks, drawing, and junk sculpture—ones that captured his imagination and focused his energies. Building began to consume his days. His fidgeting fingers quickly became adept at putting small pieces together, crafting interesting objects and designs. Susan fueled his interests by providing regular opportunities to pursue these activities, as well as by providing materials, resources, conversation, and other related experiences to enrich and extend them. She connected to what he already knew, helped uncover his curiosity and questions, advised and supported him in their pursuit. This approach strengthened his skills and expanded his knowledge.

Over the course of several months Akeem built a set of aviation vehicles accompanied by a book illustrating the history of flight; a series of Lego buildings and drawings reproducing important architecture in New York City, and a set of action figures with a companion descriptive catalogue. This action figures catalog, "Man after Man," illustrates not only his sophisticated artistic ability, but also his ability to plan and sustain an extended, tightly organized piece of work. The 28 pages in his book (see Figure 6.4) follow a common pattern: a highly detailed sketch of a character with some unique characteristics, described in a carefully printed caption that explains the character's traits, habitat (these range from the Amazon to Greenland, from the rain forest to the treetops and the mountains), and interesting facts or questions, i.e., "Did you know SixFist is BarBell's brother?" "Did you know Ice Gadget pays for the damages of good/bad battles?" Akeem's capacity to plan, organize, and draw connections, to maintain correspon-

Figure 6.4. Excerpt from Akeem's action figures catalog

dence between his drawings and text, to create a logic for a world popu-
lated by innovative characters is clear in this work.

At times Akeem was so involved in these projects that he chose to give
up recess to continue working on them. One staff member who supervised
children during lunch time recollects:

> I'll never forget an image of Akeem standing at the lunchroom door,
> wolfing down his sandwich, hopping from one foot to another, wait-
> ing for his teacher to pick him up so that he could return to his class-
> room to finish *writing (!!)* his book on the history of flight.

Susan kept track of Akeem's progress through regular entries in her
journal, documenting what he did, how he did it, the issues that arose for
him in the course of his work, the areas of his strengths, and those areas in
which he needed help. In one journal entry, after Akeem had been in her
class for several months, she wrote:

> During a unit on space he constructed a space shuttle out of a seltzer
> bottle, cardboard pieces, and other items. He referred to books for
> help with his work. He even sat through a meeting without disrupting
> the rest of the class. Others now seek him out for advice on building.
> It appears that he is valued for his talents.

Based on what she learned from her careful observations and from
reflecting on the documentation in her daily records, Susan not only helped
Akeem to change, she changed her thinking and her teaching as well. She
came to realize that a classroom limited only to traditional forms of academic
expression excludes different types of children as well as different types of
knowledge. She became poignantly aware that children who have diverse
strengths and interests often feel that because there is no room in school for
the kinds of activities they value, there is literally no room for them either.
By demonstrating that other forms of work—paint, clay, construction, etc.—
are just as important as math or writing, Susan extended the range of what
was valued. As a result, Akeem and the other children began to understand
the inclusive message. They began to feel that there was a place for them
in the classroom and the school.

The student teacher who worked in his classroom during this time
reflects on the changes she observed in Akeem as he experienced Susan's
classroom environment:

> There are children who "can" and children who "can't" here just as there are
> in any given classroom. But the difference in this room is, if Akeem is not
> a writer, he *is* a builder. And Stephen, who happens to be a writer, is *not* a
> builder. There is value placed on each individual's abilities alongside a con-

cern for, and an educational emphasis placed on, overcoming their current inabilities. No one here is a "failure." Everyone is an acknowledged success in one area or another.

A room without the abundance of art supplies and collection of odds and ends that support his self expression would exclude Akeem. His experience in his other school proves how hard this can be on a child. (Miller, 1990, pp. 32, 21)

As Akeem received recognition for his work, his demeanor began to change. The surly look began to fade. The disruptive episodes all but disappeared. The desire to be part of his classroom surfaced. He began to choose to stay with the group for meeting times. He even started to participate in quiet reading time (a period during the day when students selected their own books and read independently) and to allow the reading specialist to work with him. It appeared that the validation he had experienced from doing what he was good at transferred to his most vulnerable areas. His interests had been strengthened and unleashed by having the opportunities to pursue them (Carini, 1986). He began to take risks, try what he couldn't do, ask questions when he didn't understand.

Akeem's strengths, resources, and areas in need of support began to emerge as his teacher learned about him through her ongoing observations of his language and his work. The details she recorded revealed Akeem's strengths and affected the way she thought about him. She stopped reacting to him as "the troublemaker" and began to regard him as a builder, a doer, a maker of things; as artistic and adept at mechanical tasks. She also had greater insights into his learning style—his interests, his tastes, his approaches, his pace, and the areas in which he needed greatest support. She used this information to support him as he struggled with reading and other areas of learning that he found most difficult.

In reading, for example, Susan's ongoing assessment efforts allowed her to determine that while Akeem had a grasp of phonetic skills, he had little understanding of what he was reading. Because he relied on phonics almost exclusively, he would often get mired in the text and unable to decode the print, lacking other strategies that could support him, such as using pictures for clues, reading on to the end of the sentence, substituting a word that would make sense, looking to the syntax of the sentence. His lack of resources for getting meaning from reading, combined with his generally low level of self-esteem, left him frustrated and angry and kept him from persisting to take the risks needed to learn new things.

In addition to these observations, which diagnosed the areas in which Akeem needed support, Susan also discovered an idiosyncrasy that gave her direction for how to help him. She noted that whenever Akeem began a book, he was most interested in its illustrations. Even when he was supposed to be reading the text, he would generally fixate on the pictures, noting the most intricate of details in them. This understanding led her to guide him toward books that contained beautiful, detailed drawings. She learned to allow him plenty of time for soaking up the pictures before attempting the words. It was this approach and these kinds of books that Akeem eventually began to seek out independently, that engaged his interest and attention, and that ultimately helped him break into independent and fluent reading. In these excerpts from her daily notes, reading support teacher Karen Khan gives a sense of how she worked with Akeem:

> Today we read two chapters. I read the first page. He went on. He built momentum as he went along. I provided unknown words at first. Then I suggested several strategies: pointing to the words as he goes along (sometimes he needs this but sometimes he doesn't); going ahead to try the rest of the sentence when he doesn't know the word; using the pictures for clues. I also pointed out different endings of root words such as "er," "ing," and "ed." At the height of his momentum, he was almost reading fluently! Then he slowed down. It seems that he needs to concentrate so hard that he gets exhausted.

As teachers worked with Akeem in this way, he integrated new understandings, new ideas, new competencies, and new skills into his prior ones. He began to uncover hidden strengths and talents. He began to actually enjoy school (one teacher observed him skipping his way down the block to school one morning) and to eagerly seek out new opportunities for work. His feelings about school, taken from a yearbook at the end of his 5th grade year, had changed:

> If you don't know something in another school it's your problem. Here you can work it out. Instead of reading about something, you do it. And because you want to learn about something, you learn more. (The Bronx New School, 1991, p. 15)

In spite of the changes that took place in Akeem's learning, his standardized test scores did not improve dramatically over the three years that Bronx New School teachers knew him. Although they increased slightly each year, he essentially remained a low test-scorer. The tests did not reveal what a thinker and questioner he had become; what a risk-taker he was; what an inventive, artistic sculptor and drawer he was; what a gentle, funny, considerate person he could be. They did not demonstrate his progress or give information that would support further teaching for him. They did not show, for instance, that over time he had tapped into many more reading strategies than he had utilized before; that he was able to read a wider range of materials with greater success; that he had begun to try instead of giving up when attempting something that did not come easily; that he was building resources to carry him further in his struggle with literacy and learning.

The only story they told was that Akeem did not answer the multiple choice questions on tests in the way that inauthentic configuration of normed questions posited that an "average" 3rd or 4th or 5th grader should.

Fortunately, the observations of Akeem documented by his teacher and the samples of work collected in his portfolio *do* reveal these aspects of growth and development not demonstrated by the mass-administered, standardized tests. They provide information about many different types of knowledge as well as many different ways of acquiring it. They give a fuller, more contextualized picture of change. They keep track of the process, expose the nuance, and provide information to those charged with helping the child make the learning journey more productive.

Akeem is currently completing the 8th grade. While academics are still not easy for him, his effort and regular attendance are reflected by his record of practically all A's on his spring report card. He continues to draw and design on his own, is connected to his strengths and to his interests. These understandings appear to serve him well as he makes plans to attend a high school oriented toward art and design. He hopes to become an architect or an engineer. Susan's ability to help him find himself, with the aid of the array of lenses she could employ to gain insight, certainly made an important difference in his success as a learner and a doer.

THE DESCRIPTIVE REVIEW OF A CHILD

The *Descriptive Review of a Child* (Prospect Center, 1986) is another assessment strategy used at the Bronx New School that helped Akeem's teachers in their struggle to find ways of supporting his growth. In the review, faculty collectively engage in a structured, descriptive process for addressing an issue, question, or concern about a child. Its creators at the Prospect Center in Vermont describe the review as follows:

> The primary purpose of the *Descriptive Review of a Child* is to bring together varied perspectives, in a collaborative process, in order to describe a child's experience within the school setting. An underlying assumption of the Process is that each child is active in seeking to make sense of her or his experiences. By describing the child as fully, and in as balanced a way as possible, we begin to gain access to the child's modes of thinking and learning and to see their world from their point of view: what catches their attention; what arouses their wonder and curiosity; what sustains their interest and purpose. To have access to that understanding of a child or children, offers a guide to the education of the child's fullest potential. Recommendations can be made which draw upon and support the child's strengths, interests, and power to make and do things.
>
> The perspectives through which the child is described are multiple, to insure a balanced portrayal of the person, that neither over-emphasizes some

current "problem" nor minimizes an ongoing difficulty. The description of the child addresses the following facets of the person as these characteristics are expressed within the classroom setting at the present time:

The child's physical presence and gesture
The child's disposition
The child's relationships with other children and adults
The child's activities and interests
The child's approach to formal learning
The child's strengths and vulnerabilities.

(Prospect Center, 1986, pp. 26–27)

The presenter of the *Descriptive Review* is most often the child's classroom teacher, although teachers at the Bronx New School eventually progressed to having several co-presenters who had unique and important understandings of the child, either from different perspectives or from different time periods. Some schools also include the child's parents or family members in the actual review itself.

Prior to their presentations, a previously determined chairperson (this position is always rotated) discusses and defines a focusing issue or question with the presenter(s). For example, the focusing theme for Akeem was his two distinct postures—motion and stillness—and how they could best be accommodated in the classroom. Finding the focusing issue was not always easy but led to thinking, discussion, and reflection among teachers that in and of itself often led to new insights. As Schon (1983) suggests in *The Reflective Practitioner:* "Problems of professional practice do not present themselves ready-made, but rather the [practice] situation is complex and uncertain, and there is a problem in finding the problem" (p. 129).

Prior to the review, the chairperson of the review process obtains background knowledge and history of the child relevant to the issue to be discussed. The chairperson uses this information in a brief opening presentation of his or her findings. This opening presentation also includes a reminder to participants of the *Descriptive Review* format of its protocol—no gossip, no innuendo, no judgmental language—and of its purpose: to support the growth of a child by focusing on his/her strengths. A note-taker is assigned to document the entire process for the school's and the child's permanent records.

To verify, validate, and illustrate each description, the presenter(s) set up a display of the child's work for the review. After they speak, the chair gives an overview of their presentations by highlighting themes and issues that emerged from the portrait of the child the presenters constructed. Then other participants are invited to comment and reflect on what they have heard in a round-robin fashion (no cross-conversations allowed). The chair once again reflects back to all that has been said and invites the presenter(s) to respond, if they choose. Finally, participants are requested to make suggestions about changes in approaches, classroom environment, or teaching practices that might better address the needs of the child.

Rather than looking at the child as the problem and expecting the child to make all the changes, the *Descriptive Review* process calls for the school to be responsive to the needs of the individual child and to assume responsibility for problems and their remedies. This is not to say that the child's responsibility is ignored. It is indeed addressed, but cast in a different light—of building capacity through support of strengths rather than of remediating weaknesses or punishing shortcomings.

An excerpt from a *Descriptive Review* of Akeem illustrates how this works:

Akeem's favorite activities are drawing and construction of all kinds. He has built space shuttles from seltzer bottles, cardboard cartons, straws, tape, bottle tops, and the like and created a robot with moving parts from similar materials. He also likes to draw. His drawings are expressive of a young child, with a creative and imaginative approach. He is fascinated by powerful machinery such as space ships, airplanes, electronic robots. He also enjoys the more fanciful side of such things and has spent time constructing a Bat Cave, Bat Mobile, and Bat Helicopter. He is deeply involved with ideas of power, strength, force, and defense. He tends to favor materials he is accustomed to using and with which he has some skill. If he does not like what he has created, he expresses anger and disappointment. He instantly crumbles it into a tight wad and rams it into the wastebasket. Sometimes he will begin work again immediately. At other times, he will simply not try anymore.

His approach to a new topic is typified by the following example: On the day Akeem's teacher introduced outer space to the class as the next area of study, she spent some time talking with everyone about space travel, the stars, planets, and the like. She also made many books on these topics available to the children and spoke about them in detail. Right after the discussion Akeem went directly to the construction corner of the room. He searched through the cartons for material and began building almost immediately. He seemed to have a picture in his mind. He worked deliberately. Once his work began to resemble a space vehicle, he opened a book on the space shuttle for a reference. This shuttle was the focus of Akeem's work periods while the class studied space. He also did a blueprint of it. While working on both parts of the project, he used books as references, relying primarily on labeled diagrams to help him. He also built a plastic plane that actually flew. Its body was a seltzer bottle, and its wings were made from plastic odds and ends. He rigged a rubber band in the bottle and attached it to the plane's propeller. When the propeller was spun and the rubber band twisted tight, the plane flew.

Akeem approaches most subjects as he did outer space. He appears most comfortable when he can, at some level, physically construct a subject or process for himself. He is very uncomfortable with reading and writing. There seems to be something about a page full of print that fails to connect with him. These processes offer no pieces he can handle and try to fit together. The same difficulty is seen in his math work. One day, he was trying to do a division problem and looked completely lost. He brightened up when presented with unifix cubes. Having the bits and pieces to handle there, as in his construction work, made what had seemed impossible possible.

He is increasingly able to do this for himself—transform what is difficult for him into a medium he can handle more comfortably. He made a game for multiplication that had pieces he could hold in his hands and move around and fit or match together. He also needs physical involvement in a task to help him figure it out. When figuring out the diameter of a circle, he crawled around a taped circle on the meeting area rug with a tape measure, to get the diameter.

Akeem cannot seem to truly learn while sitting still or as part of a group. He needs to be able to move about to make that imaginative or intuitive leap. He is an active, strong, but vulnerable child. His continued presence in the classroom (he is never absent) testifies to his enduring efforts to fit into this place called school.

The kind of observation called for by the *Descriptive Review* format offers understandings which set the tone for a learning environment providing for the needs of each child, respecting the individuality of each child, making each child visible. This is especially powerful in schools that serve diverse communities and that are endeavoring to include all children in the ranks of successful learners. A teacher explains:

The value of an education will never be missed by visible and included children. They will be too excited by their own wonderful ideas to give up on learning. (Miller, 1990, p. 35)

The chair concludes the *Descriptive Review* with a summation of what has taken place. New perspectives on the child, as well as new ideas for work with the child, are gained by all. The notes of the event are placed in the child's folder, providing the school with a written document that becomes part of its permanent record.

The *Descriptive Review* process, through observation, documentation, and the presentation of these observations, enables the people charged with supporting the growth of children to gather and organize empirical information for the purpose of assessing growth and disclosing new meanings. It is not an expedient assessment instrument. It requires preparation time, time to actually do the review (one and a half to two hours), and administrative juggling for the time to be arranged either during or after the school day. Despite these difficulties, however, school staff who have participated in the process have described it as time well spent. One teacher said:

As a child is described through the *Descriptive Review* process we can literally see the child emerge before us. We get a sense of his physicality, his tastes, his style, his pace, his interests, and his particular strengths. We can note continuities and repeating themes in the child's work that provide us with direction as to how to support him.

Another teacher notes how the time spent on discussing the issues of one child can enhance understandings of all children:

The *Descriptive Review* process, by focusing in depth on the issues of one particular child, gives us understandings and deeper sensitivity to the intricacies of the process of growth and development for all children. In this sense, it is time well spent. Through it we learn about teaching and about learning in general.

There are few occasions in most schools in which a group of adults convenes to talk about what might be done to support a child who is struggling. Teams are sometimes convened when a child is in trouble, when a special education placement is sought, or when a transfer or expulsion is considered. The *Descriptive Review,* however, stands in contrast to the kind of discussion about a child that typically occurs at such meetings, where the focus is on the child's deficits and inabilities, on the inconveniences to the school and teachers to try to educate him in an inclusive setting, on the behavioristic schemes that are to be created to treat the child's problems (remedial work if the problems are academic; rewards and punishments if the problems are seen as behavioral). Instead, the *Descriptive Review* is as wide-ranging as the interests of the child and the vantage points of the adults; it is explicitly educative and constructive; and it is focused on bending the knowledge of teachers and the capacities of the school to the renewed support of the child.

The *Descriptive Review* is more than an assessment instrument for student growth. While it describes the nuance and details of a child's growth, its real power lies in its ability to directly affect the ways in which helping adults can better support that growth. In addition, it serves as a record of school practice and it documents the discussion of important staff development issues. Finally, it serves to build a sense of community in the school as a whole because it provides a common language, common perspective, and common framework for teaching and learning.

REPORTING SYSTEMS

Progress reports, family conferences, and other communication vehicles were developed at BNS to share the vivid and detailed information about student work and progress collected through the assessments with families and the wider school community.

Progress Reports

In lieu of traditional report cards, listing a set of letter or number grades, a progress report was prepared for each student twice during the course of the school year. The progress report is a narrative summary of growth describing each child's development over time. Informed by teachers' detailed observations and documentation of students' work, it is meant to be used in much the same manner as the *Descriptive Review*—to be descriptive, not evaluative (judgmental); to focus on the child through the lens of strength; and to frame vulnerabilities as areas in need of support rather than as problems to be remediated. A family conference to discuss the contents of the report was held soon after each was completed—at the end of the first term in February, and at the end of the school year in June. A space at the end of the report was reserved for comments from both the student and the family about any aspect of the report and for sharing additional ideas or information.

These reports were a continual work in progress. As a result of family input and teacher dialogue, they underwent changes every year, evolving from a combination narrative and checklist, complete with a numbered assessment code for each discipline (see Figure 6.5), into a full narrative, minus the checklists and assessment code, without the separation between the disciplines. (See excerpted sample in Figure 6.6.)

These changes were made after the first year of the school, when faculty discovered that families and students reacted to the assessment codes as if they were grades. Although the ratings were meant only to give a sense of each child's place in the continuum of development, families interpreted them quite differently. They responded to the assessment code as if their child had been evaluated and this caused them to subsequently lose sight of the true nature and purpose of the reports—that they were intended to give a detailed portrait of the child, framed in the perspective of the continuum of growth and development, and presented through the light of support, not judgment. An example of this positive way of framing a child's development can be seen in this excerpt from Kevin's* report:

II. Social/Emotional Development: Kevin is well-liked by both adults and his peers. He expresses himself freely and with confidence both during the group meeting and 1-1. He is most focused in his work and productive when working with a small number of children in close proximity to a supportive adult. His difficulty in controlling the impulsive urges to touch other children's work frequently instigates a conflict, as does his tendency to become easily distracted during meeting and work times. Both his classmates and I will continue to support his growth in these areas. Kevin remains always an "idea person," not only with regard to his own work, but in terms of his ability to act as a catalyst for ideas for the rest of the classroom.

Figure 6.5. Bronx New School Report Form

THE BRONX NEW SCHOOL
REPORT FORM

Name: _____   Date: _____

Teacher: _____   Grade: _____

ASSESSMENT CODE: The following code has been developed to describe your child's progress:

   N/A Not Applicable
   1) Needs a lot of help; a serious concern
   2) Needs reminders; making progress
   3) Handles this well
   4) This is an area of strength

I. **Projects, themes, special interests:** Please refer to the above assessment code. Also, see accompanying curriculum letter.

   _____ Asks appropriate questions
   _____ Actively seeks to make sense of things; experiments
   _____ Takes risks with new things, new skills, new experiences
   _____ Observant, notices details, watches carefully and patiently
   _____ Participates in class discussions

COMMENTS:

II. **Social and behavioral:** The following issues, which we have discussed in conferences, cover important aspects of our child as a learner and as a member of the school community. Please refer to the assessment code.

   _____ Relationships with classmates and schoolmates
   _____ Working in groups, sharing with others
   _____ Relationship with adults and other "authorities"
   _____ Handling of regular daily classroom rules and routines
   _____ Responsibility toward materials, clothes, environment
   _____ Focus, concentration, sticking to a task over time, attentiveness to work
   _____ Standing up for her/his own rights, protecting her/himself in appropriate ways
   _____ Helping out others, sympathy for others
   _____ Handling work-related frustration, acceptance of mistakes

COMMENTS:

III. **Language development and self expression:** Please refer to the assessment code.

_____ Comfort describing ideas, feeling, events
_____ Skill at describing ideas, feelings, events
_____ Attentiveness to what others are saying
_____ Ability and interest in conversation
_____ Vocabulary

COMMENTS:

IV. **Reading:** Reading is NOT a subject matter. It is a tool of learning. The
attached sheets describe the different stages of literacy development. All of
these stages are important in becoming a reader.

Your child can presently be described as _____ reader.

Titles of books read recently:

COMMENTS ON READING:

V. **Writing:** Writing development is intricately linked to reading development.
As your child's reading skills develop, so will his/her writing skills. As your
child's writing skills develop, so will her/his reading skills. Please see the
attached sheet to describe your child's stage of development in writing.

Your child is at Writing Stage _____.

Please refer to the assessment code for the following items:

_____ Use of writing time
_____ Thinks up ideas for writing
_____ Attitude toward writing
_____ Handwriting
_____ Drawings

(cont'd.)

Figure 6.5. Bronx New School Report Form (cont'd.)

COMMENTS:

VI. **Math Assessment:** Please see the attached sheet to explain the stages of development in mathematical thinking.

Your child is at Stage _____ as a mathematical thinker.

_____   Interest in the use of numbers in the world around him/her
_____   Interest in connection between things
_____   Sorting and classifying
_____   Sees patterns and relationships
_____   Understands appropriate mathematical terms
_____   Counting
_____   Computation
_____   Estimation
_____   Measurement—non-standard: with cubes, blocks, string, etc.
_____   Measurement—standard: with rulers, inches, centimeters
_____   Surveys and graphs
_____   Application of math skills to other projects and activities

COMMENTS:

VII. **Homework:** Please refer to the assessment code.

_____   Turns in homework on time and completed
_____   Puts in effort—creative, imaginative, beyond what is required
_____   Done neatly and carefully

TEACHER'S SIGNATURE _____

DIRECTOR'S SIGNATURE _____

CHILD'S SIGNATURE _____

PARENT'S/GUARDIAN'S SIGNATURE _____

                              _____

COMMENTS:

Please return this report with your signatures and comments. We will make a copy of it for your records after it is signed.

Framing the information in the perspective of a growth continuum was particularly helpful to parents who wanted or needed information regarding the question, "How is my child doing in relation to other children his/her age?" This need for comparative information was especially prevalent in families whose children were progressing differently than what they thought of as "the norm." They needed to know if their children were "okay" and, if not, what was being done to help them.

For example, many families worried a lot about their child's reading. This is understandably a highly charged concern because the consequences of problems in this area can be literally life-threatening for some students (Kohl, 1991). As in many schools using a developmental and holistic approach to reading instruction rather than sequenced basal readers, some families at the Bronx New School were apprehensive about whether their children were progressing properly. The process was different from what they remembered, and this difference often made them uneasy, even though memories of their own schooling were frequently unpleasant.

Families experienced even more anxiety if their children were not reading independently by the beginning of the 2nd grade, which is not an uncommon phenomenon for many children within the normal range of development (Bussis, Chittenden, Amarel, & Klausner, 1985), given the differential development of children's visual/perceptual skills. In these cases, the BNS approach to documentation, developmental assessment, and reporting was particularly important, as the following experience of Margaret* and her mother demonstrates.

Margaret, who at the time of this writing is a 5th grader who reads fluently and is a competent student, was slow to move into reading when she was younger. She was an otherwise attentive, inquisitive, and involved student who worked well with others and enjoyed school. She loved being read to, writing stories in her own "invented" spelling, and making detailed drawings to accompany her work. In spite of evidence that Margaret was progressing, her mother could not help but compare her daughter with the accomplishments of other children who seemed to read better. To make matters even more complicated, Margaret's mother also constantly compared her to her older sister who, when attending their traditional neighborhood school—replete with work books, basal readers, and ability groups—had begun to read at a much earlier age.

Teachers tried to assure Margaret's mother that she possessed many strengths and that, in addition, she was making steady gains in reading. The teachers' lengthy progress reports, based on their observational records and the collected samples of Margaret's work, which were shared at numerous family conferences and conversations, helped Margaret's mother see Margaret's strategies for learning and what the teachers were doing to support her. This evidence helped her mother finally to accept that her daughter was indeed making progress, that although she was figuring out how to read more slowly than did some others, it did not stop her from learning a lot and loving the process, and that she was being supported sufficiently by her teachers. About midway through Margaret's 2nd grade year, several months after she began to read independently, her mother looked back and reflected on the process:

> It wasn't until Margaret became an independent reader that I came to appreciate and understand what the Bronx New School's philosophy really meant—that each student has a particular way of learning. I couldn't relax enough while Margaret was still struggling to appreciate what the process really entailed. I was too anxious, never having experienced this before. I didn't trust that all along Margaret was learning and putting the pieces together. But having experienced it now, I see how much the conferences, the progress reports, all the evidence collected about what Margaret could do and how she could do it was used by the teachers to support her learning. Now I understand much more about teaching and learning.

This story points to a tension that is inherent in the effort to provide assessment that simultaneously serves the purpose of teaching and learning as well as of public accountability. The tension is between norms of development meant to ensure that student problems will be addressed in a timely fashion and the pressures created by these very same norms to have children move in lockstep fashion, creating dangers of stigmatizing anyone who simply works at a different rhythm. In many schools it is not unusual for children to be retained in a grade, or to be referred to special classes, because they have not attained established standards within a determined amount of time, even though this expectation contravenes what is known about actual developmental stages and progress. How to create standards that lessen the chances of students falling through the cracks—while also allowing them flexible time frames in which to grow—presents a challenge that schools must sensitively and knowledgeably address. As teachers become increasingly knowledgeable about development and learning and more observant of their students' concrete abilities, they are better able to reconcile these competing concerns intelligently and productively.

Demonstrating individual growth within the context of the developmental span was the Bronx New School's way of addressing the tension created by accountability concerns. An example of how this was done can be seen in the first section of a progress report reproduced in Figure 6.6. As it explains the child's strategies, characteristic approaches, accomplishments, and behaviors, it also places this information in the context of the entire continuum of development.

Progress reports done in this fashion provide families with detailed information about the child that they know (in some respects, better than anyone)

Figure 6.6. Bronx New School Report Form (Kevin)

THE BRONX NEW SCHOOL
LA NUEVA ESCUELA DEL BRONX

Progress Report

Name: _Kevin Jones*_   Date: _2-18-91_

Teacher: _____   Grade: _2_

I. Themes, interests, approaches to learning:

Kevin has a strong interest in discovering "how things work," an interest that has been reflected in his many constructions and electrical and mechanical projects. He is interested in learning about Space and other science themes presented in the new *True Books* and *Magic School Bus* series. Humor is a strong motivating force for learning!

With regard to literacy development, Kevin is well-launched on reading! He uses a broad range of reading strategies—picture and context clues, sounding out words, and breaking larger words down into smaller, known parts. He rereads to self-correct and to maintain momentum. His miscues are generally meaningful, especially when he is tuned into the illustrations—rather than getting "stuck" on trying to sound out a single word. He can read books from the *I Can Read* series with increased confidence. He continues to be very attuned to all classroom print, charts, and black board messages and is always eager to read them aloud.

In his writing Kevin continues to draw or diagram first, then writes with the purpose of explaining or elaborating his drawing. He writes by sounding out words, using classroom print and the other children as spelling resources as well. He borrows ideas and themes from books he's read or from the stories of his friends and then adapts them to his own purposes. Humor frequently plays an important role. He is becoming increasingly aware of the need for punctuation and capitalization. Kevin takes particular delight in dramatizing his stories in puppet shows. He also loves to write on the computer using the Bank Street Writer Program.

Kevin's interest in working with computers carries over into Math where he uses the "Racing Car Math" program on almost a daily basis to practice simple addition and subtraction facts. His number sense has improved greatly. The Hundreds Board has been of particular help to him in working out computational problems and in understanding the relative values of numbers and their relationships. A sense of place value is slowly emerging, although Kevin still prefers to count by 1's, usually with the aid of the Hundreds Board. He can read and interpret story problems and knows when to add or subtract. He can tell time to the hour and 1/2 hour. His sense of spatial relationships is well-developed and he enjoys working out complex construction and mechanical problems using building materials—like figuring out how to design a working elevator or how to precisely fit a Lego train between two platforms or through a tunnel.

from the perspective of the teacher—what the child is like in the context of peers in the classroom setting. Such reports also give concrete and detailed information about the curriculum and teaching methods used and the child's development with those methods, thus teaching families a lot about both the school's approaches and the child's learning process. This enables them to support their child in a more informed and comprehensive way, something they greatly appreciate, as can be seen in the following comments by parents.

> The developmental information in the reports is absolutely essential in order for me to better understand my child's developmental stage. I appreciate the lengthy comments provided by the teachers. ("Feedback," 1990, p.1)

> The progress reports which we've received in the last two years clearly and fully described how our son was progressing in school. We really appreciate the time and effort which the teacher puts in these reports. ("Feedback," 1991, p. 5)

Family Conferences

Family conferences, a concept developed by the Ackerman Institute and used at several similar New York City schools, followed on the heels of the narrative progress reports. The family conference is a meeting between the teacher and the significant people in the student's life, including the student. It is a scheduled event, usually lasting anywhere from 15–30 minutes (sometimes longer if needed) to discuss the progress of the child as well as questions and concerns of family members. The child's work is on hand so that families have firsthand contact with the concrete evidence of the child's growth over time.

After several years, conferences at the Bronx New School evolved so that the students themselves actually prepared and conducted the conference presentation. Students presented their work to their families, demonstrating how they had grown, what they considered to be their best work, what areas they needed to work on more, and what was still "in progress." Student, teacher, and family members then discussed the student's future plans.

Information sharing that takes place at a conference is meant to flow in two ways. In addition to the information provided by the school, a substantial part of the family conference is devoted to the family telling teachers about the child's home interests and activities. They talk about the kinds of things people in the family do for relaxation and recreation, the books the child likes to read or the TV programs the child likes to watch, and the responsibilities the child has at home. This kind of information gives valuable clues about how to support learning in school. Connecting home events to school learning in this way is one of the reasons why all family members are generally invited to attend the family/school conference. Sometimes even a sibling can provide insights into the learning style or behavior of a student.

Through the experience of family conferences, a sense of community was built at the Bronx New School. Including the child in the conference strengthened trust, demonstrating that there were no behind-the-scenes secrets; that nothing would be done "to" the child without frank, collaborative discussions ending in mutual consent. Inviting the family to be contributors as well as receivers of knowledge increased their trust in the school as well. In the following quotation, one parent reflects on this in a letter to her local newspaper.

> [At the Bronx New School] I learned that parent involvement could be very rewarding—not for the right to negotiate which teachers my children would get or to lobby for good evaluation reports about my children, but so I might have the opportunity to help shape the quality of their education, and participate in workshops to learn about a philosophy of education that was different than the one I was raised with. This allowed me to share in my children's school experience and carry over at home the principles taught in school. Furthermore, I had the opportunity to broaden my own network of friends among the parents and staff who shared my vision for our children (Einbender, 1991, p. A15).

Other Communication Contexts

A context of continual communication between teachers, students, families, and community provided still other ways in which information about student learning and progress could be shared. In addition to recording individual children's work, teachers also documented the inquiry process of the class as a whole. Some teachers recorded the content of their daily class meetings that took place prior to and after work time. On extra-large chart paper, they would note:

1. Children's prior knowledge and understandings about a topic
2. Children's questions about it
3. Children's observations from activities or experiments in relation to it
4. Answers and comments in response to the original questions
5. New questions arising from the inquiry.

This record served to chart the journey of their inquiry. It also served as a document of their curriculum.

Exhibitions of student work were organized regularly at the conclusion of individual classroom studies. Classrooms were temporarily transformed into "museums" containing exhibits of student-made books, experiments, artwork, constructions, puppet shows, videos, musical performances. At exhibitions, students display and explain their work to classmates, schoolmates, family members, and school faculty.

Another way that information got shared was through curriculum letters that teachers wrote and sent home regularly, on a weekly, biweekly, or monthly basis. The letter reproduced in Figure 6.7 illustrates how planned activities and studies intersected with inquiry that emerged from students' interests and experiences.

The school's director also sent a weekly newsletter to families. Apart from informing the community about the events taking place in the school, the newsletter regularly discussed broader current educational issues, such as standardized testing, and explained specific educational practices, such as whole language, invented spelling, or new methods for teaching mathematics. The excerpt from one of these, presented in Figure 6.8, helps explain the school's philosophy and how it connects to the curriculum. This kind of reporting does more than provide information about events, or seek to reassure parents that "things are under control"—it also helps to develop parents' deeper understanding of the educational process and of their children's experiences, so that they can become full partners in the enterprise. The sense of a growing community is clear and palpable.

Even the school's Parent/Teacher Association published a newsletter to give voice to parent comments and concerns. In one issue, the "Feedback" column asked parents about the schools' strengths and weaknesses and about their feelings on homework and the upcoming progress reports. They received the following comments:

> We think reading and math are (the school's) strong points. Various class projects based on themes like architecture or sea life have helped our son to think creatively and to explore other related topics like how pollution and net fishing have affected our ocean life. It has made him socially conscious, too. [He gave part of his Christmas money to Greenpeace.]

> The school gives validity to the children's thoughts, expressions, and creativity.

> [One strength is] the degree of communication with parents.

> I appreciate the basic attitude which underlies all—that our children are valuable resources worthy of respect. It is my impression that they are treated kindly, which is not necessarily the case in other schools where I have worked. I'm glad that I am valued as a parent and seen as an ally, rather than "the enemy." In other schools, parents who want to take an active part in their child's education are often viewed with resentment and suspicion by teachers and other staff. I also appreciate the varied and stimulating activities (many books, recorder lessons, cooking, great trips). The parent meetings are an invaluable resource!

Figure 6.7. Teacher letter

March, 1991

Dear Family,

As I reread my two notebooks of our class meetings this year, I am impressed with the range of interests and knowledge of the class. Our main overall theme is still The Way Things Work and The Environment. The Way Things Work has been studied by building with various materials such as Capsella, Lego Technic, and Construx as well as with found materials. We discussed sinking and floating, the density of metals and liquids and materials and their relationship to the design and function of objects, such as boats. Our trip to the Intrepid inspired an in-depth study of airplanes and aerodynamics. Historic, present and future airplanes were created from cardboard and found materials. We gained a better understanding of simple machines through the exploration of Lego Technic. We talked about and worked with pulleys, gears, belts, and levers.

The Environment, endangered animals and extinction became important when we took our sessions at the Bronx Zoo. Recycling became part of our class. We made paper. A group of children got involved in a Trash Decor Exhibit and Sale, where we made $67. With that money we adopted 2 manatees, an acre of rainforest, and a whale. We began researching some of the answers to questions the class raised. Some children did clay models of endangered species. Man After Man is a theme that has captured the imagination of several children. This is an area inspired by Douglas Dixon, an anthropologist. He talks about man-altered humans who are adapted to specific environments.

We spend Wednesday afternoons with our wonderful architecture student, Alberto. We visited the new school site several times during its construction and built a scale model of our new room, including furniture.

Lots of other projects have occurred simultaneously throughout the year. Some of the children studied acids and bases. Think Big came back again by popular demand. MC Snake, our class pet, stimulated a lot of questions about snakes and reptiles which led to research and experimenting. The Gulf War inspired us to make a Peace Quilt out of needlepoint.

In math, we studied patterns and functions in numbers. We learned how to read charts and graphs. We learned how to use the Hundreds Board and multiplication tables. We explored palindromes and math riddles. We tackled division and higher numbers. We are currently working on fractions and decimals. The children have recently decided to have a combined quiet reading and writing time the first hour of the day. They work on different writing interests. We have published two newspapers and are currently working on a magazine.

As you can see, our days are busy. We are a class in constant dialogue and conversation. Our interests and ideas are many, as are the ways in which we express them. It has been a delight and a challenge to work with this class. I look forward to the rest of our year together.

Susan

Figure 6.8. Teacher letter

THE HAVING OF WONDERFUL IDEAS:

The vacation respite gave me an opportunity to read and think and deepen my understanding of the work we are doing in our school. You know, we are actually forging a new kind of educational environment—a school that views the "having of wonderful ideas" as the essence of learning. I'd like to share some thoughts on this matter with you.

Rather than trying to "cover" curriculum, in our school we are helping children to "uncover" parts of the world that they would not otherwise know how to tackle. We do this by providing children with real and purposeful materials, experiences, and questions in ways that suggest many things to be done with them. By offering children these opportunities, we believe that they cannot help but be inventive. They cannot help but learn.

Our educational goals are to give children first-hand knowledge of the world; to develop an interest in further exploration of the world; to give them confidence in their ability to find out about the world on their own; to help them know how to make discriminating use of secondary sources—books, experts, television, etc.—to continually learn more.

We help children to learn by accepting their ideas; by providing a setting that suggests wonderful ideas to catch their interest; by letting them raise and answer their own questions; by letting them realize that their ideas are significant; by encouraging them to feel good about themselves for having wonderful ideas.

We try to stimulate kids to have excitement, puzzlement, surprise, anticipation, uncertainty. We are delighted to hear them say "Ooh, I got it!" or "Gee, how can I do it?" We value them noticing something new, wondering about something, framing a question for oneself to answer, sensing contradiction in one's own ideas. We try to accept and provide lots of occasions for honest attempts and for wrong outcomes.

We view "wrong answers" as legitimate and important elements of learning. Wrong answers help children come honestly to terms with their own ideas. They are often very productive. Any wrong idea that is corrected through experience provides far more depth than if one never had a wrong idea to begin with. For example, you will have mastered an idea far more deeply if you have considered alternatives, tried to work them out where they didn't work, and figured out why it was that it didn't work. What you do about what you don't know is, in the final analysis, what determines what you will ultimately know.

We trust that children (people) have a natural desire to learn. We believe that active learning will lead to independent learning. We believe that active learning will awaken your child's interest in the world and develop your child's confidence in his/her abilities. We believe that this is the best way to prepare your child for a life-time of exploration and growth.

To ensure ongoing communication and accountability to parent concerns and student needs, the school developed a variety of formats in which families could meet with teachers and with one another to discuss the never-ending issues, questions, and concerns that arise in the course of building a school. Class meetings were led by each classroom teacher twice a year to familiarize parents with the routines and expectations of each particular classroom group. All-school meetings took place monthly, serving as forums for discussion of the school's philosophy and values.

Just as the school's assessment strategies provided many ways to look at how students learn, all of these communication structures tried to provide the school community with multiple opportunities to learn about professional practice, to express concerns, to request explanations, to offer suggestions, or to share knowledge and information. In this way school community members participated in shaping the school's policies and practices.

SUPPORTS FOR AUTHENTIC ASSESSMENT

Structuring Time for Communication and Assessment

As a new school, BNS was able to invent new approaches to structuring school time and activities without having to undo existing attachments to a "master schedule" or to traditional procedures. Recognizing that planning, assessing, and reflecting on students' learning are crucial aspects of successful teaching, BNS looked for ways in which teachers could have more time for the professional responsibilities involved in their assessment processes—recording, organizing, reviewing, reflecting on, and summarizing their data—as well as for the professional development needed to help them learn how to observe and to teach in new ways.

The staff reorganized the school's weekly schedule so that each Friday, the director, along with other support personnel, supervised the children during an extra-long lunch and recess period. This gave teachers almost a 2-hour period in which they could focus on assessment-related tasks. In addition, classes were occasionally combined for special projects so that teachers could be relieved for a day or half-day to work on records. Some district funds were also obtained to reimburse teachers for a portion of the time they spent on assessment tasks.

The assessment processes themselves created "new" time in class because they helped teachers shift to a "facilitator" role, replacing the role of "instructor" always at the center of the classroom. Because assessing students as they are actively engaged in different kinds of learning tasks creates a concomitant need to teach in ways that allow active engagement of students, a part of the traditional time problem is alleviated naturally as teachers create learning settings in which students are working rather than listening to the teacher. This frees teachers more to watch, record, and reflect on their students' work. As they look for direct evidence of many forms of student work, teachers provide more opportunities for students to engage in these many forms. This in turn requires them to structure their classrooms so they can provide a fuller range of independent activities. One Bronx New School teacher explains it this way:

> When a classroom is set up as a workshop in which children can work independently and in which the teacher assumes the role of facilitator rather than as the central figure around which all interaction occurs, the teacher is freed to engage in the essential task of observing and recording children's behavior and their work. While tremendous preparation, scheduling and thinking is required to get this process started, once it begins, it takes on a momentum of its own and results in changes in children's thinking, behavior, and dynamics. The children begin to function more autonomously. Subsequently, the teacher is freed up to move about the room, to jot down notes, and to conference with individuals or groups for purposes of assessment and instruction. In this conception of the classroom, assessment, in a sense, *is* the essence of teaching.

When Bronx New School teachers changed in this way, they indeed had more time for collecting assessment data. As they talked and learned about how to keep records and then experienced the effects of this on their teaching, they also came to feel that the time they devoted to this work was well spent. These notes, excerpted from a teacher's journal, discuss the benefits of their new approach to assessment:

> The day is so completely different! There's a calmness in the room. Everyone is busy. K. is calm. J. is happy, excited about working with bubbles. G. loves illustrating and drawing. S. is organizing a dummy for a magazine. N. is working on gliders. H. is working with balloons to figure out motion.
> The meeting today was the best so far. The technique of notetaking seems worth developing. I don't quite know how to do this well yet—but I feel it's right because of the way things are at worktime. The work seems to generate itself. The children are beginning to emerge.

Teacher Dialogue and Professional Collaboration

Teachers had occasions to talk with one another about what they saw and what they thought at weekly, after-school faculty meetings, at semiannual, all-school retreats, and at regular conferences with one another and the director. Here they questioned assumptions and asked questions of themselves and others in much the same way that they tried to encourage this in their students. Together they explored themes central to understanding their teaching; posed problems; discussed dilemmas that they were finding difficult to answer; questioned knowledge they found to be problematic; defined the kind of evidence they sought in order to document and explore issues; and suggested ways they could link up diverse experiences.

The following notes from a weekly staff meeting give an example of the kinds of conversations that promote and deepen educational understandings:

> Our discussion focused on the question: What are the values we hold dear and promote?
> Other questions emerged: How do we assess these values? What inadequacies/pitfalls do standardized tests have in regards to them? How can we best prepare our students for the tests since they are a city/state mandate? What are the implications of test results inside and outside this school?

Other meetings provided occasions to discuss still other issues that arose in the course of daily teaching practice: the practicalities of keeping records and storing information, the mysteries of a particular child and how to find his/her strengths, the difference between using observation for the purpose of facilitating a child's *own* learning agenda versus observing for the purpose of getting him/her to perform the *teacher's* predetermined agenda. Everyone's plate was always full of food for thought.

These conversations spilled over to teachers' interactions at lunch, in the hall, and after school. Staff were excited to be refining and deepening their practice, evolving the school's outlook and philosophy. Through shared understandings of the children they knew, they were coming to better know learning and curriculum. The teachers themselves speak about this process:

> The conversations and dialogue we had together helped me a lot. At the end of the day I would leave the children with only those crazy last ten minutes as a memory. But then, as I was cleaning my room, I'd talk to B. and she would ask me questions that would push me to look back and reflect on all the other things that happened. This helped me to see the children in a different light and gave me food for curriculum building for the next period of time.

Another teacher had this to say:

> This is a place where teachers have the opportunity for the kind of support and reflection that they are trying to give to children. We are involved in an ongoing process of actively making knowledge about teaching and learning and about children's learning. What it takes to do this is to always be observing, always reflecting, always evolving. This underscores for me what it means to be a community of learners.

The kind of professional development discussed here is different from the staff "training" that takes place in many schools. It is not packaged or preconceived but process-oriented, evolving from teacher dialogue and reflection. It is based on the assumption that a teacher's learning, like that of a student's, is never finished but is always in the making.

DEALING WITH STANDARDIZED TESTING

In spite of the nourishing professional environment that innovative teaching and assessment practices provided for teachers, children, and families at the Bronx New School, standardized testing still exerted a powerful impact on everyone's life. Children at the Bronx New School (and in other similar places) are still required to take city, state, and federally mandated standardized tests.

Despite all that has been written about their damaging effects (Darling-Hammond, 1989, 1991; Neill, 1989; Oakes, 1985), the voice of these tests still rings loudest to the public with respect to assumptions about school accountability. As long as they continue to be the predominantly accepted form of assessment, tension for teachers and schools will exist. Teachers will be torn between two responsibilities—enacting developmentally appropriate, multifaceted, learner-centered teaching and adequately preparing students for the often inappropriate, one-dimensional, decontextualized recall of facts and skills that the tests demand.

As Lauren Resnick, a nationally renowned expert on learning, explains in her argument for the creation of more authentic forms of assessment:

> We've got a terrible model of what knowledge is, and what we care about, built into those tests: Collections of decontextualized and decomposed bits of knowledge that do not add up to competent thinking. . . . We have the assembly-line version of knowledge: Break it into little bits so any nincompoop can fill in the bubbles. . . . [T]he only way to get going on what we need to do [educationally] is to attack directly what is one of the most powerful dampers to the kind of change we need. Talk to teachers who have caught on to the idea that the kind of teaching required in a "thinking curriculum" is possible, and then ask them, "What is the biggest barrier to it?" Their answer every time is, "Those standardized tests are coming, and I'm afraid my kids won't pass them." . . . The pressures to drill to the test are

overwhelming, and they are overwhelming mainly in the schools that serve our poorest children. (Education Week, 1992, p. S6)

The seemingly unresolvable tension between knowledge as it is used in real performance contexts and knowledge as it is asked for on standardized tests creates great anxiety for school people, even those most committed to innovative teaching and assessment practices. Teacher after teacher spoke about these tensions in an interview session with the school faculty. Others spoke of the limited information the tests provide.

> It was very painful to subject children to the tests. Some of my kids had grown tremendously through the course of the year. They made great progress in becoming independent readers but were still unable to read a passage out of context without picture clues. The records I kept of them could show this growth. But I knew it wouldn't show up on the tests.

Another teacher spoke of the tests' demoralizing effect:

> The experience of taking the test was terribly demoralizing for many children. Sometimes I felt like all the growth in self-esteem and self-confidence that took place in the course of an entire year went down the drain in the two or three hours of taking the test.

Yet another addressed their developmental inappropriateness:

> The tests are so frustrating! They often ask children to do things that they are not ready to do, that developmentally they are not capable of doing. For example, there's research to document the fact that most second graders really don't comprehend and can't conceptualize place value. Yet second graders are expected to do place value problems on the math test. What do you do? You can't force children to learn something they aren't ready for. And if you teach them the tricks so that they can do the problems on the test, that gets in the way of their thinking and makes it more difficult for them to *really* understand when they would otherwise have been ready.

Another worried about the disjuncture between standardized test events and children's growth and development, which is uneven and takes place over long time spans:

> The problem with the tests is that they can't really reflect growth and development. At best they can only measure isolated, decontextualized skills or facts at one moment in time in a child's life. But decisions—high-stake ones that may determine or significantly affect that child's future—are made on the basis of that one or two hours on one day in the child's life.

Despite convictions about the inadequacies of the tests, Bronx New School teachers were painfully cognizant of the consequences the tests can have for their students. While test results would not significantly affect children's lives in this particular school, the scores still signified achievement to many families, to the school district, and to the world at large. So an effort was made to prepare students for them. All teachers agreed that the best preparation was to continue developing a learning environment that fostered skill acquisition in as meaningful and purposeful a context as possible. The tests were *never* to drive the curriculum.

A conscious differentiation was made between real learning—for example, how to read or how to think mathematically—and test preparation. Several weeks prior to the testing date, teachers exposed children to the format of the tests. They taught them how to fill in the bubbles on a separate answer sheet. They also taught strategies for answering multiple choice questions. Children were constantly reassured that their test scores would not affect their life in the school and that what happened on the test would be viewed as merely a few hours of one day in the course of the year. They were continually reminded of the tests' limitations in demonstrating what students know and can do and that ongoing records of student work really provide this information.

Despite these anxieties and the pervasive belief that tests placed significant limitations on learning, students at the Bronx New School actually performed quite well on them. The areas in which they showed the greatest strength were the sections that allowed them to demonstrate their abilities to "problem-solve" in mathematics and to make sense of text in a holistic way. The older the children, the better the scores. It seemed that as the children progressed through the grades, the limiting format of the tests became less of a hindrance in allowing them to demonstrate what they knew and what they could do.

AUTHENTIC ASSESSMENT'S IMPACT ON FAMILIES

Many families were staunch advocates of the teaching and assessment practices being developed at the Bronx New School. As they witnessed their child's educational experience they appreciated the differences that life at the Bronx New School had created. Many noted how happy their children were about attending school, how the school supported the diversity of children's backgrounds and talents, how the teaching approach encouraged curiosity and a love of learning, how segregation of children with special needs was replaced with special attention and special supports within the context of the mainstream community. They also understood how the school's assessment practices and reporting structures provided them with more information about their child than they had ever received from traditional test scores and report cards. Some of their views are expressed in the following excerpt from a parent letter to the local community newspaper:

As an active parent in our school, I have watched it turn into a true community of learners. I watched children take control of their own learning. I
watched children learn to respect each other in a cooperative learning environment. I watched children with special needs being mainstreamed. I
watched children learn to resolve conflicts in a non-violent manner. I
watched children, through the creative use of discarded materials, build
bridges, skyscrapers and planets. I watched creativity flourish in so many different ways. I watched children from diverse racial, ethnic and socio-eco-
nomic backgrounds living, loving and learning together. (Flynn, 1991, p.A15)

Despite widespread agreement with these sentiments, some families at the
school remained uneasy about their individual children's progress in this nontraditional environment that was different from what they had known before.
Although elated by the growth and development they witnessed in their children, these parents needed to talk, share, compare, ask questions, and express
concerns, doubts, or anxieties with one another and with school faculty. The
school staff was aware of this tension. They soon realized that the best way to
address it was to provide many forums for discussion, not only of authentic
assessment but of the educational values, goals, and practices on which all of
these practices are based. The various communication formats mentioned earlier—the Director's weekly Notes, teachers' curriculum letters, class meetings,
all-school meetings, PTA News, progress reports, family conferences—were
created precisely for this reason. They helped families to learn about learning,
encouraging and supporting them to recognize the strengths of their child, to
share with the school their knowledge of their child, their culture, and their
community, and to work together with the school to support children's growth
and development. A homework assignment directed to parents of students in
a 2nd/3rd grade class, reproduced in Figure 6.9, was used by the teacher to
explain aspects of her teaching philosophy and methodology.

The Director's weekly Notes also explained the purposes of some
school practices. For example:

How do children learn writing in the whole language approach? In
the whole language approach, children begin to write from the first
day of school. Teachers allow, accept, and encourage them to write
personal thoughts, notes, letters, cards, and stories. Children can do
this because they are allowed to represent their compositions through
pictures, marks, and scribble, because writing is viewed as the communication of messages.

Children can tell stories at any age but they have difficulty when
they are young with conventional symbolic representation (conventional letters) and spelling. Sometimes the teacher is a scriber or
recorder of children's stories, but often students are encouraged to
use their own invented representations to "write" their own stories.
This helps them to make phonetic sound-symbol connections that
they can also use in their reading.

Figure 6.9. Homework assignment

Jan. 10, 1991

Dear Families,

Tonight's H.W. involves reflecting back on our trip to see "Blue Planet" yesterday. For hesitant writers, drawing a picture *first* of something they were struck by and then writing about it (or simply describing the drawing) can help. Or ask your child to *tell* you about what they saw before writing. Verbalizing their ideas before writing them down helps the child realize he or she has something worth saying.

Now the actual writing—the hard part for many of us.

* If your child starts right in, not needing your assistance—let him go. *But,* when he is done, gently ask him to go back and check it over. Do all the sentences *end* with a period (or question mark)? Do they all *begin* with a capital letter? Questions about spelling?
* Help with spelling by:
   * Encouraging them to listen for the first letter sound.
   * Giving them words that *rhyme* with the one they're searching for. For example, they're trying to spell *"stand."* Run this list by them: land, band, hand, st___? (You can also refer to them as "word families." This is the *AND* family.)
   * If you write them down, your child will begin to see the pattern.
   * Reversals are *normal* in beginning writers, i.e., "saw" for "was"; "fo" for "of"; "paly" for "play"
   * Encourage them to write the words as they *hear* them when said slowly, i.e., Man - hat - tan for "Manhattan". (Of course not *all* words are this cooperative.)
   * When your child is desperate for a word—give it to him—this should not be a battle.
   * If none of the above seems to help your work with your child—let him write as he feels and *please* write a note on the back to let me know.
   * Remember, writing *will* come just as learning to read did! Trust your child!

Thanks—

Sue

When children read back their pictures and scribbles, we are invited into *their* world of symbols. We learn what they understand about language, what they can do with it, and how we can help them to develop. Because they see conventional text everywhere—on signs, labels, in their dictated stories, as well as in the literature stories we read to them several times a day—they gradually integrate more conventional spelling and grammar forms into their writing. Older students also learn spelling, grammar, and usage during the process of writing. Spelling ability grows proportionately to the amount of writing and reading in which students engage. Spelling, grammar, and usage are further refined when students edit their own stories and those of their classmates. When needed, students receive individual and small-group lessons on these conventions.

As conversation about teaching and learning spread throughout the school community, families increased their understandings and their commitment to learner-centered education. This conversation soon spread beyond the boundaries of the school to connect them with others involved in school reform initiatives. Families began to speak at conferences and forums and to write articles about their experiences. This excerpt from an article in one of the city's major newspapers, part of the parents' efforts to save the school when it was threatened with consolidation, gives a sense of the depth of their conviction and understanding.

> [Before my daughter came to the Bronx New School], when she entered first grade, her natural love of math and her pleasure in playing with numbers was squashed by a well-intentioned teacher who was ignorant of the way children really learn. You see, my daughter knew without thinking that 3 + 3 = 6. But she wrote the 6 backward, and the answer was marked wrong. So she thought that 3 + 3 equaled something other than 6. In fact, she wrote all her numbers backwards and so all her answers were marked wrong. Her ease with computation was destroyed. For children at that stage of development, backwards or forwards is all the same thing. That confusion sorts itself out in its own time. But children in our school system are not trusted to learn in their own time. They must learn according to the timetable of "experts" who measure and quantify these things. At the Bronx New School, children learned how to learn rather than how to endure one more tedious day. [When my daughter came there she] slowly began to regain her self-confidence and curiosity. I felt such relief knowing that she was valued for her uniqueness and was being encouraged to take control of her learning—to trust herself as she was trusted by her teacher. (Danzig, 1991, pp. 48, 90)

A COMMUNITY OF LEARNERS

This story of assessment at the Bronx New School gives rise to some thoughts about teaching, learning, and the development of community. It illustrates how observation and documentation of student work can be used for assessment purposes. In contrast to traditional standardized assessments, which consider but a single dimension of what a student can do at an end-point of learning, this kind of assessment is longitudinal, multidimensional, and richly textured. It allows for many forms of expression of many kinds of knowledge. Rather than comparing students against one another, it is both self-referenced and theory-referenced (Johnston & Harmon, 1992). It compares students to their past work, developing a portrait of individual growth over time, grounded in a developmental continuum.

This account of the Bronx New School illustrates the ability of authentic assessments to inform and support the teaching and learning process. In contrast to norm-referenced, standardized tests, which rarely yield information useful to teaching, authentic assessments provide understandings that help students from diverse backgrounds and experiences identify and meet their own standards as well as achieve the goals defined by their community.

The accounts of teaching and learning presented here strengthen the view that no two people have the same background, learn in a like manner, or take away the same knowledge from the same experience. Standardized teaching and assessment *don't* address this fact, while learner-centered curricula—grounded in the learner's own interests, purposes, and prior experiences and understandings—*do*. Curriculum that does this is, by nature, intricately connected to assessment and can be defined as "opportunities for inquiry," in which the learner is the primary constructor and integrator of knowledge who can be guided best by the in-depth knowledge teachers gain through their observations of students and their work. Such a curriculum focuses on the attainment of a common set of broad and comprehensive goals for all students, while allowing for each individual's different approaches to learning.

This study also points to the importance of a learning environment designed to provide multiple kinds of learning experiences and multiple forms of expression of that learning. Such an environment is richly provisioned with many different kinds of materials, is activity-based and inquiry-oriented. It accommodates students of different ages who possess varying strengths and abilities. It encourages continuous dialogue among peers, and it places both teacher and students in the role of learner.

Many different forms of assessment can be used to examine and learn from student work. Akeem's story, for example, illustrates how multiple indicators of growth and development can reveal student strengths, which are a central resource for supporting learning. Building on strengths ensures that students' diverse abilities get recognized and used.

The tension between standards and standardization is another issue raised by this case study. Standards provide common ground and common goals, while standardization requires uniform formats and outcomes that deny the uniqueness of each learner. In the course of doing their work, Bronx New School teachers resolved this tension by developing standards of practice—shared outlooks that allow for a variety of learning formats and a range of student outcomes. As teachers developed similar ways of looking at children and the learning process, they came to agreement about broad, common goals for student achievement. Within this context, personalized teaching methods and assessment instruments, as well as diverse demonstrations of learning outcomes, can be encouraged and can flourish. A common language and culture emerges and learning standards are defined.

This struggle cannot take place without collaboration and conversation among teachers and the school community. Assessment-related discussions, as well as experience with the assessments themselves, help teachers to refine their perceptions of students' skills and abilities. Ongoing dialogue leads to a continuous examination of teaching strategies, of classroom activities, and of goals and standards for learning. This enhances teaching effectiveness and professional growth, contributes to a sense of professional renewal and empowerment, and serves as a catalyst for the development of a shared vision.

Including the families of the school community in these discussions and experiences provides a meaningful way for families to be involved in the life of any school. Bronx New School families were valued as partners in the educational process. Their knowledge of their children was used by teachers to inform and enhance the learning that took place in school. In return, teachers continually presented information about child development, about learning, and about teaching methodology that further enhanced families' understandings of how best to support their children's growth. The result of this partnership was an informed community better equipped—both individually and publicly—to advocate for quality education.

These stories of families, teachers, and children at the Bronx New School bring to life John Dewey's (1938) conception of a "community of learners." In this vision, all members of the learning community are valued and respected for their knowledge, their contribution, and their needs. Each voice is listened to and each voice is honored. Authentic assessment practices and learner-centered teaching, woven together into the fabric of a school, are central to the realization of this vision.

NOTES

1. Students' names have been changed and are denoted by an asterisk. Teachers' names are unchanged.

2. Teachers in the Bronx New School were known to the children and parents by their first names. We have preserved that convention here.

7

MAKING ASSESSMENT WORK FOR STUDENTS AND SCHOOLS

The case studies in this volume illustrate how powerfully teachers and principals can use assessment practices as a means to help themselves become more successful with students and more accountable for learning—both their own ongoing learning and the learning of their students. In these schools, the interaction of teaching, learning, and assessment practices creates the grist and the energy for developing learning organizations. This is made possible by the fact that the schools have restructured roles, relationships, time, and courses to allow for serious collective work on the part of both students and staff.

By working on standards and assessments, looking carefully at students' work and progress, and working to develop supports for student success, teachers are engaged in constant learning about the needs and talents of their students, about the effectiveness of their teaching strategies, and about the nature of teaching and learning. By working toward challenging standards on authentic tasks, students are engaged in constant learning about the nature of high-quality work, about themselves as learners and workers, and about the phenomena they are studying. By working collectively to create and evaluate assessments, by rethinking schoolwide practices so that they enable students to work on and succeed at complex, extended performances, and by communicating in new ways about students' work, schools are engaged in constant organizational learning about the effectiveness of their practices.

Another powerful theme in the cases is how these schools' teaching, learning, and assessment practices are able to support high standards without standardization—to promote excellence in the context of diversity. They illustrate what Howard Gardner (1991) calls the pursuit of "individually configured excellence," enabling students to find and develop their unique talents, to build from their experiences and strengths a strong scaffolding for extending their work and thinking. The schools' teaching and assessment practices acknowledge and nurture students' strengths and interests in ways that enable students to develop habits of high-quality performance that are expressed in many different forms.

The power of authentic assessment as a learning tool and as a support for high levels of student attainment depends on several factors that require much more fundamental school restructuring. First, in order to use assessments to support student, teacher, and organizational learning, schools must function as communities; that is, they must create an environment in which faculty, with parents, work collectively to define goals and standards, to shape policies and practices, and to inform each other's work. Within such a community, restructured uses of time, roles, and responsibilities are needed to sustain authentic teaching and assessment practices, to enable strong relationships with students so that teachers can come to know their minds well, and to support teacher work and learning on problems of practice. None of these schools are structured like traditional schools; their practices and their successes would be impossible within the confines of traditional schedules, grouping arrangements, egg-crate classrooms, and the isolated departments and grade levels typical of large bureaucratic schools. Faculty empowerment and shared decision making are important for developing and sustaining these new roles and relationships, as is committed leadership.

In addition, members of school communities must be engaged in the development and use of the assessments. This is because teacher learning about the deeper structures of curriculum, the nature and nuances of student thinking, and the connections between teaching efforts and student performances derives substantially from firsthand, constructivist encounters with assessment development, and from the subsequent evaluation of student work. Assessment reforms can increase student success only if they change both the kinds of tasks students are asked to engage in and the kinds of inquiry schools and teachers are called on to undertake as they bring assessment into the heart of the teaching and learning process. Thus, the locus of assessment development and implementation is as important as the nature of the assessment tools and strategies. Assessments that are externally developed and scored cannot transform the knowledge and understandings of teachers—and of school organizations—even if they are more performance-based than are current tests (Darling-Hammond & Ancess, in press).

ASSESSMENT AND THE BUILDING OF LEARNING ORGANIZATIONS

Teacher learning is a recurring theme in these and other studies of schools engaged in authentic assessment. Over and over again, teachers explain how their understanding of learning generally, and in particular of the learning approaches and styles of individual students, is enhanced by opportunities to look at student work deliberately and collectively with other teachers, sometimes with parents, and frequently with the students themselves. As work with the *Primary Language Record* and the *Descriptive Review of a Child* illustrates at the Bronx New School, careful observation of even a few students in-depth can help teachers to learn about all students. This kind of learning about student thinking and performance also occurs in secondary school exhibitions, where juries of teachers are able to carefully examine the work of individual students who present and defend their projects or portfolios.

In many cases, engagement in these assessment strategies helps teachers develop a curricular vision for their teaching as well as a focus on how to connect learners to those learning goals. The more teachers learn about their students from new assessments, the more aware they become of how to change teaching practices to better meet their students' needs.

Articulating values and goals for schooling and developing assessments that demonstrate if and how students meet those goals helps teachers clarify and develop their thinking about teaching, about student learning, and about curriculum development. When school communities engage in these tasks together, they create common understandings and shared meanings. This kind of concrete communication about student learning, rare in most schools, is a prerequisite for developing the shared vision that is essential if any change is to succeed. Such communication, "vitally social and vitally shared," is critical to the building of a community (Dewey, 1916, p. 6). By building on a foundation grounded in vivid, concrete conversations about students and learning, communities can proceed to develop shared norms and standards for their practice.

The process of developing standards of practice requires that teachers take a close look at their teaching strategies, at curriculum, at the environments they construct for learning, and—perhaps most important—at the students themselves. As teachers talk together about these aspects of their work in light of what they have learned from observing their students, they begin to understand learning more deeply. They find themselves developing new ideas, new ways in which to implement their ideas, and new structures that will support their practices.

The process of developing assessments and evaluating student work is, in itself, a powerful form of professional development—one which recognizes that growth results from teachers engaged together in dialogue and reflection rather than from "experts" who deliver information at training sessions or one-shot workshops. This kind of professional development takes teachers out of the role of passive receivers of information and places them instead in the position of collaboratively and actively constructing knowledge about teaching. It replaces delivery of packaged "teacher-proof" curriculum units and lesson plans with the provision of opportunities for teachers to synthesize (individually and collectively) what they observe about students, what they know about human development and learning theory, and what they know about curriculum content and skill development. This kind of professional development also takes teachers out of the role of being passive recipients of others' decisions and places them instead in a position of directly acting together on decisions that can affect their students' futures and their own work. When teachers are empowered in these ways they become engaged in their work and a professional culture is created. Dewey (1916) called it a "democratic community of learners."

This is part of the answer to the questions: "Why would teachers want to take on all of this?" "What are the rewards of taking on the 'extra' functions once handled by commercial test developers, textbook makers, and district offices?" The simplest answer is that creating with colleagues, learning and inventing, and experiencing ever greater success with students actually do prove to be their own rewards. CPESS teacher Edwina Branch described the rigor and commitment accompanying the collegial process of assessment development.

> Teachers pushed each other to answer "Why are we doing this?" "And what do we want kids to get out of it?". . . I can't imagine right now trying to teach without thinking about assessment all the time. It's easier to be in your own little world and not to be accountable to anybody. But it's not the best thing for the kids, and it's not really the best thing for my teaching.

Noting that the level of conversation about learning at CPESS is leagues beyond what had been the norm in her previous school, Branch observes that she feels sorry for other teachers who do not have the opportunity to participate in such a discourse about teaching and assessment. "Going through the process . . . made me what I am [as a teacher]. I think that makes all the difference in the world."

In these schools and in many others, assessment development has become an opportunity for teachers to become both problem-framers and problem-solvers, taking hold of the destiny of their school and collectively steering its course to enhance student success. Their willingness to submit themselves to a rigorous process of inquiry, evaluated by the outcomes of their students, makes them reflective decision makers about how and what students learn, what strategies and supports are necessary for high levels of learning, and what changes are needed for these things to occur.

Concerns about what's best for students come to the fore when the students and their work are at the center of the conversation. Authentic assessment can help teachers not only to focus more clearly on students but also to include students and their parents in a more inclusive learning community. In all of these schools, portfolio development and performance assessments involve students in reflecting on their learning. This process helps both students and teachers better understand how students think and what they know, demonstrating respect for student knowledge and acknowledging them as partners in teaching. Students develop greater responsibility and commitment to the learning process as an outgrowth of this involvement. Families are also engaged in the process of assessing student growth. The parent conferences for the *Primary Language Record* and the graduation committees at Central Park East Secondary School (CPESS) illustrate how family input into assessment enlarges and enriches teacher understandings of their students. It enables teachers to view their students through a variety of lenses and contexts while enabling parents to view their children in new ways, better able to appreciate both the processes of development and the efforts and goals of the school.

As teachers' discussion throughout the case studies reveals, the proliferation of feedback emerging from authentic assessment practices engages teachers deeply in the dilemmas of their practice and profession, creating a need for communication with colleagues. As teachers seek out the time to communicate about their students and their practice, as schools find the time and space in their schedules for such communication, a school culture characterized by opportunities for continuous improvement takes root.

Peter Senge (1992) explains why the development of learning organizations requires the opportunity for both reflection and action and the replacement of external controls by internal processes for assessment and decision making:

> (M)aking continual learning a way of organizational life . . . can only be achieved by breaking with the traditional authoritarian, command and control hierarchy where the top thinks and the local acts, to merge thinking and acting at all levels. This represents a profound re-orientation in the concerns of management—a shift from a predominant concern with controlling to a predominant concern with learning. (p. 2)

Learning, he goes on to explain, builds on intrinsic motivation—people's innate curiosity and desire to improve their work, which is encouraged when they have the opportunity to discover, experiment, observe the results of their actions, and continually refine their approach. The engine for continual improvement that is created through this process is removed when goal-setting, planning, and evaluation are conducted outside the organization or by those at the top of a bureaucratic hierarchy. It exists when the hands-on work of simultaneously thinking and creating is spread throughout the organization and motivated by shared goals and vision (Senge, 1992).

Actually, the lesson is much older. The Eight Year Study, conducted by the Progressive Education Association in the 1930s, illustrates the significance of participatory decision making about matters of real substance. During those years, a group of 30 experimental schools individually created "break the mold" forms of education, including integrated forms of instruction and authentic forms of assessment. The study demonstrated, from its evaluation over 8 years of nearly 1,500 matched pairs of students from experimental and nonexperimental schools, that on virtually any dimension of student development and performance—from academic honors to civic social responsibility; by the judgment of professors, teachers, or others—the students from experimental schools outperformed those from traditional schools (Smith & Tyler, 1942).

Most important, the study found that the more successful schools were characterized not by the particular innovation they had adopted but by their willingness to search and struggle for valid objectives, for new strategies, and for new forms of assessment (Chamberlin, Chamberlin, Drought, & Scott, 1942, p. 182). It was the *process* of collective struggle that produced the vitality, the shared vision, and the conviction that allowed these schools to redesign education in fundamentally different ways. If the processes and outcomes of education are defined by those outside of schools, schools and community members are deprived of the opportunity to engage in the kind of empowering and enlivening dialogue needed to create learning communities.

Despite superficial recognition that local involvement is critical to improvement, the current policy dialogue is largely characterized by plans for the use of externally developed and imposed assessments as levers for externally imposed rewards and sanctions (Hornbeck, 1992; O'Day & Smith, 1993). Though hierarchical controls and punitive forms of management have not produced high-quality schooling in the past, those committed to top-down governance feel that relaxing prescriptions could undermine accountability and reduce standards. The success of the schools we examined in creating high standards without standardization—indeed, the fact that they could not have done it otherwise—should inform the policy debate.

CREATING STANDARDS WITHOUT STANDARDIZATION

Students in these case-study schools overwhelmingly represent those groups that conventionally score low on traditional, high-stakes, standardized assessments: low-income and working class students, many classified as at-risk, with limited English proficiency, or identified for special education. Traditional tests and tracking schemes often trap these students in an iterative cycle of low scores and low-level learning opportunities in schools and classes where they are taught in ways that mimic the rote learning and passive format of multiple choice tests (Oakes, 1985). Systemically denied access to rigorous and interesting content, along with opportunities to develop intellectually, they are imprisoned in a "Catch 22" cycle of intellectual deprivation: In order to get access to an excellent education, they must first demonstrate the kind of performance that results from an excellent education.

As Kornhaber and Gardner (1993) note, excellence is developed "in meaningful contexts over an extended period of time." They also note that individuals who develop excellent performances do not start out with this capacity.

> Instead, they engage in a series of efforts, which include many small victories and defeats, which ultimately enable them to meet high standards in a discipline. To help young people excel, schools need to create conditions that foster sustained engagement and encourage reflection on one's own and others' efforts. (p. 3)

In these schools, where assessment and instruction work together to provide students with access to challenging forms of learning, opportunities to successfully develop higher order skills, and options to find the most effective means possible to demonstrate their knowledge and mastery of skills, we see excellence under construction. Classroom interactions, student work, exhibitions, and hallway conversations provide widespread evidence of in-depth learning, intellectual habits of mind, quality products, and student responsiveness to rigorous standards. The cases demonstrate that students frequently denied the opportunity to engage in complex content and higher order skills do in fact master them when they are given the opportunity to do so. Students at CPESS and Hodgson learn deeply when they develop extensive projects and publicly demonstrate and defend their knowledge. Students at International High School recognize the intensive learning they have achieved when they complete the in-depth mastery statement at the close of their *Motion* portfolio. Elementary school students at P.S. 261 and at the Bronx New School develop habits of sustained engagement and a sense of standards as they assemble portfolios of their best work, reflect on their reading and what it means for them, and revise their writing.

Authentic assessment as practiced in these five schools illustrates that excellence is not dependent on standardization. Standardization, based on unidimensional views of success and on acknowledging a narrow spectrum of performance as worthy or legitimate achievement, precludes for many students any possibility of excellence. Because diverse ways of demonstrating excellence are neither permissible nor possible on narrowly constructed standardized tests, many students are denied the opportunity to exhibit the full range of their knowledge and skills. They do not have vehicles with which to demonstrate the "varied array of mental competencies, strengths, or 'intelligences'" that they possess, and most schools miss opportunities to develop these wide-ranging abilities (Kornhaber & Gardner, 1993, pp. 2–3). Because the case-study schools have developed assessments that legitimize multiple ways of knowing, and that acknowledge diversity and the contextual nature of learning, human experience, and performance as the norm, access to achievement, success, and "individually configured excellence" become possible.

Assessments that acknowledge multiple forms of excellence promote educational equity because they release learning and performance from the stranglehold format that characterizes standardized tests, giving students access to more valid and varied means by which to demonstrate their abilities. The graduation portfolio at CPESS, for example, permits students to demonstrate their knowledge and skills in a variety of ways so that they are free to find the best means to show what they know: research papers, projects, essays, original artworks, videotaped performances, and written and oral examinations. Because the learning experiences that produce these products and performances offer diverse opportunities for sustained and deep engagement, they are rich with possibilities for excellence. By allowing students to select how they will demonstrate their abilities, these assessments increase students' access to excellence without compromising high standards.

The assessments we examined make more rigorous demands on students than do the low-level recall skills that characterize standardized tests. The criteria and processes for judging student learning in these high schools require students to demonstrate critical thinking and to defend their work before juries of experts from different disciplines, as well as before peers. The multiple perspectives these assessments bring to bear increase the possibility that the complexities of learning will be respected, that assessors will strive for rich understanding as a path to judgment, and that the validity of diverse modes of performance will be acknowledged.

When diversity is the norm, it also becomes legitimate for schools to create and acknowledge diverse "contexts for engagement" (Kornhaber & Gardner, 1993, p. 10). In these schools, assessment creates many contexts for engagement. These are apparent in the accounts of P.S. 261 and Bronx New School teachers looking for arenas of student interest and strength that will enable initial successes upon which further engagement and learning can be built. Assessment at International High School supports an effective ESL strategy that provides collaborative contexts for engagement, starting with the unique experiences and language skills of immigrant students and promoting content acquisition in concert with language development. At Hodgson and CPESS, faculty guidance as students select and develop project and portfolio topics consistent with their interests and strengths promotes a personalized context characterized by high levels of student ownership and motivation for sustained engagement.

These studies suggest that the responsiveness and flexibility inherent in assessments that are real "performances of understanding" (Kornhaber and Gardner, 1993) can release students, teachers, and schools from the shackles that standardization clamps on teaching and learning. By encouraging curriculum, teaching, and assessment practices that support students in developing high-quality, individualized products and performance, using the best possible means to demonstrate what they know, these schools have lifted the ceiling standardization has imposed on student achievement. As typically low-scoring students have had expanded access to knowledge and opportunities to learn, their productivity and motivation have increased and the quality of their work has risen. Student and teacher testimony from all of these case-study schools, along with samples and documentation of student work and achievement, support this conclusion.

Faculty in all of the schools describe how authentic assessments have raised teachers' expectations of students and heightened teachers' standards for their own performance. As standards are better articulated and supports for high-quality products and performances are put in place, both teachers and students raise their sights. The processes of revision and of peer, expert, and self-assessment embedded in the CPESS portfolio and graduation process, in the Hodgson Senior Project research paper, in the *Motion* debriefings, and in the *Beginnings* autobiographies help students to internalize habits of excellence. The opportunity and the expectation of ongoing revision to meet standards help students to learn that "the work is not done until it is done right" (Wiggins, 1989), enabling them to understand what a good performance entails and to grow ever closer in attaining it.

The public nature of many of these assessments holds them up to scrutiny, promoting effort as well as equity and accountability. Students and their parents know the criteria and process for judgment. They are not secret or beyond question. Students know what constitutes excellence and what they must do to attain it; they have recourse to the judges and to their judgments. Shared exemplars of student work communicate the nature and the diverse range of high-quality performances to staff and students alike. When the process involves teachers and students across classes and grades in judging work—as in the CPESS and Hodgson committees—the development of shared understandings and standards is enhanced, while the possibilities for individually appropriate modes of expression are preserved.

Authentic assessment also increases opportunities for the achievement of excellence because of its power to affect teacher knowledge about how to teach diverse learners well. This theme reverberates throughout all of the studies: At The Bronx New School and P.S. 261, the use of the *Primary Language Record* has informed the pedagogy of teachers, expanding their teaching repertoires and extending their reach to successfully engage students whose efforts to achieve literacy have been marked by frustration and failure. At Hodgson, International, and CPESS, teachers consider students' performances, projects, and portfolios as indicators for assessing, revising, and improving their pedagogy and curriculum. They have found an increasing number of strategies and entry points to help a wider range of students reach more challenging learning standards.

Standards for teaching practice are not developed in the abstract. They emerge from careful observation of and reflection on what students bring with them to the learning situation, what they do, and how they do it. Practices that are responsive to students' potentials reflect sensitivity to their interests, histories, and cultural backgrounds, to their current contexts for learning, and to their families. When teachers look closely at students at work, they can see students' many strategies, paces, and styles of learning; their different strengths and experiences; the different ways students express what they know; and the kinds of teaching strategies and contexts that are effective for helping students get meaning out of what they are doing. With these observations, supported by information that parents provide, teachers can find ways to create bridges between students' experiences and challenging curriculum goals.

The example of the community of Bronx New School teachers collaboratively struggling to construct an individually responsive context in which Akeem could learn how to read, write, and become a productive member of the school community is particularly emblematic of a school in which authentic assessment practices provide a student with access to achievement and excellence. In the case of Akeem, we see how powerful the iteration between assessment and instruction can be. We see the possibilities for success that are released when teachers and a school embrace the norm of diversity as a starting point for instruction. Because these teachers are in the habit of responding creatively to the contextualized needs of their students, they invent, develop, and adapt instructional approaches and learning tasks, expanding their repertoire and professional knowledge base. They had means to help them get to know Akeem well enough to successfully guide him toward success. They got to know him well by observing him in many different contexts, by problem-solving collaboratively, and by assessing his interests, his competencies, and his successes in order to increase his learning opportunities. They were able to provide the sustained support that is a condition for the achievement of excellence.

Such approaches to supporting student learning develop standards for teaching and learning without standardization. These strategies build the capacity of teachers and schools to be responsive to the unique needs and circumstances of their students. They move beyond recipes and teaching packages to a way of thinking about teaching and learning based on inquiry about human learning and about individual students, and on individual and collective problem solving. Finding effective contexts and strategies for student engagement requires that teachers understand learners and learning rather than relying on uniform prescriptions for teaching practices. The policy implications are that investments in building teachers' capacity are more useful than are standardized teaching and testing procedures that are certain to be inappropriate for many students. To support high standards of excellence, schools must find ways to support teachers in individualizing the contexts for student success.

Contexts for Authentic Assessment: The Need for Restructuring

None of the schools in these case studies is conventionally organized and structured, although two of them, P.S. 261 and Hodgson Vo-Tech, were conventionally structured at the time their current principals assumed leadership. This suggests that form follows function. In addition, their authentic assessment practices are not prepackaged implantations. Their emergence at these schools is one feature of a more extensive reform effort that aims to transform school from a bureaucratic institution into an educational community, bound by commonly constructed goals, values, beliefs, and commitments about how children should be educated and how schools need to be organized to achieve these goals.

This suggests that authentic assessment is not just another external program that can be imported into a school that behaves as though it is a warehouse of programs, stacked side by side, securely isolated from one another, and having little expectation of significantly impacting the school culture. Quite the contrary, assessment in each of the case study schools embodies and reinforces the school's set of commonly shared values. It is both a means and an end, a way of life and a way of doing business that is purposely change oriented. Authentic assessment can survive, thrive, and be powerful only as schools become dynamic, consciously evolving communities.

Since the research for these case studies was completed, the organization and structures of International and Hodgson have significantly changed due to the impact of new practices. As of September 1993, the entire faculty of International agreed to restructure the school into interdisciplinary, thematic clusters fashioned on the model of the *Motion* team. The entire school is now embarking on formalizing its authentic assessment practices. At Hodgson, vocational clusters have been created and academic interdisciplinary teams have increased, as has special education mainstreaming. Advisories are in place throughout the school. Changes at both schools are a result of teacher and principal collaboration. At CPESS, clusters within two of its divisions have, in a number of instances, subdivided into triads where three teachers work intensively with 80 students for two years. Closer teacher/student relationships and interaction are goals of all three schools. The process of self-renewal means ongoing adjustments, fine tuning, reorganization, and restructuring. Authentic assessment is one major catalyst for this journey.

The schools illustrate what Schon (1987) calls "communities of practitioners": They are developing "professional norms and structures . . . conventions, constraints, languages, appreciative systems, a repertoire of exemplars, systematic knowledge, and patterns of knowing in action" (pp. 7, 36–37). In these case study schools, common norms undergird new structures that enhance: *personalization*—opportunities for teachers to know students well and to communicate regularly with colleagues to reflect critically, share, and problem-solve; *ownership*—allowing students and teachers to have a stake in their learning; *contextual authenticity*—embedding learning in authentic tasks that link to students' experiences; and *recognition of diversity*—resulting in a high degree of teacher–student interaction around individualized work and personal and social development. All of these increase opportunities for deep engagement in school and school work.

In all of the schools we have studied, authentic assessment practices have encouraged faculties to rethink traditional allocations of time and traditional organizational structures to support these norms. Time is structured into the school day and week for teachers to meet with one another and with students. Block schedules give teams of teachers the authority and flexibility to organize the day and week so that students have opportunities to engage deeply for sustained periods of time in the tasks they are pursuing. Because the work demanded of students is more intense and challenging than are passive forms of learning, all of the high schools have developed flexible time frames for classes featuring blocks of time longer than 45 minutes. Interdisciplinary clusters of courses enable more integrative forms of teaching, with longer periods of time for extensive project and research work. Teaching teams have more control over the use of time within blocks, so that they can regroup for different learning and teaching goals to provide small- and large-group instruction as needed, and to team teach.

Teachers have reorganized their classroom structures to allow for increased and intensive interaction with individuals and small groups of students. Subject matter is organized more broadly so that students have opportunities to make connections between and among the disciplines, and so that they have opportunities to encounter problems in increasingly authentic contexts. At the same time, more intensive focus is placed on skills that promote intellectual development. At International High School, for example, teachers have adapted their practice so that students can work collaboratively in groups. This practice corresponds to the school's belief that students will develop their language capacity though conversation and that the inability to speak English should not be a barrier to content acquisition. At CPESS, teachers work with students in seminars and advisories to develop the skills needed for exhibitions. At Hodgson, teaching of academic courses is increasingly being restructured for active learning and group work so that students can develop the skills they will be required to demonstrate in their senior projects. At P.S. 261 and the Bronx New School, increased use of individual and small group learning activities nurtured by closely observant teachers enables students to work from their interests and strengths toward common curriculum goals.

In the elementary schools where documentation of learning is a key assessment tool, time for observing and recording children's growth within the daily structure of the classroom can also be a challenge to arrange. Making this kind of time available has required a shift in thinking about the teaching process. These shifts inevitably move teachers away from the conventionally conceived role of instructors—who constantly direct behavior and dole out information—to the role of facilitators who create learning opportunities and then step back to allow students to engage their own work, observing students' work and thinking and using these observations to inform their teaching. The classroom environment also changes to allow for more student autonomy, more activity and dialogue among students, and thus more time for teachers to be observers of children.

Interdisciplinary teams that manage the allocation of time for their own students and teachers also use the resulting scheduling flexibility to establish regular opportunities for collaborative teacher planning and communication. Several of the high schools have creatively squirreled time for regular meetings by establishing external learning opportunities for students through community service programs, internships, and courses on college campuses. Others have created time for collegial work by rearranging course schedules, adding time to each school day to allow an early dismissal or special "club" time for students one day a week (during which teachers work together), or rearranging school staffing patterns to "buy" more teacher time that enables shared planning time.

Other changes include reallocation of staff so that virtually all adults are working directly with students on advisement and academic tasks. In contrast to typical American school staffing patterns in which only half of professional staff work closely with students as classroom teachers (Darling-Hammond, 1990c), these schools organize themselves for more personalized and intensive adult–student relationships. When schools reconfigure themselves into smaller, self-contained learning clusters, the need for nonteaching personnel, such as deans, assistant principals, guidance counselors, attendance officers, and pull-out program staff, diminishes. Instead, these roles are assumed by teachers who take responsibility for a greater range of functions for fewer total students, with whom they work more intensely. Time is built into the schedule so that teachers can assume these roles: There are periods for advisories and team planning, and there is time built in for mentoring.

The resulting stronger relationships enable teachers to know students and their families better and to address their individual needs more quickly and effectively. As a consequence, teachers, along with students and their families, solve problems before they give rise to learning failures, nonattendance, disciplinary issues, and other outcomes of students' inabilities to adapt to or be noticed by a depersonalized school structure. The authentic assessment systems of the case study schools irrigate these new structures with information about how students are doing, increasing the likelihood that teachers can make sound pedagogical judgments about how to challenge and support students.

Authentic assessment development and practice has helped these schools reframe the reform debate by changing the fundamental question of restructuring from "How can we achieve our goals within the current structures?" to "What kind of structures do we need to establish in order to achieve our goals?" These schools have seen their structures as porous, flexible, and changeable in the service of their goals. Structures become servants to school goals, rather than school goals remaining servants to school structures. These schools have toppled the hierarchy of regularities—the immutable "master schedule" (indeed, the "master" of possibilities within most high schools), the standardized time frames for classes, the rigid role definitions, and the fragmented instructional program—that have been obstacles to serious learning and higher levels of performance (Sizer, 1984).

THE IMPORTANCE OF PARTICIPATION AND LEADERSHIP

These case-study schools illuminate features of leadership, and of faculty and parent participation, that support innovation. Each of the schools is collaboratively managed and in each case the principal encourages a culture of inquiry that provides a context for adult engagement. School leaders have encouraged multiple opportunities for professional growth in various forms and shapes, inside and outside the school community, for teachers at all stages of development. Each understands the ebb and the flow of change, respects swells of enthusiasm and the undertow of resistance, and tolerates the directional cross currents, eddies, and still waters that characterize their faculty's engagement in change. All the while, their commitment to their vision remains steadfast.

These school leaders have created learning organizations by scheduling meeting time for teachers to regularly discuss and debate policy and practice issues on teaching, learning, assessment, and school organization; by encouraging teachers to make recommendations and plans for change; by enabling teachers to enact their ideas; by creating new connections and conversations with parents; and by their own active participation in these conversations and initiatives. They have sought to transform their schools into knowledge- and capacity-building organizations that can be guided by a culture of professional accountability emphasizing self-regulation rather than external, hierarchically determined constraints and edicts.

The approaches to change undertaken in all of these schools have encouraged teachers to think together about children, teaching, and learning rather than mandating specific behaviors or practices. There was, in each case, a recognition that the ways in which teachers are asked to work are likely to be reflected in how they work with their students. If teachers are simply told what to do and expected to follow a script, they are likely to make similar demands on their students. Their understanding and ownership of ideas foisted upon them will be shallow, and their own experience of change will negate the goals of the change process. If, on the other hand, teachers work in an atmosphere permeated with respect for individual growth and development, where they are encouraged to dig down deep, to ask new questions, create new answers, and figure out new approaches, they are likely to work with their students in the same ways. It was after the International school faculty developed portfolios and peer coaching for their own faculty evaluation process, for example, that they found they could engage these ideas deeply with their students. A school leader's attitude and approach can determine whether a new idea becomes simply another new technique that comes and goes or a change that profoundly affects the quality of teaching throughout the school community.

In addition, the faculties built parental support for and understanding of their work by including them in the life of the school: through direct parent participation in exhibitions and assessment conferences, and through parent workshops, the distribution of educational articles, and displays of students' authentic work—all of which offer parents the opportunity to learn more about their children's development and the work of the school. Reaching out to parents in these ways, together with the ongoing communication that many of the assessments encourage and require, contributes to creating an informed parent body that can be active on behalf of quality education.

That is not to say that there are not always areas of resistance, legitimate concerns, and ongoing issues for debate. Significantly, in all of the schools, resistant or skeptical faculty have been won over to innovative practices by three factors: the improved quality of student learning and performances they have witnessed; the persuasive arguments of a critical core of peers; and opportunities to collaborate with colleagues. Faculty empowerment has led to student empowerment. And teacher empowerment in governance is used for educational purposes that affect student outcomes. Without the structured opportunities for communication developed by teachers and principals, the adoption of these innovations and the increased opportunities for success that they provide for students would have been difficult to achieve. Certainly, they could not have taken root in the school culture so as to come to define education in these schools as they have.

THE IMPORTANCE OF NETWORKS

A final critical factor has been the schools' participation in supportive networks. Each of the high schools is a member of the Coalition of Essential Schools (CES) and the four New York City schools belong to the Center for Collaborative Education (CCE), the New York City Coalition affiliate. While these networks have provided common ground for sharing practice and for exploring new possibilities, each school has interpreted and enacted the CES principles in quite different, contextually appropriate ways. That the reforms at Hodgson and the structures at CPESS were inspired by the CES principles (International came to the CES/CCE network after having discovered, in its structures and practice, a commonality and compatibility with the CES/CCE principles) demonstrates the applicability of the CES principles to diverse reform initiatives. It also underscores the importance of ensuring that practitioners invent models—rather than replicate models—that are embedded in and embody their knowledge of their local contexts.

Interestingly, in the CCE network, elementary and secondary schools learn from one another in novel ways as the results-oriented concerns of secondary schools interact with the developmental concerns of elementary schools. From the child-centered stance of elementary schools, the emphasis for teaching and assessment is on the process of learning and on nurturing children's growth and development in responsive ways. This is done out of a concern for supporting student strengths and potentials and for ensuring that the achievement of specific results is not used as a means of limiting future learning opportunities for those who proceed in different ways. In the best of places, this approach coincides with student outcomes that are also of high quality.

Secondary schools, on the other hand, must focus on results. They have traditionally been more involved in evaluating content learning and less involved in supporting the process of human development. The high schools in these studies have sought to do both through the creation of more personalized learning environments. Though their assessments still focus predominantly on curriculum outcomes, they do so in broader ways than do traditional assessments, revealing not only what students know and can do but what they think, who they are, and who they want to become.

Because authentic assessments ask teachers to think both about students as developing people and about what they can do in light of conceptions of competent performance, they help redress what can often be an imbalance between concerns for development and for results. As a network enables practitioners to consider these issues across schooling levels, each learns important strategies from the other. Elementary school work is strengthened as communities reflect on their values and purposes, articulating their expectations for what students should be able to do and developing public criteria for their standards and expectations. Secondary schools also benefit from exposure to the child-centered focus of the elementary grades. Their environments and their students' learning are enhanced by observation and discussion of student learning, focusing on students in more holistic ways that extend beyond content knowledge.

The network is a vehicle for reconsideration of practice from many vantage points, centering around a hub of common values supporting learner-centered practice. This makes connections between and among like-minded practitioners both possible and mutually profitable. As the CES network builds communities of practitioners that can learn with one another, it expands the possibilities for the kinds of conversations that practitioners need to have if teaching, assessment, and school structure are to be organized for student success, and if we are to assure all children an education characterized by excellence and equity.

REFERENCES

Alvarez, A. (1991). Primary language record. *School Voices 2* (1), 11.

Archbald, D. A., & Newman, F. M. (1988). *Beyond standardized testing: Assessing authentic academic achievement in the secondary school.* Reston, VA: National Association of Secondary School Principals.

Bailey, T. (1989). *Changes in the nature and structure of work: Implications for skill requirements and skill formation* (Technical paper no. 9). New York: National Center on Education and Employment, Teachers College, Columbia University.

Barrs, M., Ellis, S., Hester, H., & Thomas A. (1988). *The primary language record.* London: ILEA/Centre for Language in Primary Education.

Boyer, E. (1983). *High school.* New York: Harper and Row.

Bradekamp, S., & Shepard, L. (1989). How best to protect children from inappropriate school expectations, practices and policies. *Young Children, 44* (3), 14–24.

The Bronx New School (n.d.). *The Bronx New School/La Nueva Escuela Del Bronx 1988–1991,* p. 15. New York: Author.

Bussis, A., Chittenden, E., Amarel, M., & Klausner, E. (1985). *Inquiry into meaning: An investigation of learning to read.* Hillsdale, N.J.: Lawrence Erlbaum.

Calkins, L. (1986). *The art of teaching writing.* Portsmouth, NH: Heinemann.

Carini, P. (1986). Building from children's strengths. *Journal of Education. 168* (3), 13–24.

Carnevale, A. P., Gainer, L. J., & Meltzer, A. S. (1989). *Workplace basics: The skills employers want.* Alexandria, VA: American Society for Training and Development.

Center for Collaborative Education (n.d.). *Essential principles.* New York: Author.

Central Park East Secondary School (n.d.). *A public high school: Central Park East Secondary School.* New York: Author.

Central Park East Secondary School (1990). *Senior institute handbook.* New York: Author.

Central Park East Secondary School (1991). *Senior institute handbook.* New York: Author.

Central Park East Secondary School (1991, October). *CPESS Newsletter # 5.*

Centre for Language in Primary Education (1990). *The reading book.* London: Inner London Education Authority.

Chamberlin, D., Chamberlin, E., Drought, N., & Scott, W. (1942). *Adventure in American education (Vol. 4): Did they succeed in college?* New York: Harper and Brothers.

Chittenden, E., & Courtney, R. (1989). Assessment of young children's reading: Documentation as an alternative to testing. In D. S. Strickland & L. M. Morrow (Eds.), *Emerging literacy: Young children learn to read and write* (pp. 107–120). Newark, Delaware: International Reading Association.

Clay, M. M. (1985). *The early detection of reading difficulties (3rd ed.).* Auckland, New Zealand: Heinemann.

Coalition of Essential Schools (1990, March). *Performances and exhibitions: The demonstration of mastery (Horace, Vol. 6., No. 3)*. Providence, RI: Coalition of Essential Schools.

Cohen, S. (1990). Grading limited English proficient students. In *Insights: Thoughts on the process of being international* (pp. 30–33). Long Island City, NY: International High School.

Danzig, R. (1991, August 28). A parent's SOS: Save our school. *New York Newsday,* pp. 48, 90.

Darling-Hammond, L. (1989). Curiouser and curiouser: Alice in testingland. *Rethinking Schools, 3* (2), 1, 17.

Darling-Hammond, L. (1990a). Achieving our goals: Superficial or structural reforms. *Phi Delta Kappan, 72* (4), 286–295.

Darling-Hammond, L. (1990b). Instructional policy into practice: The power of the bottom over the top. *Educational Evaluation and Policy Analysis, 12* (3), 233–242.

Darling-Hammond, L. (1990c). Teacher professionalism: Why and how. In A. Lieberman (Ed.), *Creating collaborative cultures in schools: Building the future now.* New York: Teachers College Press.

Darling-Hammond, L. (1991). The implications of testing policy for educational quality and equality. *Phi Delta Kappan, 73* (3), 220–225.

Darling-Hammond, L., & Ancess, J. (in press). Authentic assessment and school development. In D. P. Wolf & J. B. Baron (Eds.), *Ninety-third Yearbook of the National Society for the Study of Education.* Chicago, IL: University of Chicago Press.

Darling-Hammond, L., & Wise, A. E. (1985). Beyond standardization: State standards and school improvement. *Elementary School Journal, 85* (3), 315–336.

Davidson, A. (1985). *Monitoring reading progress.* Aukland, New Zealand: Shortland Publications Ltd.

Dewey, J. (1916). *Democracy and education.* New York: Macmillan Co.

Dewey, J. (1938). *Education and experience.* New York: Macmillan Co.

Drucker, P. F. (1986). *The frontiers of management.* New York: Harper & Row.

Duckworth, E. (1987). *The having of wonderful ideas and other essays.* New York: Teachers College Press.

Dunetz, N. S. (1990). From isolation to collaboration. In *Insights: Thoughts on the process of being international* (pp. 3–5) Long Island City, NY: International High School.

Educational Testing Service (ETS) (1989). *A world of differences: An international assessment of mathematics and science.* Princeton, NJ: Author.

Education Week (Eds.) (1992, June 17). The Roundtable: A new "Social Compact" for mastery in education. *Education Week* [Special Report].

Einbender, P. (1991, August). CSB 10 must act [Letter to the editor]. *The Riverdale Press,* p. A15.

Elkind, D. (October, 1989). Developmentally appropriate practice: Philosophical and practical implications. *Phi Delta Kappan,* 113–117.

FairTest (1989, Fall). Alternatives implemented in North Carolina. *Examiner,* 3.

Feedback: A regular column of feedback from parent. (1990, June). *The Bronx New School News: The voice of the PTA,* p. 1.

Feedback: A regular column of feedback from parents (1991, February). *The Bronx New Schools News: The voice of the PTA,* p. 5.

Feeney, K., & Hann, P. (1991). *Survey of reading performance in year 2: Summer 1991.* Lewisham, England: Lewisham Education.

Flynn, T. (1991, August 15). Destructive net [Letter to the editor]. *The Riverdale Press,* p. A15.

Fowler, W. J. (1992). *What do we know about school size? What should we know?* Paper presented at the annual meeting of the American Educational Research Association, San Francisco, CA.

Garcia, G., & Pearson, D. (1994). Assessment and diversity. In L. Darling-Hammond (Ed.), *Review of Research in Education, Volume 20.* Washington, DC: American Educational Research Association.

Gardner, H. (1983). *Frames of mind: A theory of multiple intelligences.* New York: Basic Books.

Gardner, H. (1991). *The unschooled mind.* New York: Basic Books.

Godowsky, S., Scarbrough, M., & Steinwedel, C. (1991). *The Senior project: An exhibition of achievement.* Hodgson Vocational Technical High School.

Goodlad, J. I. (1984). *A place called school: Prospects for the future.* New York: McGraw-Hill.

Goodman, K. (1982). Analysis of oral reading miscues: Applied psycholinguistics. In F. Gollasch (Ed.), *Language and literacy: The selected writings of Kenneth Goodman, Vol. 1* (pp.123–132). Boston: Routledge & Kegan Paul.

Goodman, K. (Ed.) (1979). *Miscue analysis: Applications to reading instruction.* Urbana, IL: National Council of Teachers of English.

Goodman, Y. M., & Burke, C. L. (1972). *Reading miscue inventory manual.* New York: Macmillan Co.

Goodman, Y. M., Watson, D. J., & Burke, C. L. (1987). *Reading miscue inventory: Alternative procedures.* New York: Richard C. Owen Publishers.

Gottfredson, G. D., & Daiger, D. C. (1979). *Disruption in 600 schools.* Baltimore, MD: The Johns Hopkins University, Center for Social Organization of Schools.

Graves, D. (1983). *Writing: Teachers and children at work.* Portsmouth, NH: Heinemann.

Green, G., & Stevens, W. (1988). What research says about small schools. *Rural Educators, 10* (1), 9–14.

Haller, E. J. (1992). *Small schools and higher order thinking skills.* Paper presented at the annual meeting of the American Educational Research Association, San Francisco, CA.

Haney, W., & Madaus, G. (1986). *Effects of standardized testing and the future of the National Assessment of Educational Progress.* Working paper for the National Assessment of Educational Progress (NAEP) study group. Chestnut Hill, MA: Center for the Study of Testing, Evaluation and Educational Policy.

Harris, J., & Sammons, J. (1989). *Failing our children: How standardized tests damage New York's youngest students.* New York: New York Public Interest Research Group.

Hawkins, D. (1965). Messing about in science. *Science and children, 2* (5), 5–9.

Hirschy, D. (1990a). Address to the faculty of Grover Cleveland High School, Buffalo, New York. In *Insights: Thoughts on the process of being international* (pp. 15–19). Long Island City, NY: International High School.

Hirschy, D. (1990b). The new schedule. In *Insights: Thoughts on the process of being international* (pp. 6–9). Long Island City, NY: International High School.

Hornbeck, D. (1992, May). The true road to equity *Commentary, Education Week, 11* (33), pp. 32, 25.

Howley, C. B. (1989). Synthesis of the effects of school and district size: What research says about achievement in small schools and school districts. *Journal of Rural and Small Schools, 4* (1), 2–12.

Howley, C. B., & Huang, G. (1991). Extracurricular participation and achievement: School size as possible mediator of SES influence among individual students. *Resources in Education,* January 1992.

Hudson Institute (1987). *Workforce 2000: Work and workers for the 21st century.* Indianapolis, IN: Author.

International High School at LaGuardia Community College (n.d.-a). *Educational Philosophy.* Long Island City, NY: International High School.

International High School at LaGuardia Community College. (n.d.-b). *The International High School mission statement.* Long Island City, NY: International High School.

International High School at LaGuardia Community College. (n.d.-c). *Personnel procedures for peer selection, support and evaluation.* Long Island City, NY: International High School.

International High School at LaGuardia Community College, The Curriculum Committee (1987–88). *Beyond high school graduation requirements: What do students need to learn at the International High School?* Long Island City, NY: International High School.

International High School, Middle College High School, & LaGuardia Community College (1991). *The Motion program.* Long Island City, NY: International High School.

Johnston, P. H., & Harman, S. (1992). Snow White and the seven warnings: Threats to authentic evaluation. *The Reading Teacher, 46* (3), 250–252.

Kamii, C. (1985). *Young children reinvent arithmetic.* New York: Teachers College Press.

Kamii, C. (1989). *Young children continue to reinvent arithmetic.* New York: Teachers College Press.

Kantrowitz, B., & Wingert, P. (1989, April 17). How kids learn. *Newsweek,* pp. 50–57.

Kohl, H. (1991). *I won't learn from you!: The role of assent in learning.* Minneapolis, MN: Milkweed Editions.

Koretz, D. (1988). Arriving in Lake Wobegon: Are standardized tests exaggerating achievement and distorting instruction? *American Educator, 12* (2):8–15, 46–52.

Kornhaber, M., & Gardner, H. (1993). *Varieties of excellence: Identifying and assessing children's talents.* New York: National Center for Restructuring Education, Schools, and Teaching (NCREST), Teachers College, Columbia University.

Madaus, G. F., West, M. M., Harmon, M. C., Lomax, R. G., Viator, K. A., Mungal, C. F., Butler, P. A., McDowell, C., Simmons, R., & Sweeney, E. (1992). *The influence of testing on teaching math and science in grades 4–12.* Chestnut Hill, MA: Boston College, Center for the Study of Testing, Evaluation, and Educational Policy.

Martin, B., & Carle, E. (1967). *Brown bear, brown bear, what do you see?* New York: Holt.

McDonald, J. P. (1992). Steps in planning backwards: Early lessons from the schools. *Studies on Exhibitions (No. 5).* Providence, RI: Coalition of Essential Schools, Brown University.

McDonald, J. P. (1993). Planning backwards from exhibitions. In *Graduation by exhibition: Assessing genuine achievement*. Alexandria, VA: Association for Supervision and Curriculum Development.

McKnight, C. C., Crosswhite, F. J., Dossey, J. A., Kifer, E., Swafford, S. O., Travers, K. J., & Cooney T. J. (1987). *The underachieving curriculum: Assessing U.S. school mathematics from an international perspective*. Champaign, IL: Stipes Publishing.

Medina, N. J., & Neill, D. M. (1988). *Fallout from the testing explosion*. Cambridge, MA: FairTest.

Meier, D. (1989, September 8). In education, small is sensible. *New York Times*.

Meier, D. (1992). School days: A journal. *Dissent (Spring)* pp. 213–220.

Miller, J. (1990). *Educational transitions*. Unpublished master's thesis, Sarah Lawrence College, Bronxville, NY.

National Assessment of Educational Progress (NAEP) (1981). *Reading, thinking and writing: Results from the 1979-80 National Assessment of Reading and Literature*. Denver, CO: Education Commission of the States.

National Association for the Education of Young Children (NAEYC) (1988, January). NAEYC position statement on developmentally appropriate practice in the primary grades, serving 5 through 8 year olds. *Young Children, 43* (2), 64–84.

National Association for the Education of Young Children (NAEYC) (1991). Guidelines for appropriate curriculum content and assessment in programs serving children ages 3 though 8. *Young Children, 46* (3), 21–38.

National Association of State Boards of Education (NASBE) (1988). *Right from the start: The report of the NASBE task force on early childhood education*. Alexandria, VA: Author.

National Council of Teachers of Mathematics (1989). *Curriculum and evaluation standards for school mathematics*. Reston, VA: Author.

National Research Council (1982). A. K. Wigdor & W. R. Garner (Eds.), *Ability testing: Uses, consequences, and controversies*. Washington, DC: National Academy Press.

New York State Council on Curriculum and Assessment (1993). *Building a learner-centered curriculum for learning-centered schools*. Albany: New York State Education Department.

Neill, M. (1989, October 30). Standardized tests. *The New York Teacher*, p. 8.

Oakes, J. (1985). *Keeping track: How schools structure inequality*. New Haven, CT: Yale University Press.

O'Day, J. A., & Smith, M. S. (1993). Systemic school reform and educational opportunity. In Fuhrman, S. (Ed.), *Designing coherent education policy: Improving the system*. San Francisco: Jossey–Bass.

Podl, J. & Faculty from Hodgson VoTech High School, Watkinson School, and Thayer Jr./Sr. High School (1992). Planning backwards: Stories from three schools. *Studies on Exhibitions (No. 7)*. Providence, RI: Coalition of Essential Schools, Brown University.

Prospect Center (1986). *The Prospect Center Documentary Processes: In Progress*. North Bennington, VT: The Prospect Archive and Center for Education and Research.

Resnick, L. B. (1987a). *Education and learning to think*. Washington, DC: National Academy Press.

Resnick, L. B. (1987b). Learning in school and out. *Educational Researcher, 16*, 13–20.

Rugger, K. (1990). A teacher's odyssey. In *Insights: Thoughts on the process of being international* (pp. 36–41). Long Island City: International High School.

Schon, D. (1983). *The reflective practitioner.* New York: Basic Books.

Schon, D. (1987). *Educating the reflective practitioner.* San Francisco: Jossey Bass.

Senge, P. M. (1992, March). Building learning organizations. *Journal for Quality and Participation.* Reprint. Framingham, MA: Innovation Associates.

Shepard, L. (1993). Evaluating test validity. In L. Darling-Hammond (Ed.), *Review of Research in Education, Volume 19.* Washington, DC: American Educational Research Association.

Sizer, T. (1984). *Horace's compromise: The dilemma of the American high school.* Boston, MA: Houghton Mifflin.

Sizer, T. (1992). *Horace's school.* Boston, MA: Houghton Mifflin.

Smith, E., & Tyler, R. W. (1942). *Adventure in American education, Vol. 3: Appraising and recording student progress.* New York: Harper and Brothers.

State University of New York (SUNY) (1993). *College expectations: The report of the SUNY task force on college entry–level knowledge and skills.* Albany: Author.

Sternberg, R. J. (1985). *Beyond IQ.* New York: Cambridge University Press.

Sturz, H. (1988, July 4). The editorial notebook: What's happening at International High? *The New York Times.*

Wiggins, G. (1989). Teaching to the (authentic) test. *Educational Leadership, 46* (7), 141–147.

Willson, V. P. (1992). New Castle County, Delaware: Senior projects anchor for adulthood. In *Learning Work: Redefining Vocational Education.* Washington, DC: Education Writers Association.

Wilson, S. (1990). A conflict of interests: Constraints that affect teaching and change. *Educational Evaluation and Policy Analysis, 12* (3).

ABOUT THE AUTHORS

JACQUELINE ANCESS is currently a senior research associate at the National Center for Restructuring Education, Schools and Teaching (NCREST), Teachers College, Columbia University. Her research has focused on authentic assessment, learner-centered restructuring, and school accountability. Formerly she served as the Director of Secondary School Changes Services for the Center for Collaborative Education, the New York City affiliate of the Coalition of Essential Schools. For over 20 years, Ms. Ancess worked for the New York City Board of Education, beginning as a junior high school English teacher in the South Bronx. In 1981 she became the founding director of Manhattan East Junior High School in District 4, East Harlem, for which she received the New York Alliance for the Arts, School, and Culture Award in 1985. Ms. Ancess was a senior district administrator for three New York City school districts, where she was responsible for initiating, supporting, and supervising over 20 innovative elementary and secondary schools and programs.

LINDA DARLING-HAMMOND is currently William F. Russell Professor of Education at Teachers College, Columbia University, and Co-Director of the National Center for Restructuring Education, Schools, and Teaching (NCREST). She is actively engaged in research, teaching, and policy work on issues of school restructuring, teacher education reform, and the enhancement of educational equity. She is author or editor of six books, including the *Review of Research in Education, Volumes 19 & 20, The New Handbook of Teacher Evaluation, Professional Development Schools: Schools for Developing a Profession, A License to Teach: Redesigning Teacher Education and Assessment for 21st Century Schools,* and *Authentic Assessment in Action.* In addition, she has authored more than 100 journal articles, book chapters, and monographs on educational policy issues.

Dr. Darling-Hammond is currently President-elect of the American Educational Research Association (AREA), a member of the National Board for Professional Teaching Standards, and a member of the National Academy of Education. She is Chair of New York State's Council on Curriculum and Assessment and of the Model Standards Committee of the Interstate New Teacher Assessment and Support Consortium (INTASC). She has also served on the boards of directors for Recruiting New Teachers, the Spencer Foundation, the Carnegie Foundation for the Advancement of Teaching, and the National Foundation for the Improvement of Education. She began her career as a public school teacher and was co-founder of a preschool and day care center.

BEVERLY FALK is Associate Director for Research at the National Center for Restructuring Education, Schools, and Teaching (NCREST), at Teachers College, Columbia University. She has taught in early childhood through graduate education settings, has been the director of an early childhood center, the founding director of a public elementary school, and a program coordinator and consultant for several school districts. Dr. Falk's current work focuses on reforms of both practices and policies pertaining to learner-centered curriculum and authentic assessment. She has co-authored several articles on school leadership and professional development and is the editor of the Fall '94 volume of Kappa Delta Pi's *Educational Forum*.

Index